Nursing and Social Policy

Nursing and Social Policy

Care in Context

Pippa Gough

RGN, RM, HV, MSc, PGCEA

Professional Officer Health Visiting and Community Nursing,
United Kingdom Central Council for Nursing, Midwifery and
Health Visiting

Sian Maslin-Prothero

RGN, RM, DipN [Lond], Cert Ed, MSc

Senior Education Manager – Open Learning, Avon and
Gloucestershire College of Health, Bristol, UK

Abigail Masterson

RGN, BSc, PGCEA

Lecturer in Nursing, Institute for Advanced Nursing Education,
Royal College of Nursing, London, UK

Foreword by Jane Robinson

Professor and Head of Department of Nursing and Midwifery
Studies, University of Nottingham

Butterworth-Heinemann Ltd
Linacre House, Jordan Hill, Oxford OX2 8DP

A MEMBER OF THE REED ELSEVIER GROUP

OXFORD LONDON BOSTON
MUNICH NEW DELHI SINGAPORE SYDNEY
TOKYO TORONTO WELLINGTON

First published 1994

British Library Cataloguing in Publication Data

A catalogue record for this book is available from the British Library.

ISBN 0 7506 1872 8

Library of Congress Cataloguing in Publication Data

A catalogue record for this book is available from the Library of Congress.

Composition by R. H. Services, Hertford, Hertfordshire
Printed and bound by Biddles Ltd, Guildford and Kings Lynn.

Dedication

This book is dedicated to:

Bryan
Paul, Charlotte and Jack
Mike and Sylvia.

Contents

Contributors

Pippa Gough   RGN, RM, HV, PGCEA, MSc is a registered nurse, midwife and health visitor and has worked in a variety of clinical settings, both here and in Africa. She holds a Masters in Science degree in Policy Studies from the School of Advanced Urban Studies at Bristol University and a PGCEA from the University of Surrey. She worked as a teacher of health and community studies at the Avon and Gloucestershire College of Health before moving to the King's Fund Centre where she was involved in the Nursing Developments Programme. While at the King's Fund Centre, Pippa set up the national Nursing Developments Network. Currently she is Professional Officer for Health Visiting and Community Nursing at the United Kingdom Central Council for Nursing, Midwifery and Health Visiting.

Sian Maslin-Prothero   RGN, RM, DipN (Lond), Cert Ed, MSc is a Senior Education Manager (Open Learning) at the Avon and Gloucestershire College of Health, Bristol. She trained as a general nurse in Oxford and later qualified as a midwife. She practised as a nurse and midwife in both the UK and Australia. On her return to England she worked with older people. During this time she undertook a part-time Diploma in Nursing course. Sian worked as an unqualified nurse teacher before becoming a nurse teacher in Bristol. By the time the book is published she expects to have successfully completed a Masters in Science degree in Gender and Social Policy. She is particularly interested in issues relating to women, black populations, nursing and caring and creating an environment of equality of opportunity.

Abigail Masterson   RGN, BSc, PGCEA is currently a lecturer in nursing at the Institute of Advanced Nursing Education, Royal College of Nursing. She undertook a BSc degree in Nursing at the University of Edinburgh, a PGCEA at the University of Surrey and is currently completing an MN at the University of Wales, Cardiff. Nursing the older person is her clinical practice speciality and her research interests include health promotion in nursing and nursing policy.

Jean Neave BA (Hons), MSc, RGN, RM, RHV, FWT, HVT, PGCEA is a Senior Educational Manager at North West London College of Nursing and Midwifery.

Hannele Weir currently teaches sociology in St Bartholomew, Princess Alexandra and Newham College of Nursing and Midwifery in London. She has worked as a nurse and health visitor in Finland, Norway and the United Kingdom.

The views expressed in this book are those of the individual contributors, not of their organizations.

Foreword

New demands for teaching the academic disciplines related to nursing have been created by the development of Project 2000 programmes in nurse education. Existing textbooks may be inappropriate because they were not written with the particular, applied needs of nurses in mind.

In *Nursing and Social Policy: Care in Context*, the authors have begun to address this problem by presenting a balance between the theoretical origins of social policy and its immediate, practical application to nursing as an applied discipline. They bring a freshness of approach to the subject matter derived partly from their experience of observing policy in action as it affects patients and clients in their care, and partly from their own personal experiences as nurses working in a health care system. Hence, at the very outset they reject an approach to the study of social policy which tends to splinter people's lives into different services and interventions and instead adopt an analysis which aims to be 'person focused'. The student of nursing will find in this book summaries of the historical background to current policy initiatives plus more detailed attention to issues such as health, class, the family, women, race, older people and disability – all of which are of major concern to nurses. Useful further reading is suggested throughout the text. True to its nursing focus, the concluding chapter is concerned with policy for, and of, nursing.

Several years ago, when struggling to make nursing intelligible as a policy issue to nurses, I made a plea that readers should participate themselves in refuting or rejecting the ideas I was presenting (Robinson, 1991). To see this challenge taken up and

advanced in this book is enormously rewarding for the development of ideas is an ongoing, organic process. I commend *Nursing
and Social Policy* to all students who wish to understand nursing
practice within its wider social context, and am confident that it
will spark off a commitment in many readers to continue to pursue
in greater depth many of the important policy issues which it
raises.

Reference

Robinson, J. (1991) Power, politics and policy analysis in nursing. In
Perry, A. and Jolley, M. (eds), *Nursing: a knowledge base for practice*,
Edward Arnold, London

Jane Robinson
Professor and Head of Department of Nursing and Midwifery Studies
University of Nottingham

Abbreviations

AIDS	Acquired Immune Deficiency Syndrome
ANA	American Association of Nurses
BMA	British Medical Association
BUPA	British United Provident Association
CHC	Community Health Councils
CRE	Commission for Racial Equality
DoE	Department of Employment
DHA	District Health Authority
DMU	Directly Managed Units
DoH	Department of Health
DHSS	Department of Health and Social Security
EC	European Community
EMS	Emergency Medical Service
EOC	Equal Opportunities Committee
HMSO	Her Majesty's Stationery Office
FHSA	Family Health Service Authority
GCSE	General Certificate in Secondary Education
GHS	General Household Survey
GNC	General Nursing Council
GP	General Practitioner
HIV	Human Immunodeficiency Virus
ME	Management Executive
MENCAP	Mentally Handicapped Adults and Children
MIND	National Association for Mental Health
MPA	Medico-Psychological Association
MP	Member of Parliament
NAWCH	National Association for the Welfare of Children in Hospital

NCVO	National Council for Voluntary Organizations
NDU	Nursing Development Units
NHS	National Health Service
NHSME	National Health Service Management Executive
OSCAR	Organization for Sickle Cell Anaemia Research
OPCS	Office for Population and Census Surveys
RCN	Royal College of Nursing
RHA	Regional Health Authority
SAUS	School of Advanced Urban Studies
UKCC	United Kingdom Central Council for Nursing, Midwifery and Health Visiting
WHO	World Health Organization
YTS	Youth Training Scheme

Introduction

Pippa Gough, Sian Maslin-Prothero and Abigail Masterson

A common theme over the last decade in nursing literature has been a concern to explore and elucidate a knowledge base for nursing (Benner, 1984; Perry and Jolley, 1991; Vaughan and Robinson, 1992). Key to this discussion has been the concept of shared and borrowed knowledge (Schultz and Meleis, 1988) – a concept which has been brought sharply into focus with the introduction of Project 2000. Attempts to develop this curriculum have included knowledge from a variety of other disciplines, including Social Policy.

For too long nurses have failed to acknowledge that their work exists within the wider policy context – a context which shapes and influences those decisions that control and ration health resources and ultimately impacts on the way in which nursing care itself is delivered. In order to control the future direction of the profession, nurses must be able to challenge adequately the public policy agenda, which has persistently neglected issues directly concerning their practice. One way of doing this is to encourage a policy acumen among nurses which would allow them not only to create an analysis of social policy in a coherent way, but also to develop proactively their own analysis for policy.

The aim of this book therefore is to stimulate an interest and awareness within the nursing profession of the fundamental importance and relevance of social policy to its everyday practice and organization of work. We feel this book will be useful to all nurses, midwives and health visitors in every area of practice. In particular, students in pre- and post-registration education will find it a valuable resource in terms of its accessibility as an introduction to social policy and as a guide to further reading. At the end of each chapter several questions are given, which can be used as triggers for discussion or for written work. These will enable the reader to see the relevance of social policy to her practice and to highlight the unique nursing per-spective. Additionally, lists of material for further reading give guidance as to where some issues dealt with in the text are con-sidered in more detail as well as giving pointers to other areas of interest.

Much of the contemporary literature to do with nursing emphasizes the holistic nature of nursing interactions – inter-actions which are informed by an awareness of the whole person and the physical, mental, emotional, social, societal and spiritual dimensions of that person's environment and community.

This book aims to reflect this philosophy of holism in the way in which aspects of social policy are examined, and the book is laid out. For the most part, each chapter avoids focusing on one particular welfare service, e.g. education, housing, personal social services, and the way in which this impacts on a person's life, but rather it is concerned to show how any one person, group or community is affected by policy decisions about what, how and by whom State services are, or are not, delivered. Consequently, chapters have been created around certain policy issues such as welfarism and families, issues of class, race and ethnicity, gender, age, disability, illness and so on. By taking this approach we realize that we may possibly have laid ourselves open to the criticism that we have generalized and stereotyped the experiences of different groups in relation to social policy issues. After all, any discussion of a particular group is bound to be somewhat contrived – the experience of being black in contemporary British society is different for women than it is for men, just as the experience of being old is likely to be different for working-class groups than for those who come from the ranks of the middle or upper classes.

Our intention here has not been to 'problematize' certain social groups. Rather, we feel that there are issues pertinent to some groups, sociologically and statistically which need explanation and discussion within a separate context. For example, although class cannot be discussed without reference to other bases of power, such as gender, age and so on, there is a case to be argued that class, class culture and status, as a source of domination, needs discussion on its own and as a separate issue.

Above all, we have attempted to avoid a traditional policy analysis which tends to splinter people's lives into different services and interventions – a crime of which nursing has often been found guilty. This book, in line with a well-rehearsed nursing philosophy, aims to be 'person focused' – and for this we make no apology.

The plan of this book

Within the first chapter, we feel an important starting point is to attempt to define what social policy is and the extent of its area of investigation. For the purpose of this book the term social policy will encompass not only an examination of the Welfare State, which traditionally and historically has formed the basis of this discipline, but also policy at the interface of the State, the private and voluntary sectors and the domestic sphere. Where reference is made to Social Policy as an academic discipline the term is treated as a proper name and initial capitals are used, as in the example given here. When talking about policies as a whole, for example social security benefits or health policies, then the reverse is true.

A necessary part of exploring Social Policy as a discipline is to take a historical perspective. We do this in brief and aim to point the reader towards fuller exploration by other authors and specialist texts. We take as our starting point the Poor Laws of the last century, when health and welfare became issues of public debate, and arguably necessitated social policy formulation for the first time.

Particular emphasis is given to the tools and methods of study, that is the type of questions asked, the variety of problems that are addressed and the potential applications of the discipline.

In chapter 2 the focus is on how policy is made and implemented. The organization of central government, the functions and powers of Parliament, the role of the Civil Service and the part other dominant groups play in the policy process are examined. Nursing's success or otherwise in accessing, influencing and deciding the political agenda is a central theme.

No single theoretical approach in Social Policy, or the social sciences as a whole, can be usefully assessed on its own. In chapter 3, therefore, we explore and compare a number of mainstream perspectives on welfarism and State action all of which attempt to explain the aims and values contained within the provision of welfare as well as the distribution of economic and political power within society and its systems of government. This critical assessment of State action, in the context of public policy, is helpful in enabling the student to understand the world from a variety of differing views. None of these theories holds the complete explanation as to 'what is really going on' in the complex world of political activity, nor can our grasp of reality be enhanced by the constraints of any one, single world view. Consequently, clarity in analysis *of* and *for* policy is dependent on a wide theoretical focus, an introduction to which is provided here.

Chapter 3 also concentrates on the concept of power, a full understanding of which is vital to any analysis of the policy process. An examination of the definitions and differing dimensions of power draws on the work of key theorists in this field, namely Dahl (1961), Bachrach and Baratz (1970) and Lukes (1974). We link this discussion to the earlier examination of elitism and pluralism which are fundamentally concerned with identifying the true basis of power and vested interest in society and government.

Fundamental to this examination is the idea of a 'system of domination', as described by Dearlove and Saunders (1984), in which a power relationship becomes routinized and rules with unequal outcomes are obeyed as a matter of course. It is this analysis that helps us to make more sense of the complexities of racism, sexism, ageism and class-based domination within the policy arena – issues which are addressed repeatedly throughout the book. Later chapters contrive to show how power operates overtly, but more often covertly, to keep the needs and interests of subordinate groups off the public policy agenda. The idea of nursing as one of these subordinate groups is explored.

Chapter 4 starts with an examination of the multidimensional nature of health, and the difficulty in attempting an overarching definition of a concept which ultimately is so subjective and personal. The problems presented by this lack of a working definition for policy purposes are explored. A short historical review of health policy encompasses the origins of the National

Health Service, and some of the important intervening health policy initiatives up to the current day. In terms of nursing, we place considerable emphasis on those initiatives which have enhanced or damaged the development of the profession, for example the lead role given to nursing in primary health care as a result of the Alma Ata declaration (WHO 1978); or the Griffiths reorganization in 1984. This ongoing struggle for power is a theme we return to in chapter 12. Current policy concerns examined include the creation of Trusts and the provider/ purchaser scenario and community care policy – policy which has split health and social care. The Health of the Nation (DoH 1992) and the changing role of the State in health care are discussed in detail. Similarly issues of ownership of health policy and consumerism are also addressed. We take a very broad definition of health which reflects the nursing perspective and this encompasses poverty, housing, environment, education and global issues.

Caring is the central theme of chapter 5, although this will also be touched on in other chapters. We examine assumptions made about caring within policy, and explore aspects of paid and unpaid care, including nursing. Due to demographic changes there are more women working, and this has implications for both the carers and the cared for. We demonstrate how social policies reinforce sex-role stereotypes, with the consequent failure to compensate adequately those with the burden of care. The concept of care in the community has become ideologically more attractive since the inception of the Welfare State. We concentrate on the implications of this ideological shift for families, carers and the economy.

Chapter 6 briefly explores the formation of gender identity through the process of socialization, and the way in which gender divisions are perpetuated in the labour market through horizontal and vertical segregation, reflecting the pervasive influence of sexism. We place particular emphasis on health and social services policy, and, with reference to nursing, we examine the sex imbalance in the profession which reflects gender divisions in caring generally. We discuss nurses' lack of power historically, a fact which is particularly associated with women, and arguably results in a tendency to be reactive rather than proactive, in decision making. We feel that an analysis of how and when nursing becomes an issue of public debate is crucial to the 'gender and policy' discussion.

Chapter 7 explores the paradox of state intervention, particularly that of the welfare state, in the lives of families and by definition in the lives of women, in contemporary society. It has been argued that on one hand welfarism provides the material and financial resources necessary to sustain health, and therefore self-sufficiency, through enabling family members to work. Yet, on the other hand, social policies are seen as ways in which capital and men gain control of the domestic sphere and of women's work. In other words there is state organization of domestic and family life, which can be seen in the provision of nursery education, primary schooling, enforced health care and so on. An examination of primary health care interventions links into this argument.

We attend to the issues surrounding policy and race in chapter 8, concentrating on their complexity, specifically with respect to the idea of a system of domination (Dearlove and Saunders, 1984) as described in chapter 3. The associations between the formation of policy, power and social class are identified and the need for appropriate support and provision of care for black populations is discussed. Questions are raised as to who decides what is available and who provides services for these populations. Discussion centres on issues in housing, employment and health policy, which are particularly pertinent and which elucidate the multi-dimensional nature of the problems. Links are made with chapters 5 and 6 which deal with aspects of caring and gender. The nursing perspective remains an underlying theme.

The focus of chapter 9 is exclusively older people and the way in which ideology can influence the policy process and marginalize the needs and demands of this growing group. Ageism, and the myths and ideological values contained therein, are explored in depth. We include an examination of the Marxist ideas of the value of economic productivity and the way human beings become disposable commodities once their usefulness to capital has expired. Older people make extensive use of the health service and pensions and are often used as an emotive vote winner.

The potential political power of older people is considered and the future policy challenges in this area are reviewed. A brief historical perspective reveals how provision for older people, and particularly older women, has always been poor and lacked coherence across the provider agencies.

In chapter 10 we consider welfare provision with respect to disabled people. Here we argue that disability is a social constuct, reinforced fundamentally by social policy. The rise of the institution, in which nurses have played a large part, as a mechanism of both social provision and social control has been key to structuring both perceptions and experiences of disability. This form of 'care' has also facilitated the exclusion of disabled people from the mainstream of social life. The case is put for nurses to stop seeing disability as an individual problem that requires individual adjustment but rather to put collective effort into 'curing' the current disablement of society.

Issues concerned with class and social policy are considered in chapter 11. Sociological theories of the concept of class are explored in some depth as a basis for understanding the role of welfarism within class societies. Against this background the relationship of nursing to the State and the use of class as a basis of professional power are examined. The chapter ends with a discussion as to the relevance of a class analysis of welfare in our postmodern age. With respect to nurses being able to identify and target class-related causes of ill health, the relevance is obvious. However, further examination of the deep-rooted shift from uniformity to diversity within society reveals a rejection of structural analyses based on class and their replacement by the new politics of identity. Within the policy arena this is reflected in the move away from universalism and the creation of diverse, individualized and differentiated services – a trend which must be pursued by nursing.

In chapter 12 we pull together the wider discussions of social policy which have been pursued in previous chapters, in order to examine more closely its relevance to nursing practice. We set out by arguing that nurses have failed to acknowledge the wider policy context and have thus failed to influence the decisions that control and ration health resources. In this chapter we debate ways in which the future policy agenda for nursing could be addressed, including the need for a paradigm shift and the development of a world view that places nurses as political actors in the mainstream of the policy process.

In the final chapter we summarize the essential characteristics of earlier chapters and revisit our reasons for writing this book. We reaffirm our beliefs in the fundamental importance of a knowledge base for nursing which includes social policy and we urge nurses to address this deficit with haste.

References

Benner, P. (1984) *From Novice to Expert: Excellence and Power in Clinical Nursing Practice*, Addison-Wesley, Menlo Park, CA

Bachrach, P. and Baratz, M. S. (1970) *Power and Poverty*, Oxford University Press, New York

Dahl, R. A. (1961) *Who Governs?*, Yale University Press, New Haven

Dearlove, J. and Saunders, P. (1984) *Introduction to British Politics*, Polity Press, Cambridge

Department of Health (1992) *Health of the Nation*, HMSO, London

Lukes, S. (1974) *Power: A Radical View*, Macmillan, London

Perry, A. and Jolley, M. (eds) (1991) *Nursing: A Knowledge Base for Practice*, Edward Arnold, London

Schultz, P. and Meleis, A. (1988) Nursing epistemology: traditions, insights, questions. *Image – Journal of Nursing Scholarship*, **20**(4), 217–21

Vaughan, B. and Robinson, K. (eds) (1992) *Knowledge for Nursing Practice*, Butterworth-Heinemann, Oxford

World Health Organization (1978) *Primary Health Care. Report on the International Conference on Primary Health Care*, WHO, Geneva

1

What is social policy?

Abigail Masterson

Introduction

We shall begin by clarifying the nature of social policy. To do this we will address questions such as: what distinguishes a social policy from any other kind of policy; what sort of questions does the study of Social Policy attempt to answer; what is involved in policy investigation and analysis; and why is it crucial for nurses to study Social Policy. Finally we will explore the early history of the development of social policy in Britain, placing particular emphasis on health and related social policies.

Defining social policy

Social policy is a term widely used but in fact extremely difficult to define. Often the meaning given to it is largely a matter of convenience or convention (Marshall, 1975). In the Social Policy literature there is a wide variety of definitions ranging from the very specific to the very broad. Sooner or later, it seems that everyone who writes about social policy offers a definition and discussions concerning the exact nature of anything can often become pedantic and tedious. We hope to avoid such tedium by adopting a pragmatic rather than purist approach.

Let us then explore a range of definitions to identify clearly the essential charachteristics of what we know as social policy.

Titmuss begins his definition of social policy by discussing the words 'social' and 'policy' separately. He defines 'policy' as 'the principles that govern action directed towards given ends' (Abel-Smith and Titmuss, 1974i) and goes on to note that it is only sensible to have policies about things that are open to change. Using the weather as an example, he points out that it would not make much sense to have a policy about the weather as nothing much can be done to change it. 'Social' he takes quite simply as being concerned with people and society. Bringing these two ideas together, it can be seen that social policy is something to do with taking deliberate action to achieve a change in individuals and/or society. Even though the purpose or goal may not always be easy to discern, the idea that social policy involves purposive behaviour seems a necessary part of its definition (Anderson, 1990). Social policies then by and large do not just happen, they are instead intended to accomplish specified goals or produce certain results.

Hill and Bramley (1986) identify several key elements in what they see as social policy, that is there must be decisions involved, and that social policy is situational and context dependent. By saying this they imply that although the decisions taken about social policy are important, it is equally vital to identify how things actually turned out and the historical and social context in which the policy was made. This is because what was intended to happen may not always be the same as what really happened. The reasons for such discrepancies between intention and outcome will be discussed more fully in chapter 2.

Social policy may not always be about action. Social policy may involve some overt action to deal with a problem or perceived problem on which action was demanded, or conversely it may involve a decision to do nothing. A contemporary example of this is homelessness. Despite the increasing numbers of people sleeping rough or living in temporary accommodation, the government has chosen not to intervene actively through the provision of more public housing or by changing the benefit system to enable homeless people to access other forms of housing more easily. Such governmental inaction then often has major social consequences for society or some groups of people within it.

Inaction however differs from non-decision making (Bachrach and Baratz cited in Hill, 1984). In non-decision making governments, rather than opting to do nothing, as in the homelessness example, actually limit the scope of decision making to 'safe' issues by manipulating the dominant value system to ensure that certain problems or needs are prevented from becoming policy issues. Non-decision making is also suggested as being one of the mechanisms that maintains the current unequal distribution of power in society. Power is addressed more fully in chapter 3.

Charles and Webb (1986) propose that social policy springs from observations and ideas about how society ought to be. Social policy is thus normative, that is it contains values and beliefs about how society should be ordered and the ideal relationships between certain groups in society, advocating change when the reality conflicts with such values and beliefs. Social policy is therefore seen as having a deliberate social-engineering function.

Marshall (1975) states that 'welfare' (or the general good) is the central concern of social policy. This focus on welfare has led to a continuing interest in attempts to define social need and consideration of the most appropriate ways of meeting such need. Consequently health, personal social services and social security are usually accepted as being the domain of social policy.

Some writers have suggested however that social policies do not in fact arise out of such humanitarian concerns but are a response to the existence or threat of social unrest. Therefore policies identified as social should not be considered purely and uncritically as if they were dreamed up and implemented with only the welfare of the public in mind. And other policies, not conventionally identified as social policies, such as agricultural policy or economic policy, often make a comparable or even greater contribution to welfare (Hill, 1988).

It has also been suggested that to describe something as 'social policy' or as part of social policy may say as much about the perceptions of the writer as it does about the particular policy (Jones, 1985). Virtually every aspect of public policy can be interpreted as possessing some social policy significance. The rationale then for labelling a particular policy a social policy would appear to be pretty arbitary.

Social policy has been frequently identified purely with central government. However, the policies which result from: international agencies and agreements, social services, the Health Service, local government and professional groups such as nursing and medicine should arguably also be included (Ham and Bramley, 1986). In addition, as social policy is perhaps primarily concerned with analysing the provision of services, now more than ever the examination of the private and voluntary sectors should also be emphasized (Bulmer, Lewis and Pichaud, 1989).

To sum up then, the exact nature of a social policy is very difficult to define. It usually involves some action or inaction on the part of central government or others, that results in a change in society. Particularly in its early days social policy contained both an implicit and explicit commitment to the creation of a better society. Other public policy however may also have social implications. Finally social policy refers also to the social consequences, deliberate and otherwise, of actions and inactions of groups other than central government such as local government, professional groups and the private and voluntary sectors.

The goals of social policy

From the opening discussion it can be seen that the area of investigation with which the study of social policy is concerned can be extremely broad. An analysis of the principles and practice of welfare provision in the areas of health, housing, income maintenance and education has always been central to social policy investigation. Other areas, as diverse as the family, criminology, unemployment and even development of the Third World, however, are also currently legitimately included (Bulmer, Lewis and Pichaud, 1989).

Early study of social policy often involved a desire for social improvement and greater national efficiency, notions which are still strong in much of the present work in this area. Abel-Smith (1989), in this vein, identifies what he sees as the four main goals of contemporary social policy. The first goal, and the oldest, being what Sidney and Beatrice Webb (late-nineteenth-century Fabian Socialists) called 'a minimum of civilized life', that is, the abolition of extreme poverty and the establishment of an effective minimum income. Prevention is the second goal and refers to the key role of social policy in the promotion of health. The third goal Abel-Smith identifies is countering discrimination. The final goal suggested is the humanization of services by making them more user friendly and responsive to individual wishes.

All four of these goals are of key relevance and importance for nurses, and so are major themes of this book.

Why study social policy?

One response is to say that it is important, that we and those we care for are all affected in many ways by social policies, and thus we should know something about them. This is certainly the case, but a more systematic response is needed. Anderson (1990) has developed a useful framework that identifies scientific, professional and political reasons which is adopted here.

Scientific reasons

Social policy is studied in order to gain greater understanding of its origins, the processes by which policies are developed and implemented and the consequences of such policies for society. In this way our understanding of political processes and political behaviour is increased. Policies must be understood as products of politics, and attention must thus be given to the roles of MPs, civil servants, pressure groups, economics and the electorate (Hill, 1988). For instance, through studying Social Policy it is possible to begin to discover how health policy and nursing is affected by the distribution of power in society. The nature, importance and distribution of power will be explored further in chapter 3.

Professional reasons

As nurses, our daily working lives, and those of the clients we work with, are defined and controlled by social policy. Therefore studying social policy can help us gain a fuller understanding of the organizations and systems that we work in and how they interlink with others. Successful nursing care of an older person with mobility problems, for example, may require knowledge of the current workings of personal social services, social security and housing policy. These areas will be expanded upon further in chapters 9 and 10. The study of social policy thus helps nurses determine the best care alternatives for patients and clients. Nurses have an important evaluation function too in assessing the effects of social policy. Achieving policy change is never easy, but for nurses a knowledge of possible policy alternatives and an understanding of how social policy is made and implemented is invaluable.

Political reasons

Some policy analysts do not believe that the study of social policy should strive to be neutral or impartial. Rather, they contend that the study of social policy should be directed toward helping to ensure that favoured policies are adopted to attain the 'right' goals. An example of this would be nurses lobbying for a change in the educational preparation of nurses as a way of encouraging a greater emphasis on the importance of primary health care in health policy. The study of social policy, as it has developed in Britain, has often been concerned with examining the extent to which the Welfare State meets people's needs (Hill, 1988). This he goes on to suggest has, at times, led to a greater preoccupation with criticisms of policies than with attempts to discover why they take the forms they do.

There are many reasons then for nurses to study social policy. There is the practical, self-centred reason that social policy affects us all and that we should therefore know more about it and understand it. And there is the professional concern that nurses, given the opportunity and preparation, can and should play an active and effective part in the policy arena.

Tools and methods of study

The study of social policy draws on many different academic disciplines and has evolved hand in hand with state social provision in the UK. Bulmer, Lewis and Pichaud (1989) note that there are few academic departments of social policy at American universities and only recently has the subject developed a separate identity in Germany.

Social policy does not possess its own theory or an exclusive set of analysis tools and historically the methods used were largely empirical and pragmatic, involving the collection of facts and evidence about social phenomena such as poverty (Williams, 1989). As the discipline developed, however, it increasingly drew insights, tools and methods from other disciplines. Sociology, for example, has developed a substantial amount of knowledge and theory in areas such as social control, socialization and social change which has been useful in trying to understand the effects of alternative social policies and the behaviour of policy makers and implementers. The discipline of economics attempts, among other things, to identify the best allocation of scarce resources such as health care. Such insight has informed policy recommendations and evaluation. Psychology offers research and statistical techniques that have been used to evaluate the effects of social policies. Anthropology, geography and history have helped to make social policy analysis less culture and time bound, thus increasing its meaningfulness. Finally, philosophy has contributed to the normative aspects of social policy in giving direction to its goals (Anderson, 1990). The theoretical basis of social policy is explored more extensively in chapter 3.

The contemporary study of Social Policy then typically involves:

(a) a description of the content of the particular policy or policy area
(b) an assessment of the impact of situational and contextual forces
(c) an analysis of the effect of institutional arrangements and political processes using a variety of theoretical frameworks
(d) an inquiry into the consequences
(e) an evaluation of the impact, both in terms of expected and unexpected or unintended consequences.

The history of social policy in Britain

To make sense of social policy today it is necessary to examine the past. This section deals with some of the key events in the development of British social policy from a nursing perspective and is thus heavily biased towards health policy development. It is not intended to be a comprehensive account of social policy development generally, as this has been covered very ably in other specialist texts. Suggested further reading is supplied at the end of the chapter.

Caring for the poor and disadvantaged

Since the sixteenth century at least, the State has had a role in the provision or planning of services for the disadvantaged in society. There were considerable population movements in Tudor times as a result of the development of sheep farming, the Enclosure Movement and some early manufacturing development (Jones, 1991). The government of the time placed responsibility for the poor upon each separate parish with the result, through the Acts of Settlement, that poor people could be returned or confined to their parishes of birth. As the country became industrialized and urbanized this system came increasingly under strain. People who were genuinely seeking work might find themselves returned to where they came from if they could not produce visible means of support, despite the country's need for labour in the new manufacturing areas. Echoes of this remain today with regard to the difficulty people have in accessing public housing and benefits if they wish to move to find work.

The most significant nineteenth-century attempt to modernize the system was the Poor Law Amendment Act of 1834. This act established a national Poor Law Commission to oversee the Poor Law, who formed the parishes into groups known as poor law unions. This system was intended to ensure uniformity of provision. Those who received help were to be worse off, or in the language of the time 'less eligible', than the poorest people supporting themselves. This Act led to the establishment of the workhouse. It was hoped that this principle of less eligibility would decrease the numbers of people requesting support and thus the cost. Thinking at the time was heavily influenced by Adam Smith's doctrines of *laissez faire* and non intervention, concepts which are considered more fully in chapter 3.

The principle of less eligibility has continued to be very influential in decisions about welfare provision and is reflected for example in the means testing of supplementary benefit and current concerns about maintaining the gap between benefit levels and the low paid.

The 1834 Act was particularly important from a health-care perspective as workhouses were to contain sick wards for inmates. Increasingly, however, such wards were also used for the poor sick of the parish due to an absence of alternative provision.

The growth of the public health movement

Poverty then was a continuing major problem but many social reformers in the nineteenth century exposed a variety of other problems which required urgent action, for example, the appalling living conditions under which many of the population existed. The social surveys of Charles Booth (1889) and Seebohm Rowntree (1901) in London and York revealed that poverty and deprivation existed on a massive scale. As people flocked to the cities in search of work, overcrowding had become a major problem. Many areas at this time did not have even rudimentary arrangements for disposing of waste or supplying clean water.

The 1848 Public Health Act was the result of concentrated campaigning by Edwin Chadwick and his supporters such as Florence Nightingale and the increasing threat posed by cholera (which did not distinguish between classes). This Act provided local authorities with powers to construct water and sewerage systems, which the developing science of civil engineering was able to facilitate. Nonetheless as the Act was permissive rather than mandatory the level of implementation was uneven (Ham, 1992). The 1848 Act is also fundamentally important in social policy terms as it identified for the first time the State's responsibility in public health matters through the creation of a central organizing body called the General Board of Health. The Public Health Act of 1875, in an attempt to encourage more comprehensive provision, pulled together previous public health legislation and obliged local authorities to provide: public health services; isolation hospitals for tuberculosis, smallpox and fevers; and medical officers of health (Jones, 1991).

The early twentieth century saw the State taking increasing responsibility for the provision of health care (Leathard, 1990). At the start of the century concern was growing about the infant mortality rate and thus the health of mothers and young children. One of the factors that provoked this concern was the poor health of army recruits for the Boer war (1899–1901); 40 per cent of the recruits, even by the minimal forces standards, were unfit for service. Another factor was the publication of letters from working women, written to the Women's Co-operative Guild, which highlighted lives of perpetual overwork, illness and suffering. Over 40 per cent of the mothers writing had had stillbirths or miscarriages (Allsop, 1984). Children suddenly became important as it was acknowledged that they represented the future. The government therefore established an Interdepartmental Committee on Physical Deterioration which reported in 1904.

Two consequences of this report were the 1906 Education (Provision of Meals) Act, which led to the establishment of the school meals service, and the 1907 Education (Administration Provision) Act which resulted in the development of the school medical service. These acts formed part of the Liberal government's wider social policy reforms, which also included the provision of old-age pensions in 1908. These reforms have been identified as the beginning of the construction of the Welfare State (Leathard, 1990; Ham, 1992). They are also important in that they embody a preventive philosophy with regard to health and health care and an explicit recognition of a link between poverty and ill health. Interestingly, from the mid-twentieth century this philosophy shifted towards one which emphasized the improvement of health through the treatment of illness in individuals (Allsop, 1984).

The establishment of midwifery and health visiting

Action was also being taken in relation to midwifery and health visiting. In the early-nineteenth century midwifery was practiced by a great variety of men and women with a wide range of skills and experiences from medical practitioners to village handywomen. Few of the female midwives would have been full-time practitioners or would have received any sort of training and their's was a low-technology craft with little use of instruments. Since the 1750s doctors had begun to expand their practice in this area and were gradually becoming accepted as the proper attendants for any complicated labour or for those who were willing to pay their higher fees. Throughout the nineteenth century training programmes were beginning to be established for midwives in many areas (Dingwall, Rafferty and Webster, 1988). After twenty years of negotiation and bargaining between the many groups involved in obstetric care the Midwives Act in 1902 made certification and training a condition of practice and established the Central Midwives Board to oversee registration.

The medical profession, secure in its own status as a result of the 1858 Act which set up the registration of doctors and laid down minimum requirements for registration, objected to midwives being given official recognition in this way. Importantly, under the Midwives Act, local supervision of registration was given to the medical officer of health.

Health visiting is usually traced back to the establishment of the Ladies Sanitary Reform Association in Manchester and Salford in 1862 (Dingwall, Rafferty and Webster, 1988). This initiative involved the setting up of child welfare clinics and the visiting of mothers of young children by 'mission women' to advise on child care. The importance of health visiting was highlighted by the Interdepartmental Committee on Physical Deterioration mentioned earlier. The 1907 Notification of Births Act aimed to develop health visiting as a local authority service.

The Maternity and Child Welfare Act led to the provision of infant welfare centres and in some areas maternity homes for mothers who required institutional confinement. The Ministry of Health which had been established in 1919 continued to be concerned at the high rate of maternal deaths and placed importance on the provision of adequate antenatal care. This resulted in an expansion of antenatal clinics and, following the 1936 Midwives Act, the development of a salaried midwifery service.

General nursing

In the early nineteenth century an extremely varied group of people were engaged in the practice of nursing. In the Poor Law infirmaries nearly all the nursing was carried out by the 'paupers themselves' and most nurses were unpaid. Even in the voluntary hospitals nursing was often seen as little more than a glorified form of charring (Maggs, 1983; Dingwall, Rafferty and Webster, 1988).

In the latter part of the nineteenth century, as a result of much lobbying and petitioning by people such as Florence Nightingale, training began to be offered at many of the voluntary hospitals despite opposition from many doctors and administrators. An inmate of the Holborn workhouse, Timothy Daly, died in 1864 as a result of filthiness and gross neglect and sparked a public outcry. This event, in addition to a growing number of disturbing reports from many voluntary workhouse visitors such as Louisa Twining, led to calls for reform (Bett, 1960).

The 1909 Royal Commission Report on the Poor Law found most of the nursing in Poor Law infirmaries still being done by the able-bodied paupers and that, even where there were nurse training schools established, the trainees were less able and from a lower social class than their voluntary hospital counterparts. Nurse training was linked to the specific work of the training hospital and the preferences of individual doctors or ward sisters. Consequently such knowledge and skills were not easily transferable to different contexts. Concern was expressed that there was no means by which the general public could judge a nurse's competence.

Within the profession there was much discussion and discord with regard to the desirability of setting up a professional register and restricting the use of the term nurse. 'Registrationists' argued that the public would be guaranteed a certain standard of expertise whereas their opponents were concerned that nurses would get 'above themselves' and thus would be unwilling to undertake many of the duties required. 'Oppositionists' were also concerned that the gender order and medical dominance in health care would be challenged (Dingwall, Rafferty and Webster, 1988). Much of this debate continues to be pertinent today with the advent of the health-care support worker and the patient-focused hospital initiative. Issues which are discussed further in chapters 4 and 12.

The nurses' case was severely hampered by the divisions in their own ranks and it was not until 1919 that nurses succeeded in gaining registration by Act of Parliament. They were led in this fight by the newly-formed College of Nursing which set out in 1916 to promote the better education and training of nurses and the advancement of nursing as a profession (Leathard, 1990). The

First World War emphasized the administrative importance of some nationally-recognized standard as the number of volunteers and the redistribution of nurses between sectors highlighted the difficulties in grading staff and matching skills to needs (Dingwell, Rafferty and Webster, 1988).

Three Nurses Registration Acts in 1919 resulted in the establishment of the General Nursing Councils (GNCs) in Scotland, England and Wales. The majority of the councils' members were elected by the nurses themselves. The GNCs laid down rules regarding curriculum content and length of training and maintained the register of qualified staff. Shortly afterwards, the College of Nursing identified the need for post basic education of nurses and set up its own Education Department to develop courses to meet this need (Leathard, 1990).

Community nursing

In 1859 the work of William Rathbone, a merchant and philanthropist in Liverpool, resulted in the emergence of the first professional community nursing service (Stocks, 1960 cited in Leathard, 1990). The idea of District Nursing however was not new. Many associations, usually with religious links, had existed for the provision of home nursing care to the poor for twenty to thirty years and the Liverpool model was probably only innovative in that it was less obviously sectarian (Dingwall, Rafferty and Webster, 1988).

In 1889, the Queen Victoria Jubilee Institute for Nursing the Poor in their Own Homes was founded. It used the money donated to celebrate the Queen's Jubilee to further district nursing and domiciliary work nationally. The Institute's name was changed to the Queen's Institute of District Nursing in 1925. The Institute sought to maintain high standards of education and practice and provide a supply of women to act as nurses for the sick poor. The view of nursing was that of a caseworker or supervisor rather than a doer. The nurse was to use her knowledge to help the patients help themselves (Dingwall, Rafferty and Webster, 1988). Gradually the service extended to all sick people and men were enabled to train from 1947. Although local authorities had the power to provide home nurses the majority were provided by voluntary distict associations funded by donations.

Care for people with mental health problems and people with learning disabilities

Before the 1830s there was relatively little formal provision in this area. The care given depended mainly on the family's resources. The better off might have more attention from domestic servants and poor people might receive help in their homes from the parish. Only a very few indeed might be placed in institutions (Dingwall, Rafferty and Webster, 1988). After the 1834 Poor Law Amendment Act and the resultant development of a national system of workhouses, people classified as 'insane' or 'defective', in the language of the time, tended to be put in either the workhouse or prison if they or their families had no money to fund care in a private institution. Following legislation in 1808 county asylums began to be set up. This provision only became mandatory in 1845. The Lunacy Act in 1890 enforced a duty on local authorities to provide hospitals for 'lunatics' as people with mental health problems or learning disabilities were then labelled.

The care available was constrained by the principle of less eligibility, the quality and availability of staff, and the slow development of knowledge in this area. At first there was little discrimination between those with learning disabilities and those with mental health problems. A medical superintendent would be in charge of each institution. The institutions were often on remote country estates and so the care of the patients varied a great deal depending on the beliefs and character of the superintendent and the patient's own class. Therapy was so called 'moral' in nature and focused on work and obedience for the poor and a gentle, secluded life for the middle classes (Dingwall, Rafferty and Webster, 1988).

Asylum staff were mainly working-class men. This was partly because of the need for physical strength in restraint and also because the institutions were supposed to be as self-sufficient as possible to reduce their costs and consequently attendants needed agricultural and workshop skills to supervise the patients' labour. As conditions were unattractive staff tended to be those who would be unemployable elsewhere (Dingwall, Rafferty and Webster, 1988).

In 1907 the Maudsley Hospital in London was endowed for the development of care and education in these specialities and a few other voluntary hospitals started out-patient clinics (Leathard, 1990). The treatment model changed from a moral to a medical approach and general nursing-type systems were introduced such as nursing uniforms and titles. Training and preparation for staff were established in some areas and attempts were made to recruit general nurses. A national certification system for nurses was set up in 1891 by the Medico-Psychological Association (MPA). The MPA was a professional association dominated by medical superintendents. The attendants thus became the first branch of nursing to secure a relatively uniform system of training and registration although this was imposed by the medical superintendents rather than being a result of their own lobbying (Dingwall, Rafferty and Webster, 1988).

The Nurses Registration Acts of 1919, discussed earlier, included provision for a supplementary register of mental nurses but this heralded a long battle between the GNC and the MPA for control of certification. The GNC only had two mental nurses among its membership and was not thought to be sufficiently sensitive to the particular needs of nurses working in this speciality. And the decision to have mental nurses on a supplementary register was seen as implying some sort of inferiority. Similar issues are echoed today in the unpopularity among mental health nurses of the United Kingdom Central Council's (UKCC's) 1992 decision to call all Project 2000 Diplomates registered nurses rather than specifying their speciality and not making provision for all specialities to have proportional representation in council. Unpopular likewise is the English National Board's decision to replace specialist educational officers with generic ones who provide curriculum development support across all specialities regardless of their own professional background and practice expertise. Colleges have also been allowed to offer a reduced selection of Project 2000 Branch programmes which has resulted in a reduction in the number of mental health and learning disabilities branches available.

In 1913, following the recommendations of the 1908 Royal Commission, the Mental Deficiency Act was passed which established Mental Deficiency Committees in local authorities to provide institutional care, guardianship, training and employment, thus formerly advocating the separation of mental health and learning disability. The First World War gave a renewed impetus to the search for physical causes of mental illness because of the discovery of syphilis as the cause of general paralysis of the insane and because the experiences of shell-shocked soldiers were related to physical and environmental stresses (Dingwall, Rafferty and Webster, 1988).

Further legislation in 1927 reaffirmed the commitment to separate care facilities. Many local authorities had continued to evade their responsibilities, an evasion made possible by the permissive rather than mandatory nature of the previous Acts. In 1929, the Mental Deficiency Committees took over responsibility for the 'pauper defectives' from the Poor Law (Leathard, 1990).

The Mental Treatment Act 1930 encouraged a different and more optimistic approach to care and treatment by allowing voluntary admissions of all classes and encouraging public hospitals to have out-patient clinics. Many voluntary agencies were also founded and offered a variety of institutional care, training, aftercare and supervision. Local authorities frequently delegated their responsibilities to such groups. The Ministry of Health exercised little control, except in the monitoring of finances. Consequently, the level and quality of provision was variable and unevenly distributed (Leathard, 1990).

General practitioners (GP) services

At the turn of the century the better off used the services of doctors whose income came largely from private practice. Under the Poor Law, the destitute sick could be seen at home by the medical officers of the Boards of Guardians but the service was often inadequate or too late. Out-patient advice and treatment were also available in some areas at voluntary hospitals, charity clinics and public dispensaries. The majority of people were treated by GPs for a fee. Friendly societies and provident clubs were formed by some workers to ensure that money would be available for members to cover such costs. Some trade unions provided similar benefits. The benefits were only available to the wage earner himself, however. Women, children, and people who were old or disabled had to make do with out-patients departments, charity clinics, paying a private fee or doing without.

The 1911 Insurance Act heralded a radical change in the State's involvement in the provision of primary health care and sickness benefit. It provided free care from GPs and sickness benefit for certain groups of workers who earned less than £160 per annum. It was a compulsory scheme financed by contributions from the worker, the employer and the State (Allsop, 1984; Ham, 1992).

There was considerable resistance from the medical profession to the passing of the Act. The doctors were fearful of State control of their work and wary of the financial consequences (Ham, 1992). These two issues of control and finance have remained key factors in the medical mind throughout all subsequent developments in health-care provision (Leathard, 1990). The doctors were only finally persuaded into the scheme by two things: the government's agreeing that the generous payment negotiated would be based on the numbers of patients on a doctor's list rather than a fixed salary, and the exclusion of higher-income groups to enable the continuation of lucrative private practice.

The 1911 scheme had important limitations. Only the insured workers were covered, not their families, and hospital care was not included. The self-employed, most non-manual workers and the unemployed were also excluded. The majority of the population therefore was outside the scheme and left without any improvements in access to GP services. Nevertheless the Act represented a major increase in the involvement of the State in the provision of health care (Ham, 1992).

Hospitals

Hospitals could not provide much in the way of therapeutic benefit until the latter half of the eighteenth century and thus tended to treat mainly the urban poor (Allsop, 1984). Those who could afford it would usually be treated in their own homes. Provision of hospitals developed mainly out of the workhouses provided under the Poor Law and the voluntary hospital system with its ancient monastic heritage.

The dissolution of the monasteries (1535–7) had resulted in the collapse of the monastic system of philanthropy. Hospitals, such as St Bartholomews in the City of London, were instead reliant on charitable donations and endowments. Doctors in the main gave their services for free.

The eighteenth century was a time of considerable activity in hospital building and many of the famous teaching hospitals date back to this time. Some voluntary hospitals, however, were only small cottage hospitals serviced by local GPs. As medicine developed in the nineteenth century, the voluntary hospitals became increasingly selective in their choice of patients, favouring the acutely ill as opposed to the chronic sick or people with infectious diseases. In 1861 there were estimated to be 50 thousand sick paupers in the workhouses and 11 thousand patients in the voluntary hospitals (Levitt and Wall, 1984).

The voluntary hospitals provided virtually all the medical teaching facilities and most of the training for nurses. Income came from a variety of sources including philanthropy and endowments, private fees and insurance (Leathard, 1990).

The workhouses therefore were left to care for the patients that the voluntary hospitals would not accept. There are still remnants of this dichotomy in hospital care today, with units for the continuing care of older people and people with physical or mental disabilities, for example, often being provided in the original workhouse buildings.

Standards in the workhouses tended to be very poor. The 'less eligibility' principle referred to earlier, meant that conditions were made deliberately unattractive as a deterrent. There was some improvement in the Poor Law hospital services following the 1867 Metropolitan Poor Act (which became the 1868 Poor Law Amendment Act outside of London). These Acts encouraged the development of infirmaries for the sick, separate from the workhouses (Ham, 1992).

The Metropolitan Poor Act was an extremely important development in social policy terms because, eighty years before the establishment of the National Health Service (NHS), it involved an explicit acknowledgement of the duty of the State to provide hospitals for the poor. Even as late as 1905, however, the majority of the sick poor received minimal care in unclassified institutions where the 'nursing' was done by pauper inmates (Maggs, 1983).

The 1929 Local Government Act marked the beginning of the end of the Poor Law and resulted in the transfer of workhouses and infirmaries to the local authorities and permitted them to provide the full range of hospital treatment (Ham, 1992). The infirmaries thus came under the control of the Medical Officers of Health alongside the other public health services (including the fever hospitals and hospitals for the care of the mentally ill and people with learning disabilities).

Increasing numbers of qualified nursing and medical staff were employed but progress was uneven as there was no compulsion. Local authorities generally levied charges for these services, fixed usually according to ability to pay. The 1929 Act however failed to remove the Poor Law stigma and class divisions. Upper-class groups still avoided local authority care where possible (Leathard, 1990).

After the First World War costs began to rise. This increase was associated with the rapid pace of medical advances and the resultant growth in the numbers of beds and staff required. Many of the voluntary hospitals were in severe financial difficulties as diminishing economic prosperity reduced donations. The proportion of patients being treated in this sector rose from 25 per cent in 1921 to 36 per cent in 1936 (Leathard, 1990).

The influence of the 1939–1945 war

During the Second World War the public hospitals were joined with the voluntary hospitals in the Emergency Medical Service (EMS). The Ministry of Health thus became responsible for the treatment of casualties and had central control over the activities of the voluntary and local authority hospitals for the first time. The government also financed this provision. Consequently, senior members of the medical profession saw at first hand the poor state of many of the local authority hospitals and some of the smaller voluntary hospitals. Concurrently some regional hospital surveys were carried out which provided documentation of the widely varying standards and distribution of services that existed. Importantly, particularly in the light of future development, the Civil Service had the administrative experience of successfully running a national health service (Allsop, 1984; Ham, 1992).

Social values had changed, 'if dangers were to be shared, then resources should also be shared'. (Jones, 1991i).

There was a new sense of altruism and a commitment to social justice. People had accepted an unprecedented degree of government intervention in their lives such as conscription and compulsory takeover of land and property. The demand for a reconstruction policy started early in the war. One generation had already fought a war after which, it was felt, the promises made to them had not been kept and there was a determination that this should not happen again. The Labour Party was also able to lobby for social reform from a position of power in the wartime coalition government. Wartime shortages had also led to many extensions in social services. For example, school meals and free milk for children were universally provided and there were special supplements for all expectant mothers (Jones, 1991). Consequently this war was instrumental in creating pressure for change, just as the Boer War had been.

The establishment of the NHS

Many of the early developments in health and social policy had occurred in a rather haphazard manner. The Dawson Committee was set up in 1919 to make proposals for the improvement of health services and recommended the provision of a nationally-organized comprehensive scheme of hospital and primary health care. Later reports in the 1920s and 1930s all highlighted the shortcomings of the existing systems and proposed greater co-ordination of services as well as the extension of health insurance cover. Crucially, however, the 1926 Royal Commission on National Health Insurance suggested that funding might eventually be derived from general taxation rather than insurance (Allsop, 1984; Ham, 1992).

Before the end of the Second World War, the government announced its intention to develop a national hospital service and followed this up by the publication of the Beveridge Report in 1942. This report made many wide-ranging recommendations for the reform and extension of the social security system, and the establishment of a centrally-organized, centrally-funded and totally comprehensive health service (Levitt and Wall, 1984).

These proposals were put into effect by the National Health Service Act in 1946 and took effect on 5 July 1948.

The Act established the pattern of the present-day health-care system in Britain. It represented a new policy commitment by the State: ie that health services should be provided universally on the basis of need alone and be financed collectively from general taxation. A full discussion and analysis of the establishment and continued development of the NHS will be given in chapter 4.

The Welfare State

The social legislation of the immediate postwar period, which is often referred to as the establishment of the Welfare State, was in fact evolutionary rather than revolutionary (Jones, 1991; Leathard, 1990). It was built on legislation dating from as far back as the sixteenth century but was made much more comprehensive and rational. A muddle of provision which had been developed haphazardly was replaced by a network of co-ordinated and centrally-controlled services. All political parties were involved in attempting to bring about a more secure and egalitarian society.

Hill (1988) in attempting to explain this phenomenon, cites the legal philosopher Dicey as identifying that at the end of the nineteenth century the government had begun to assume a role in society that had taken Britain well on the way to becoming a socialist state. The social policies that contributed to the establishment of the Welfare State can be thus interpreted as having a normative nature as highlighted earlier in this chapter.

The change in political values, from *laissez faire* and less eligibility to welfarism, may well have been prompted and encouraged by changes in the electorate. In 1885, as a result of electoral reform, a large working-class element was added to the electorate which was beginning to influence political thinking and the behaviours of politicians of all classes. The Conservatives and Liberals were increasingly aware of the need to compete for working-class support particularly with the growing threat to their futures being posed by the newly-established Labour Party (Jones, 1991). Similarly in contemporary politics the Labour Party under Neil Kinnock was perceived to be adopting a watered-down New Right ideology in an attempt to woo the expanding middle-class electorate. This change in values and its resultant effects on social policy are discussed further in chapter 3.

Conclusions

In this chapter social policy has been explored in several ways. First of all the term social policy itself was discussed and a pragmatic definition adopted which emphasized its underlying preoccupation with social change. The area of social investigation and methods of study that can legitimately be called social policy was then identified and the centrality of the assessment and examination of social need was stressed. The appropriateness of social-policy study for nurses was particularly emphasized. The final part of the chapter comprised a brief introduction to the history of social policy formulation in Britain, focusing particularly on areas of special interest to nurses and nursing.

Discussion points

1. Critically consider why the study of social policy might be crucial for nurses.
2. Evaluate the influence of war on health policy.
3. Discuss why it is necessary to take a historical perspective to fully understand the present NHS.

Further reading

Booth, C. *Life and Labour of the People of London 1889–1903*, Macmillan, 17 vols
Rowntree, S. (1901) *Poverty: A Study of Town Life*, Macmillan

References

Abel-Smith, B. (1989) Concluding thoughts: an inside view. In *The Goals of Social Policy* (eds M. Bulmer, J. Lewis and D. Pichaud), Unwin Hyman, London, pp. 313–316
Abel-Smith, B. and Titmuss, K. (1974) *Social Policy: An Introduction*, (i) p. 23 George Allen & Unwin Ltd, London

Allsop, J. (1984) *Health Policy and the NHS*, Longman, London

Anderson, J. (1990) *Public Policy Making: An Introduction*, Houghton Mifflin Company, Boston

Bett, W. R. (1960) *A Short History of Nursing*, Faber & Faber, London

Bulmer, M., Lewis, J. and Pichaud, D. (1989) *The Goals of Social Policy*, Unwin Hyman, London

Charles, S. and Webb, A. (1986) *The Economic Approach to Social Policy*, Wheatsheaf Books, Brighton

Dingwall, R., Rafferty, A. and Webster, C. (1988) *An Introduction to the Social History of Nursing*, Routledge, London

Ham, C. (1992) *Health Policy in Britain: The Politics and Organisation of the National Health Service*, 3rd edn, Macmillan, Basingstoke

Ham, C. and Hill, M. (1984) *The Policy Process in the Modern Capitalist State*, Wheatsheaf Books, Brighton

Hill, M. (1986) *Understanding Social Policy*, 3rd edn, Basil Blackwell, Oxford

Hill, M. and Bramley, G. (1986) *Analyzing Social Policy*, Basil Blackwell, Oxford

Jones, C. (1985) *Patterns of Social Policy: An Introduction to Comparative Analysis*, (i) p. 121 Tavistock, London

Jones, K. (1991) *The Making of Social Policy in Britain 1830–1990*, Athlone Press, London

Leathard, A. (1990) *Health Care Provision: Past, Present and Future*, Chapman & Hall, London

Levitt, R. and Wall, A. (1984) *The Re-organised NHS*, 3rd edn, Chapman & Hall, London

Maggs, C. J. (1983) *The Origins of General Nursing*, Croom Helm, London

Marshall, T. H. (1975) *Social Policy*, 4th edn, Hutchinson & Co, London

Williams, F. (1989) *Social Policy: A Critical Introduction*, Polity Press, Cambridge

2

Making and implementing social policy

Abigail Masterson

Introduction

In the past social policy textbooks often made a distinction between policy making, policy implementation and policy outcomes. The study of the nature and formulation of social policy has a long tradition in Britain as we showed in chapter 1. However, interest in the study of the implementation of public policy began in the United States in the early 1970s. This interest evolved from a concern regarding the missing link between policy making and the evaluation of policy outcomes and represented an important advance in terms of the academic study of social policy (Ham and Hill, 1984).

In this book then, in line with Ham and Hill, we will consider all three elements – formulation, implementation and outcome of social policy – and will highlight the importance of the considerable negotiation and bargaining which occurs at every stage in the policy process.

To understand the complexity of the policy process we must first identify and examine the role of the key players. In terms of health-related social policy such key players include: central government; Regional Health Authorities (RHAs); District Health Authorities (DHAs); Family Health Services Authorities (FHSAs); NHS Trusts; local government; specialist interest groups such as the professions; pressure groups, for example voluntary organizations such as MIND, NAWCH and so on; outside interests such as industry and commerce; international interests; and such institutions as the European Community and the World Health Organization.

Central government and the Department of Health

The State and the government are conceptually distinct (Kingdom, 1991). Usually the government is regarded as an entity consisting of secretaries of State, ministers, junior ministers and their various assistants, and of course the Prime Minister. The State on the other hand comprises a much wider set of institutions over which the government has control or at least authority, for example, the civil service, the Bank of England, the judiciary, the military, the police, local authorities, health authorities and so on. Some theorists also include the media, business and commerce, the education system and even the trade unions (Middlemas, 1979 cited Kingdom, 1991).

Formally the UK has a system of representative democracy. Elections to the House of Commons are held at least every five years and result in the election of approximately 650 Members of Parliament (MPs) (the precise number varies as constituency boundaries are redrawn every ten to fifteen years after the recommendations of the Boundaries Commission) (Kingdom, 1991). MPs are predominantly middle-aged. Over half are graduates. Most are in professional occupations or employed in business. They are almost uniformly white and very unlikely to be female.

The leader of the party which wins the largest number of seats is asked by the monarch to form a government and to become Prime Minister. From among his/her trusted supporters the Prime Minister appoints approximately one hundred people as government ministers. The most senior of these ministers, usually numbering about twenty, make up the cabinet. The government therefore is made up of both cabinet and non-cabinet ministers, the majority of whom will be MPs. The other members of government will come from the House of Lords. Occasionally people from outside Parliament are appointed to the government, but they must become MPs or be made peers. The Prime Minister determines how long individual ministers will hold office. If the Prime Minister changes or the government loses its majority in the House of Commons (usually by losing an election), the ministers, or political heads of departments, also change.

Ministers are responsible for the day-to-day running of the government's business through the major departments of State.

These departments transform the government's legislation and policies into action. Such departments include the Treasury, which is responsible for all matters to do with finance, the Department of Social Services and the Department of Health. Most of the work of the departments nevertheless is carried out by civil servants although ministers are constitutionally held responsible and accountable for this work by Parliament (Kingdom, 1991). In practice, nonetheless, the accountability is now more collective than individual.

The basis of this accountability, in the case of health, lies in the statutory responsibility of the Secretary of State for the way in which the NHS is run and funds are spent. The Secretary of State for Health also has responsibility for appointing the chairmen and non-executive members of Regional Health Authorities; the chairmen of District Health Authorities, Family Health Services Authorities and NHS Trusts; and some of the non-executive directors of Trusts. The Secretary of State has responsibility for dealing with a variety of personnel questions such as salaries and conditions of service for staff outside of the NHS Trusts and making regulations for payment by users through such mechanisms as prescription charges.

The size of the NHS budget is determined as a result of negotiations between ministers and civil servants from the Department of Health and the Treasury. The Department of Health then allocates the budget to Regional Health Authorities. Overall spending on health services and the distribution of funds to regions is centrally controlled within strict and statutorily-controlled cash limits. In contrast to local government which can raise revenue from the council tax, rents, bridge tolls and so on (albeit subject to capping by the centre), NHS authorities do not have access to significant sources of local income and are thus more subject to central control.

Ham (1992) asserts however that the extent of this central control should not be overemphasized. RHAs themselves decide how to distribute funds to DHAs. The Department of Health has limited control (although it does offer guidance) over the uses to which funds are put, except in the case of major capital building projects such as the commissioning of a new hospital. However, many of the executive positions are vetted by the Secretary of State thus giving an extra measure of central control, unlike the much more democratic local government system where councillors have to be elected. The Department of Health can also identify funds for specific purposes such as reducing waiting lists, AIDS and so on. Special funds were allocated in this way for the implementation of the NHS reforms. However, the amount of money earmarked thus is very small. Nevertheless there are enough points at which government selects or influences personnel or controls the purse-strings to ensure that the government's ideology is reflected at all stages.

The Department of Health publishes White Papers (statements of policy intentions) and consultative documents (Green Papers) proposing developments in specific areas of service provision. This form of guidance is often used to make a major statement of government policy, as in the case of the 1989 White Papers 'Working for Patients' and 'Caring for People'. Nevertheless Ham (1992) cites Haywood and Aleski (1980) to support the argument that, because the NHS authorities actually provide the services and have the day-to-day management and planning responsibilities, the Department of Health still has to work through and with these authorities to achieve its goals. Inevitably the Department is also responsible to Parliament which monitors the work of government departments through a system of select committees.

Parliament

Parliament consists of the House of Commons, the House of Lords and the Monarch but the House of Commons is the most important and powerful part. Parliament passes legislation, examines public expenditure and controls the government. This control is however necessarily limited as long as there is a cohesive House of Commons majority to support the government. The party whips are responsible for securing this majority by making sure that MPs are present and vote so that the government's legislative programme is carried through. Every week the whip notifies his party's MPs of the business for the following week, underlined according to its importance once, twice or three times and requesting their attendance. This custom led to the colloquial term a 'three-line whip' (Harvey and Bather, 1972).

While any bill except a money bill may be introduced in either house, almost all major bills originate in the House of Commons. Most legislation originates from the government and bills have to go through a number of stages before becoming law. In a normal session, about 110 days are available for legislation and all but ten of these will be taken up by the government. Nevertheless governments are always pressed for time because there are certain bills that have to be passed so that the government's work can continue. Unforeseen events and emergencies may necessitate legislation. Consequently there is little time for all the new legislation most governments would like. Priority is often given to legislation necessary to the carrying out of election pledges.

Bills have to be as well drafted as possible and are carefully drafted by civil servants to ensure they are essentially workable. Nevertheless the sheer volume of modern legislation means that there are frequent weaknesses in the wording of legislation. This may mean that law does not always have the effect intended. Law as interpreted by the courts may, because of weakness of drafting, fail to do what ministers intended. All bills go through four stages in each House before becoming law.

The first stage is known as the introduction and first reading. The first reading notifies the House and any other interests affected of the existence of the proposed legislation. At the first reading a date will be fixed for the second reading. On the appointed day the minister in charge (except in the case of private members' bills) explains the background and purposes of the government's bill and the main issues of policy involved. A debate, which may take a few days, then follows on the general principles of the bill, no discussion of detail being allowed at this stage. The traditional way of defeating a bill is either by postponement or a 'reasoned amendment'. In the normal course of events government bills are not defeated.

If the bill survives it is then referred to a committee whose task it is to examine the bill clause by clause. Amendments may be made both to improve it and make it more acceptable. The main principles of the bill however can not be altered as these have already been agreed on by the House in the second reading.

At the report stage the bill is reported to the House and the committee's recommendations either accepted or rejected, thus ensuring that the bill, in its final form, represents the opinion of the majority of the House and not merely that of the committee.

The House can also make further amendments and insert new clauses. As soon as a bill has completed its stages in the Commons it is taken to the House of Lords: the same happens in reverse if a bill originates in the Lords but most major legislation is initiated in the Commons.

The bill then passes through the same stages in the Lords. Apart from money bills, it is legally possible for the Lords to reject or amend a bill, but in practice they merely revise and perhaps delay in order to allow for full public discussion. If the bill is amended in the Lords it must go back to the Commons to be accepted.

All bills require Royal assent before they can become law but this is only a formality.

Parliamentary debates on legislation as it progresses through the Houses do provide an opportunity for the views of parties and sometimes minorities in parties to be aired, and governments will sometimes accept amendments put forward by the opposition parties. Occasionally legislation may be defeated or withdrawn but a parliamentary majority and strong parliamentary discipline ensures that such occasions are rare.

Opportunities are available for individual MPs to propose legislation in the form of private members' bills. Indeed the Nurse Prescribing legislation was put through Parliament in this way. While in theory a member may introduce any bill he pleases, in practice he or she would meet opposition from the whips if it were likely to cost the government votes or if it cut across government policy. The most important method of promoting a private member's bill is through the ballot of members which takes place every session. Usually around twenty names are drawn in the ballot but, because of pressure on parliamentary time, only a few of the MPs who are successful in the ballot stand a real chance of having their bills enacted. Even then, the MP is dependent for success on the government's not opposing the legislation.

MPs can also introduce bills through the 'Ten Minutes rule'. The MP making the motion speaks for ten minutes in favour of the bill and any other MP can speak against it for a similar time. If the House decides in favour of the motion the bill is deemed to have been read a first time.

Individual MPs are able to use Parliament in other ways. They can put down parliamentary questions, asking ministers about aspects of the work for which they are responsible. These questions will either receive written replies or be answered verbally in the House, which enables supplementary questions to be asked. MPs can also raise adjournment debates: these are often on local, constituency issues. These debates provide a chance to air matters of concern to MPs and their constituents.

Although most of the parliamentary timetable is controlled by the government, certain days are made available to the opposition to debate subjects of their choosing.

Select committees

Select committees are committees of MPs from all parties, supported by civil servants and specialist advisers, which investigate particular topics and publish reports on their findings. Their reports are often critical and adopt cross-party opinions. The establishment of select committees was in part a response to the perceived lack of power and influence of back-bench MPs (Ham, 1992). It aimed to give them what was seen initially as a token role in the policy process, however, the influence of select committees has grown (Levitt and Wall, 1992). The Health Committee was set up in 1990 and evolved from the Social Services Committee which was established in 1979 to investigate the work of the DHSS. An example of a recent report of the health select committee is the Winterton Report 1992 which focused on the future development of maternity services in Britain and emphasized the vital role of midwives. Select committees also regularly review expenditure plans and priorities. They are intended to provide MPs with a more effective means of controlling the government and to enable them to extract information about government policy.

The actual impact of these select committees on policy however is largely determined by the government's willingness to accept their recommendations. Departments are expected to pay attention to committee reports but not necessarily to act on them. Nevertheless Ham (1992) suggests that the select committees create a more informed House of Commons, force departments to account for their actions, submit ministers to a level of questioning not possible on the floor of the House and help to put issues on the political agenda. They also give MPs useful and satisfying work to do and enable outsiders to gain a better understanding of what is going on in Whitehall. Finally by extracting and producing information they provide ammunition for pressure groups to use in campaigning and lobbying.

The Prime Minister

The Prime Minister has sole responsibility for appointing members of the government and has considerable power over the awarding of peerages, knighthoods and other honours. Often this patronage is exercised in response to the influence of others but ultimately the responsibility and authority are his.

The Prime Minister is chairman of the cabinet and thus can control its agenda. He appoints the members and chairs of cabinet committees. The Prime Minister will usually chair key committees such as the defence and economic committees himself and appoint his supporters to chair the others. Much of the cabinet's work is now done by committees but little is known about their work at the time because of official secrecy.

Informal groupings of a small number of senior ministers may also be established by prime ministers to act as a so-called 'inner cabinet'. This inner cabinet may serve as a sounding board for the Prime Minister. It has been suggested that this inner cabinet might help to incorporate potential rivals into the centre of government decision making, thus neutralizing their influence (Ham, 1992). Kingdom (1991) notes, however, that this inner cabinet could also be perceived as a threat to genuine cabinet government and as devious and secretive.

The Prime Minister's position is strengthened by the support of the cabinet office. The cabinet secretary acts as a personal adviser to the Prime Minister. The cabinet secretariat prepares agendas, controls the distribution of minutes and papers in the cabinet system, takes minutes, communicates decisions made and advises on procedure. Thus it enables the Prime Minister to keep a close eye on what is taking place in cabinet committees. However, events such as the Matrix Churchill affair 1992/3 do raise doubts about the effectiveness of these monitoring systems. Nonetheless these functions do allow the cabinet secretariat a potentially huge influence on the shaping of policy. *Yes Prime Minister*, the television programme based on the books by Jonathon Lynn and Antony Jay, gives a hilarious but authentic picture of the relationship between Prime Ministers and senior civil servants. Gerald Kaufmann MP described the television programme *Yes Minister* as 'chillingly accurate . . . [and performing] a valuable public service by telling viewers something important about the way in which their country is governed' (Lynn and Jay, 1981i).

Since 1974, prime ministers have made use of their own policy unit located in 10 Downing Street. The unit's main purpose is to assist the Prime Minister in achieving the strategic goals of government. Therefore its main functions include: serving as a think-tank; giving advice; following up the implementation of policy decisions; briefing the Prime Minister on important issues; and identifying new ideas. The Prime Minister may consult other experts too. Thus Margaret Thatcher had close links with a number of right-wing intellectual groups such as the Centre for Policy Studies, the Institute of Economic Affairs and the Adam Smith Institute.

The Prime Minister thus wields immense power and is unlikely to be defeated in cabinet although he or she will be prepared to be influenced by its views or the views of leading members. If he or she should be defeated, however, there is always the possibility of the Prime Minister restructuring the cabinet and bringing in other ministers whose thinking is more in line with his or her own.

Ham (1992) and others have suggested that it is only when the Prime Minister's leadership poses a threat to the government and its future electoral chances that he or she is likely to be seriously challenged, as in the case of Margaret Thatcher in 1990 and perhaps John Major in 1994.

Ministers and civil servants

A common myth particularly in the lay understanding of the policy process is that ministers decide policy and civil servants carry it out. It is commonly accepted in academic circles however that civil servants have considerable influence over policy making. This influence can be seen to work in various ways.

The civil servants continue their work irrespective of alterations in political leadership, and often spend most of their working lives in one department. There may be great differences in ideas between civil servants and politicians over the aims of the department and the time-scale for their achievement. Ministers will usually want to establish a number of specific changes during their time in office to achieve the policies of their own party and for the good of their own careers. Civil servants, however, because of their longer association with departments are more likely to think long term.

The civil servants' familiarity with Whitehall and their particular department, together with access to information and knowledge gained over many years of service, gives them an expertise that is not easily challenged. Again *Yes Minister* gives a lighthearted but realistic representation of exactly how this familiarity and expertise can be used especially to resist change (Lynn and Jay, 1981). Ham (1992) cites Young and Sloman (1986) to argue that often the strength of a particular department's view on an issue must be overcome to achieve successful policy change.

Parties in opposition often devote little time to developing the detail of the policies they intend to carry out when in office. Manifesto proposals, for example, are often very general in nature and may be modified extensively by civil servants as they are developed into policy. Ministers may be poorly prepared and lack the administrative and analytical skills necessary to counter the weight of advice offered by the civil servants. Ministers on obtaining office may do so in departments in which they did not specialize earlier, for example as shadow ministers.

Interdepartmental committees are a key source of civil service power as they prepare the ground for ministers and cabinet committees, often to such an extent, it is said, that it is difficult for ministers to reach any other conclusion than that already decided by the officials. Although the civil service is free from overt party-political domination, civil servants have values and beliefs of their own which may of course differ from those of their ministers and thus also affect policy achievement and success (Levitt and Wall, 1992). Nonetheless the history of the Thatcher years and also the first postwar Labour government shows that even British governments can achieve great changes if they set their hearts on them.

Ministers are expected to do a huge variety of jobs such as

running their department, participating in cabinet and cabinet committee discussions, taking care of their constituents in their role as MPs and taking part in the work of the House of Commons. With so many competing demands on their time, it is certainly much easier for ministers to accept the advice they are given rather than to attempt an independent policy-making role (Ham, 1992; Levitt and Wall, 1992).

Specialist political advisers, however, have at times been appointed in attempts to enhance ministers' policy-making role. Such advisers may supply a different perspective and alternative briefings to those offered by the civil service. This was the intention in 1983 when the Secretary of State for Social Services, Norman Fowler, asked Sir Roy Griffiths, the managing director of Sainsbury's, to examine the workings of the NHS (Levitt and Wall, 1992). Ham (1992) suggests that such advisers are likely to become increasingly significant in the policy process. However, the quality of such advice has been questioned, particularly in the case of the NHS, as being too ideologically motivated and without sufficient knowledge of the NHS (Levitt and Wall, 1992).

Pressure groups

Pressure groups attempt to influence policy making at both national and local levels. Relationships between pressure groups and governments vary but Ham (1992) uses Beer's (1969) work to suggest that it is the producer groups, such as the British Medical Association (BMA) for example, which have the greatest influence over policy formulation, implementation and outcome. He argues that producer groups and governments are brought together by the desire of the groups to influence policy decisions and the need of the government for the information and co-operation such groups are able to offer for the successful implementation of policy.

The medical profession

The medical profession is involved in policy decision making at various different points and levels. Firstly, there is the profession's contribution to policy making within the Department of Health and through the Department's consultative machinery. Secondly at RHA level the profession's views are heard through members of the authority from medical backgrounds and via medical advisory committees. DHAs too have access to medical advice from doctors working in their local hospitals as well as from independent sources. The members of DHAs also usually include at least one doctor. FHSAs include a GP among their membership, receive advice from local medical committees, and may even appoint independent medical advisers. NHS Trusts usually include a medical director on their boards and rely extensively on advice received from their medical staff.

As well as having access to such authorities, the medical profession is in an influential position because of the role of doctors as direct providers of services. GPs, despite a tighter management framework and the imposition of developments such as medical audit, retain a good deal of freedom to organize their work and determine how services should be provided. Hospital doctors are salaried employees of the NHS but managers have difficulty controlling their actions, not least because of the power of 'clinical judgement'. Consequently, doctors determine what is best for their patients including the place and length of treatment, and the kinds of investigation to be carried out. Doctors therefore are the major resource consumers and controllers in health care.

A central issue in the implementation of health policy has been how to persuade or coerce doctors to organize their work in a way which is consistent with department and government priorities (Ham, 1992).

As resources have become more constrained increased attention has been given to this difficulty. Systems have been created to involve doctors in management and thereby make them more accountable for resources. The Resource Management Initiative, started in 1986, was one such attempt. It aimed to give doctors and nurses a bigger role in the management of resources (or some might argue the reduction of resources) by devolving budgetary responsibility to clinical teams. Similarly, under the 1990 NHS reforms, consultants were given the opportunity to head clinical directorates with responsibility for devolved budgets and GPs were given control of purchasing services through fundholding.

The nursing profession

The nursing profession is also a producer group and therefore should command substantial policy influence. In addition, it is often said, that nurses should be a powerful group in the policy-making and implementation process because of their numbers and their ability to command public sympathy. Nurses are responsible for the majority of professional health care given in the UK, comprise more than half of all NHS staff and consume nearly a quarter of all health service expenditure (Beardshaw, 1992). Yet nurses have traditionally not been militant or even very visible in policy terms. Some of the reasons for this are nurses' low level of political participation, our male-dominated political system and other issues such as gender and class which are explored further in the following chapters. They have tended to be ignored both by policy makers and policy analysts. Nursing and nursing issues therefore have been marginal to the debates that have shaped UK health policy (Robinson, Gray and Elkan, 1992).

Nurses, after achieving a relative peak in power terms as a result of the 1974 reorganization, have had their status and right to be represented in decision-making reduced. This movement was precipitated by the introduction of general management in 1984. In theory at least, nurses were potential candidates for general management jobs but few applied and even fewer were appointed. The Royal College of Nursing campaigned vociferously but unsuccessfully against this loss of status, despite highlighting the unique perspective that nurses are able to give. From holding posts accountable directly to health authorities, nurses became subordinate to district general managers. Many displaced senior nurses had to take up jobs with much less decision-making responsibilty and policy clout, such as in quality assurance.

The 1990 reforms have compounded this decline in policy-making power and influence. Virtually no nurses have been appointed as members of District Health Authorities. Nonetheless, as we will explore in more detail later, there has to be a non-executive nurse on FHSAs and an executive nurse member on the boards of Trusts. At local level the development of clinical directorates almost exclusively headed by doctors has also reduced the nursing profession's status and power. This situation is being mirrored in the community with nurses being placed under the ever closer control of GPs.

It remains to be seen whether or not the projected long-term shortages of staff, presently disguised by the recession, which have been cited by some authors as a catalyst for change will indeed materialize and increase nurses' bargaining and negotiating power.

Consumer groups

Consumer groups such as MIND and Age Concern are seen to have somewhat less influence than producer groups partly because their co-operation is usually not as crucial for policy makers as that of the professional groups. Information and expertise are primarily what consumer groups have to offer and consequently they have to operate through the use of influence rather than sanctions. In addition, consumers of services have been traditionally less well organized than producers; and consumers of some health services are less able to be active in applying consumer pressure. Nonetheless many organizations are consulted on a regular basis by governments and public money is given to support their activities. Such groups may also participate in advisory bodies which assist government in the development of policy. Yet not all groups can have access to governments in this way and many have to try to influence from a distance instead, using such vehicles as Parliament and the media.

Community Health Councils (CHCs) were established as a result of the 1974 NHS reorganization. Their function was to represent the views of local users of health services to the health authorities. Their establishment evolved primarily out of a concern that users of services could exert little influence on the provision and planning of services which were, up to that time, dominated by professionals.

CHC membership has been worked out principally on the basis of the size of the resident populations in districts, and ranges from eighteen in the smallest to twenty-four in the largest (Levitt and Wall, 1992). The RHA appoints the members, half of whom are nominated by the local authorities, one third by voluntary organizations and the remaining sixth by the RHAs. A limited number of people can also be co-opted. The money to pay salaries, office costs and other expenses is provided by the RHAs.

In order to be able to represent the views of the public the CHCs are first faced with the task of providing information to raise people's interest and awareness. CHC members give their time voluntarily and in addition to their other commitments. Consequently the degree to which CHCs can become known and hence be in a position to reflect the needs of local people is very dependent on the determination of the members and staff.

CHCs may appear to be pretty powerless in policy terms but they do have the right to ask for and receive information, send members to DHA meetings, visit NHS premises, be consulted about development plans and play a part in the service planning cycle, give evidence to official committees, enlist the support of MPs and use the media to articulate and publicize their views.

Nonetheless CHCs are reliant on DHAs and their staff for information and this tends to reduce their power to little more than giving a second opinion on plans. Since 1990 they no longer even have to be consulted when DHAs intend to introduce changes to local services. Their consultation is only required if their DHA deems it necessary. They have access to Trusts but do not have a right to examine GP services.

Despite the problems, CHCs, through their knowledge of the way the NHS works, and through their involvement in planning, have the potential to promote change and be advocates for local interests (Levitt and Wall, 1992).

In general, community interests do not seem to carry a great deal of weight in the policy-making process, despite government rhetoric enshrined in such documents as the Citizens' Charter (1992). It remains to be seen whether the trend to charters will have a significant effect on the way policies are implemented.

In summary then we have seen that central government promotes legislation, provides money, inspects and, on occasion, directly provides services but for the most part it needs the active co-operation of other bodies if it is to implement its policies successfully. (We will explore this in more detail when we analyse the setting up and development of the NHS in chapter 4). Central government is practically and politically restricted by the existence of power outside of the centre and by various forms of devolution and decentralization to local government, regional and district authorities, outside interests and by 'drag' and inertia in administrative institutions. Consequently we will now examine the power of such institutions.

Regions

The United Kingdom, for ease of administration, has been divided into a number of regions although at the time of writing this organizational tier is currently under review. These regions organize a range of State activities and services. Some of these regions coincide with national boundaries such as those of Scotland, Wales and Northern Ireland. They achieve a high degree of political visibility and importance as in the Scottish and Welsh Offices, for example. In England the boundaries usually represent little more than lines of administrative convenience and consequently may achieve little political prominence such as RHAs. Nonetheless over time any boundary may acquire significance and loyalty especially if it coincides with boundaries for other services or functions.

There are fourteen Regional Health Authorities in England serving populations from two million to over five million (Ham, 1992). The RHAs employ or are responsible for around one million people (4 per cent of the nation's workforce) and account for over 10 per cent of public expenditure (Dearlove and Saunders, 1991). They have a major responsibility for making policy (within guidelines established at the centre) and for allocating resources such as funding for nurse education.

RHAs are far fewer in number and larger in size than local government bodies and their members are unelected. Each authority comprises a chairman and five non-executive members appointed by the Secretary of State together with up to five executive members. The non-executives have to include a chairman of an FHSA and someone connected with a medical school in the region. Two of the executives, the general manager and chief finance officer, are members by virtue of their office. The remainder are appointed by the chairman, non-executive members and general manager acting together. Thus their accountability to local consumers is doubtful.

RHAs are accountable to the Secretary of State (Ham, 1992).

Their main work is to organize the region's health service resources in line with national and regional policy. They have, since 1989, been expected to work within a tight framework established at a national level by the Management Executive (ME) which also assesses their effectiveness in converting national policies into action. To this end in 1990 the ME negotiated a contract with each RHA concerning objectives, plans and resources in order to ensure that the NHS reforms were introduced on time and in a managed way. Other functions RHAs may carry out include service planning, staff development, information management, legal affairs and public relations.

Central government therefore has a very high level of control of RHAs. Ordinary people on the other hand are unlikely to be able to have much of a say in the activities of RHAs. Special interests, however, such as medicine, tend to achieve a relatively high degree of influence.

Since the NHS was established in 1948 it has consisted of three elements: the hospital sector; general practice and dentistry; and community health care. Until 1974 these were run by different agencies. Regional hospital boards and hospital management committees ran the hospitals, executive councils managed general practitioners and local government was responsible for community health. The 1974 reorganization brought all three branches under the control of the new RHAs in an attempt to increase efficiency and co-ordination (see chapter 4 for a more detailed discussion).

The functions of RHAs are mainly concerned with planning, resource allocation and the performance of DHAs and FHSAs. In the past RHAs provided some services directly but recently the Department of Health has encouraged them to concentrate on key strategic tasks such as the implementation of the NHS and Community Care Act. RHAs are also responsible for regulating the relationship between 'purchasers' and 'providers' of health services and ensuring that the availability and accessibility of services is maintained.

In principle the RHAs are run by their members who are appointed by the Secretary of State but in reality the full-time officers have control. In the early 1980s general managers were introduced to head regions, backed by their specialist teams and since then RHAs have been run more like private organizations.

With responsibility concentrated in just fourteen regional managers it has been relatively easy for central government to pursue its objectives without much resistance. This strong central control corresponds to the political weakness of the ordinary public. Central government finds it easier to deal with a small number of large bodies whereas to the public the RHAs seem remote and inaccessible. Similarly, while central government can extend its power and influence over bodies whose members are appointed rather than elected, members of the public are likely to find it much more difficult to have a voice when votes and support are not being competed for.

In the NHS, since the 1974 reorganization, consumer interests have supposedly been safeguarded by lay members on Regional Health Authorities and the Community Health Councils (CHCs). Yet consumer influence, despite government rhetoric, has been limited. Regional Health Authority representatives do not represent any particular group or interest. They are part-time 'amateurs' dealing with full-time 'experts' and are usually unrepresentative of the population as a whole, being mainly from the managerial and professional classes, with health-care professionals predominating. The CHCs on the other hand (as discussed earlier) are weak. They have no executive powers, tiny budgets and are frequently invisible to the vast majority of the public they are supposed to represent.

Special interests, particularly medical, are also very strong at RHA level. The doctors exert their influence in three ways. First they have strong and effective representation through the Medical Advisory Committees which are consulted frequently at regional level. Second, NHS managers are themselves often doctors. Thirdly, decisions at all levels are informed by a too infrequently questioned assumption that health care is only about curing disease.

District Health Authorities

Below the RHA level in health care there are DHAs. There has always been a tier of management at local level in the NHS. There are around 190 DHAs in England, and they were created in the 1982 reorganization. Before 1982 the regions were divided into areas, and about two thirds of these areas were divided into health districts. Under the 1982 reorganization, arrangements were simplified by amalgamating areas and districts to form DHAs. Members are appointed in a way similar to those of RHAs and the DHA works as a corporate body accountable to the RHA.

In the past the main responsibilities of DHAs were to manage hospitals and other services within the resources allocated by the RHA. The district's resident population is the basis of its financial allocation from the region. Under the NHS and Community Care Act 1990 DHAs have become purchasers of services for their residents. Their functions thus include assessing their populations' need for health care, evaluating the effectiveness of different services, and negotiating contracts with providers for the delivery of services. Providers are units, hospitals and other health-care facilities and DHAs can buy services from whichever provider is prepared to make them available. In deciding which services to purchase DHAs are expected to work closely with FHSAs, GPs, local authorities and other agencies. In the past DHAs managed hospitals and units, and carried out functions such as personnel, finance and information services but, as a result of the NHS and Community Care Act DHAs are to concentrate on their purchasing role and a number of public health functions. The NHS Trusts and Directly Managed Units have been made responsible for the other functions.

DHAs, like RHAs, have an important role in policy implementation as they may adapt national and regional policies to fit in with their own preferences and local needs. Such variation is controlled by close contact with the RHAs. DHAs must produce plans setting out their purchasing intentions and objectives, based on strategic aims agreed with the RHAs. Ham (1992) points out that, as with RHAs, DHAs have been subject to increasing control from above, particularly in implementation of the NHS reforms: thus the room for local manoeuvre has been reduced. Despite these new mechanisms of control, however, most changes in service provision need the involvement and acquiescence of a large number of individuals or interest groups and consequently regional policies may not be implemented by districts.

The local level

The powers of local government are devolved from general government: such powers can be revoked or changed by a government with an effective majority in the Commons. There is no single UK local government system. There are instead different systems in England, Wales, Northern Ireland and Scotland. Local government is seen as a check on the central State and a way of providing services that are attuned to local needs (Dearlove and Saunders, 1991). Local health officials, however, are not elected. There are also no local health committees, unlike the arrangements for social services, education and housing. Consequently this raises questions about the full existence of democracy in health and accountability to users.

Local government is responsible to elected councils and local government expenditure counts for approximately a quarter of all public expenditure. Councillors, however, are predominantly male and have mainly professional and managerial backgrounds, many in the public sector (Dearlove and Saunders, 1991). Local government raises some of its own revenue through the Council Tax (previously through rates and then through community charge or 'poll tax'). Its revenue includes user charges such as rents paid by council tenants and central-government grants and loans for major investments such as school buildings. Many Acts passed during the 1980s have sought to increase central government's financial control over local government and thus to control expenditure.

Local government then is in a position to be able to challenge to some extent the policies of central government and to provide a medium through which groups excluded from effective representation at the centre such as pressure groups and local voluntary organizations can try to secure what they want from the local public purse.

The local level of policy making and administration also contains many institutions run by people for whom we never have the opportunity to vote such as: the chief constables who control the police; the local magistrates who administer justice; and the various local authority implementation agencies such as housing and social services departments, to name but a few. Consequently, many of the decisions which affect our everyday lives are not taken by elected local councillors. To conclude there is much more to the local State than simply elected local government.

The operation of non-elected agencies within the local arena is not a new phenomenon and has grown since the mid 1970s. In 1979 the Conservative government at the centre attempted to bypass local authorities that were hostile to the aims and concerns of the Thatcher agenda through the setting up of agencies such as the Urban Development Corporations to take over planning and development in a number of urban areas. The Conservative government has seen such single-purpose agencies both as being more amenable to their policy influence and as a way of constraining local government spending.

The Thatcher government also encouraged the growth of non-elected local agencies. For example, laws that have enabled public-sector tenants to opt out of the local authority system have expanded the range of non-elected agencies in the form of Housing Trusts (Dearlove and Saunders, 1991). Since the early 1980s there has also been a substantial growth in initiatives to encourage the private sector to provide services that were traditionally provided by local government, for example provision of continuing care for older people and people with disabilities (Department of Health, 1989b).

Family Health Services Authorities

DHAs are responsible for purchasing hospital and community health services and FHSAs (which have succeeded the old Family Practitioner Committees) manage the services provided by general practitioners, dentists, pharmacists and opticians. These practitioners are independent contractors and are not employees of the NHS. Their terms and conditions of work are negotiated nationally and FHSAs are responsible for implementing the national contracts. There are ninety FHSAs in England serving populations ranging from about 130,000 to 1,600,000. Each comprises a chairman appointed by the Secretary of State, five lay non-executive members and four professional non-executives – a GP, a dentist, a pharmacist and a community nurse – appointed by the RHA, and a general manager appointed by the chairman and the non-executive members. Many of the general managers who have been appointed came from the main stream of health-services management. FHSAs work as corporate bodies and are accountable to the RHAs.

FHSAs perform a variety of functions including managing the contracts of the family practitioners, paying the practitioners, providing information to the public and dealing with complaints. They are also responsible for maintaining lists of practitioners and dealing with applications to join these lists; approving surgery locations and hours of availability; checking the standard of premises; and authorizing and monitoring the use of deputizing services. As a result of the 1990 NHS reforms FHSAs have also become responsible for new functions including: introducing medical audit; reducing drug expenditure through indicative prescribing budgets; assessing their population's need for primary health services; and allocating funds for developments to meet these needs.

FHSAs are accountable to RHAs who set objectives for them, monitor their achievements and review their plans and priorities. This should, as Ham (1992) points out, mean opportunities for closer integration of hospital and community health services and ensure greater consistency and quality of such services.

NHS Trusts

NHS Trusts began to come into existence in April 1991. They are self-governing units within the NHS and are run by boards of directors who are accountable directly to the Secretary of State. Trust boards comprise a chairman appointed by the Secretary of State, and an equal number of executive and non-executive directors. Of the non-executive members, two are drawn from the local community and are appointed by the RHA. The rest are appointed by the Secretary of State. In Trusts providing direct patient care there is also a medical director and a nursing director.

The main function of the Trusts is to manage the services for which they are responsible. They have more freedom than Directly Managed Units (DMUs) such as: being able to determine their own management structures, employ their own staff and set pay and conditions for them; acquire, own and sell their own assets; retain surpluses and borrow money, subject to annual limits. They are not completely free however. Each is required to prepare an annual business plan which is discussed with the ME and to publish annual reports and accounts and give the general public opportunity at an annual meeting to discuss them.

Industrial and commercial interests

Ham (1992) identifies at least three sets of interests that need to be considered with regard to the formulation and implementation of health policy. First there are those interests which are involved in the provision of private-sector health care services such as BUPA and the private hospital groups. This sector expanded markedly throughout the 1980s but little is known about the mechanisms by which such private providers attempt to influence the policy makers.

Secondly, there are the interests of those who supply health care goods, equipment and services such as pharmaceutical companies and manufacturers of medical equipment. For example, there are interests of manufacturers of baby milks who give 'bounty bags' of their products to new mothers despite the current professional emphasis on breast-feeding; the interests of manufacturers of stoma products who sponsor nurse advisers in hospital and community settings; and similarly, there is the effect of the pharmaceutical lobby on the limited prescribing list.

Finally there are the companies that produce goods which may be harmful to health such as the food, alcohol and tobacco industries. Ham (1992) cites Taylor's (1984) analysis of why governments have done so little to regulate the tobacco industry despite the vast amount of evidence regarding the harmful effects of smoking. Taylor suggests that the power of the tobacco industry lies in its position in the economy and its significance as a source of tax revenue. Similar analyses relating to alcohol and food emphasize the relatively weak and diffuse nature of the groups pressing for reforms, the economic and political power of commerce notably through political donations and opposition from the government departments who benefit from such industries.

International agreements and interests

It is impossible to study policy making and implementation without attending to international politics and policy-making bodies. We are an open political system and are members of a variety of organizations such as the European Community, WHO and United Nations, which have varying degrees of significance for our domestic politics and policy making. Consider, for example, the targets for 'Health for all by the year 2000', a declaration of intent to which the British government is a signatory. Additionally the recent EC regulations on lifting and handling have tremendous implications for nursing practice in Britain.

Conclusions

We have shown that health policy making involves a wide range of interests from the Department of Health through to professionals and commerce, each seeking to influence what is decided. Policy implementation too involves negotiation and bargaining between these competing demands. The medical profession maintains a powerful position and any policies which actively challenge its interests are likely to be strongly resisted. On the other hand the influence of the nursing profession has been relatively invisible. Increasingly the Management Executive and Trusts are playing a bigger part at all stages of the health-policy process.

Discussion points

1. Identify the key actors in the policy-making process.
2. Discuss why a study of policy implementation is vital to policy analysis.
3. Explain nursing and nurses' invisibility and relative lack of influence in the policy process. Critically consider:
   (a) how this influence might be increased and
   (b) the importance of increasing this influence.

Further reading

Courtney, R. (1987) Community practice: nursing influence on policy
formulation. *Nursing Outlook* July/August, 35(4), pp. 170–173
Details nursing influence at the formulation stage of the policy process
and argues for action in this area.

References

Beardshaw, V. Prospects for nursing, in Beck, *et al.* (1992) *In the Best of
Health? The Status and Future of Health Care in the UK*, Chapman and
Hall, London
Dearlove, J. and Saunders, P. (1984) *Introduction to British Politics*, 2nd
edn, Polity Press, Cambridge
Department of Health (1989a) *Working for Patients*, HMSO, London
Department of Health (1989b) *Caring for People*, HMSO, London
Ham, C. (1992) *Health Policy in Britain: The Politics and Organization of
the National Health Service*, 3rd edn, Macmillan, Basingstoke.
Ham, C. and Hill, M. (1984) *The Policy Process in the Modern Capitalist
State*, Wheatsheaf Books, Brighton
Harvey, J. and Bather, L. (1972) *The British Constitution*, 3rd edn,
Macmillan, Basingstoke
Levitt, R. and Wall, A. (1992) *The Reorganised National Health Service*,
4th edn, Chapman and Hall, London
Lynn, J. and Jay, A. (1981 and 1982) *Yes Minister: The Diaries of a
Cabinet Minister by the Rt Hon. James Hacker MP*, (i) p. 170, vol 1 and
2, British Broadcasting Corporation, London
Robinson, J., Gray, A. and Elkan, R. (ed.) (1992) *Policy Issues in
Nursing*, Open University Press, Buckingham

3

Understanding State action: perspectives on welfare and power

Pippa Gough

Introduction

As we have seen in the previous chapters, any definition of social policy involves making reference to the Welfare State and its role in the making and implementing of public policy. There is no doubt that, even in its present-day reduced and somewhat dismantled form, the State and its policies still have a profound impact on people's lives. State regulation is experienced in one form or another from birth to death – consider, for example, the initial contact with the health services, registration of birth, the payment of taxes, provision of housing, receipt of State benefits and final registration of death. Central to any analysis of social policy therefore, is an in-depth examination of the way the Welfare State works and its involvement in the making of decisions and the taking of actions which affect people's lives. This process is fundamentally about the allocation of values – values which reflect beliefs concerning the overall purpose of welfare. What these values are or how they are analysed depends upon one's political viewpoint and the theoretical approach taken. These varying perspectives of welfare are the focus of this chapter.

The chapter begins by clarifying the exact nature and composition of the Welfare State – material which is basically a summary of that offered in previous chapters. It then moves on to explore a number of perspectives, or theories, of welfare which have consituted the mainstream theoretical terrain of the discipline of Social Policy over the last couple of decades. These perspectives offer different explanations to questions such as: what is the relationship between welfare and society? What is the role of the State in the provision of welfare services? What are the goals of welfare and have these been achieved? What values and beliefs are informing the social policies that shape our personal and, as nurses, our professional lives? This is a multifaceted and complex discussion and consequently only the main tenets are sketched out here, further reading being available in specialist texts which are listed at the end of the chapter. Following on from this, the focus shifts to an examination of the part power plays in the policy process, drawing on a variety of theories about the distribution of economic and political power within society and its systems of government, and the ways that power operates, both overtly and covertly in reaching policy decisions. Power is particularly pertinent when considering the position of nurses and nursing and their ability to influence the public policy agenda. This theme of power, and the existence of 'systems of domination' is one to which we return throughout the book.

Defining the State

Central to any examination of State action is a clear understanding of what the 'State', within contemporary British society, actually is. Previous chapters have explored this concept in some detail and have shown that the State can be understood both in terms of the institutions of which it is composed and the functions which these institutions perform. Ham and Hill (1984) identify state institutions as comprising: legislative bodies, for example, Parliament and associated law-making machinery; executive bodies, such as departments of State, government offices etc; and judicial bodies which refer mainly to the courts of law. In order to sustain and uphold these institutions the political system, in common with all political systems worldwide, employs police and armed forces to ensure internal order and stability and external security. In Britain these forces are, for the most part, subordinate to the State and political structure and this, for example, differentiates this State system from military dictatorships or police states.

Traditionally, the State organizations providing the vast range of public services, that is housing, education, health, pensions, income support and so on, have been grouped together under the collective title of the 'Welfare State'. However, as explained in chapters 1 and 2, 'welfare' today is increasingly understood to mean more than State services, in that public provision is set alongside the three other sectors of private, informal and voluntary welfare. This means that discussion of the Welfare State entails consideration being given not only to decisions being taken in the State sector, but the actions of, and the interactions with, the other sectors as well.

The organizations that go to make up the Welfare State are located at national, regional and local levels and differ enormously in managerial, organizational and political structure. Additionally, the degree of autonomy exercised by peripheral bodies in relation to central institutions may vary considerably. As Ham and Hill (1984) point out, this freedom to act is important as it means that not all central policies will be implemented at a local level. In understanding welfare policy, therefore, it is important to consider the role of the local state as well as the role of the national state. A good example of this in action is the case of the community charge or 'poll tax'. Although instituted and backed at a central government and national State level, many local government agencies chose not to enforce its implementation too vigorously. The discrepancy between the political influences and values at a local State level and those at a national level became explicit during this policy episode.

As seen in the previous chapters, it is really only during this century that the state has become so involved in the provision of welfare services as well as taking on a significant role in the operation of the economy, for example through public ownership of certain industries (now rare), shielding of monopolies, subsidies and tax concessions for industrial development and so on. Until the last decade or so, much of these economic-management policies were based on the thinking of J. M. Keynes, an economist who rose to fame in the 1930s. Keynes believed that the manipulation of fiscal policy to control and shape the economy in times of boom and slump, was a proper and ethical role for the State. In this way the rise and fall of unemployment, and all the attendant difficulties of having large numbers of people out of work and impoverished, could be smoothed out. During times of recession this involved cutting taxes and increasing public works on roads or on the railway, to reduce unemployment. Alternatively, in boom times, government programmes were cut and taxes were raised in a bid to cool off the economy and stop it overheating (Green, 1987).

The next part of this chapter moves on to explore those political beliefs and attitudes that fuelled the growth of the State in this way, and those which in latter years have set about dismantling it.

Perspectives on welfare

Since the turn of the century and the rapid growth of the State sector, Social Policy as a discipline has attempted to articulate the thinking behind welfarist intervention. Up until the 1970s, much of this discussion centred on the politics of 'collectivism', or a commitment to State intervention and the universal delivery of services as a way of responding to and resolving social problems and social need. Alternatively, 'anti-collectivism' endorses the freedom of the individual from State interference, and the freedom to act in the market economy – that is an economy based on the buying and selling of commodities, the price of which is determined by a system of demand and supply. The purchase of groceries, shoes or books, for example, normally occurs within a free market (that is, with limited State controls), and this type of transaction can be said to be part and parcel of the 'market economy'.

Collectivism had its origins in early Fabianism – a movement which espoused a gradual move to socialism through State reforms and the remedying of poverty, disease, squalor, hunger and so on by providing professional welfare services and State regulation of the economy. Fabianism is fundamentally concerned with such values as equality, freedom and fellowship. As Williams (1989i) explains:

> Fabians are deeply committed to equality for the sake of social harmony, social efficiency, natural justice and the realization of collective potential. Alongside this they are humanitarians, they give priority to the alleviation of misery, and put a premium on co-operation and on democracy.

This Fabian-dominated mainstream began to be challenged from the start of the 1970s by a number of different critiques of the Welfare State which previously had been marginalized within the social-policy debate (Williams, 1989). From the political right, a powerful anti-collectivist lobby, in the form of the New Right was growing in strength in the Conservative Party (Green, 1987), while from the left, a Marxist 'political economy of welfare' perspective (Gough, 1979) was gaining credibility. A feminist critique of public policy was being developed within the women's movement (eg Finch and Groves, 1983; Pascall, 1986; Williams, 1989) and more recently a powerful critique of race-relations policies has begun to emerge (e.g. Ben-Tovim *et al.*, 1986; Gilroy, 1987; Williams, 1989).

The emergence and growing recognition of a plurality of critiques and theoretical approaches to understanding the relationship between welfare and society has given rise to substantial debate within the discipline of Social Policy. Much of this discussion has revolved around trying to describe, classify and distinguish between these explanations of State action. Williams (1989) offers a number of frameworks for distinguishing between these perspectives in terms of their welfare norms and goals, their values and the sorts of explanations they have *of* social problems and *for* social change. She suggests that all the different theoretical approaches can be loosely organized into five main groups. Basically these are: anti-collectivism; social reformism (incorporating new forms of Fabianism); political economy of welfare (Marxist critique); feminist critique; and anti-racist critique. Each of these groups of perspectives, or ways of viewng the Welfare State, can be associated broadly with a particular political tradition and particular writers or political thinkers, and these are now discussed in more detail.

Anti-collectivism

This category of perspectives has its historical roots in the nineteenth century in the form of 'classical liberalism' and is associated with the name of Adam Smith, an economic commentator of the eighteenth century who wrote *The Wealth of Nations*, published in 1776. Classical liberalism promoted the free market as being the best method of securing individual's needs and desires. In other words, people could buy what services they needed as and when they needed them. Williams (1989) suggests that from this perspective State intervention was considered anathema to social stability, creating more social ills than it resolved. The *'laissez faire'* policies of this time placed great importance on self-help and self-reliance, which was to be supported and supplemented with charity, as necessary, and a minimal welfare safety net provided through the workhouse under the Poor Law (as discussed in chapter 1). Welfare in this form was designed to act as a deterrent and was highly punitive. Much of the stigma of receiving welfare support today derives from this time.

More recent exponents of this liberalism, known as neo-liberals, eg Friedrich Hayek and Milton Friedman, writing this century, continue to espouse the values of the freedom of the individual to act in the market economy, and see State intervention as an infringement of this freedom. These ideas have fed into the policies of the New Right regimes which have held sway in the Conservative party since Margaret Thatcher's terms of office as Prime Minister (Green, 1987). New Right principles stress the need for economic freedom, distribution through the free market and reduction of State intervention – an approach which is combined with a social authoritarianism, urging individuals to stand on their own feet and break their dependency on the State. Accordingly, provision of services is ideally expected to come from the private or voluntary sector as well as through family and self-help.

From this perspective, Green (1987) argues that State welfare is seen as being paternalistic and authoritarian in dictating how needs should be met. It inhibits individual freedom in that consumers have no choice or control in the type of, and the way in which, welfare services are delivered. What's more, the individual's freedom to purchase services elsewhere is limited by having to pay the taxes necessary to fund the State machinery. The State is seen as wasteful, inefficient and even morally disruptive – through encouraging scroungers, removing motivation to work and usurping the position of the family. Additionally, the New Right suggests that the monolithic bureaucracy set up to support and operate the State has become self-serving, denying adequate choice and control to welfare consumers. A similar radical critique is directed at welfare professionalism, which contends that the professionals involved in the provision and delivery of State services, such as nurses and doctors are acting in their own interests, rather than to the benefit of the user (Green, 1987).

Williams (1989) argues that this anti-collectivist account of welfare is fundamentally flawed. It disregards those processes which render some people less able to choose and buy their education, housing, own systems of transport or health services. The social causes of problems are disregarded – if the individual is poor or sick or in debt then this is due to the individual's own actions, or inactions. The solution is seen as lying in self-help and self-reliance, rather than through a reorganization of society, or a curbing of capitalism. This perspective, and the policies derived from it over the last decade, are re-examined in the following chapters.

Social reformism/collectivism

When the new critiques of Marxism, feminism, anti-racism and anti-collectivism began to challenge the Fabian-dominated mainstream of welfare thinking, Williams (1989) suggests that the Fabianism of the pre-1970s fragmented into three strands: the non-socialist Fabians; the socialist Fabians; and the radical social administration theoretical approach. All of these perspectives have their roots in collectivism and embody varying commitments towards and reasons for State-provided welfare. Each of these strands will now be discussed individually.

The non-socialist Fabians support State intervention to provide welfare, but are pragmatists in terms of how these services are delivered and by whom. That is, they believe in a mix of public, private, voluntary and informal welfare, currently referred to as the 'mixed economy of welfare'. Writers and thinkers in this field include, amongst others, Beveridge, responsible for the setting up of the Welfare State in Britain (see chapter 1), David Owen and Keynes. Williams (1989) explains that this group share with the anti-collectivists a belief in the free market and the maintenance of capitalism, but realize that a capitalist system will create casualties, which require State support. The non-socialist Fabians see improvements in society coming about as a result of pressure-group action and encouraging collective commitment to the national interest.

Williams (1989) describes this perspective as idealist (as opposed to the anti-collectivists being individualist), in that change for the better in society is seen as being linked to changing attitudes and beliefs. Beveridge maintained that the need for the state to provide welfare was fundamentally a moral argument – that is there is a moral obligation to support the less well off in society.

Fabian socialism represents the fundamental core of the original Fabian Society, the dominant values and beliefs of which have already been described above. Fabian socialists view the system of capitalism as being unjust, amoral, unethical and undemocratic. However, unlike Marxists, a revolution is not deemed necessary to rectify this, as all inequalities can be remedied by government action and the Welfare State. This group see welfarism as being the vehicle for promoting equality of opportunity, redistribution of wealth, social harmony and eliciting actual material changes. In other words, the Welfare State and State intervention are fundamental to counter the inequalities of the private market. Williams (1989) suggests that Titmuss, Tawney and the politician Richard Crosland are the writers most associated with this perspective.

The Radical social administration view, as with all the collectivist perspectives, sees the Welfare State as being central in meeting the needs of society, but it has a Marxist underpinning. In other words class relations, the structure of society and the unequal distribution of resources under a capitalist system are the cause of social problems. The solutions lie in the radical social planning of society by means of the radical redistribution of wealth and resources according to need, combined with the pursuit of equality. For this group, public policy has predominance over economic policy as a way of re-dressing the inequalities created by capitalism. Major writers in this field include Townsend and his work on the concept of relative poverty (Williams, 1989).

Marxist critique

Drawing on the work of O'Connor (1973) and Gough (1979),

Williams (1989) describes this approach as an analysis of the 'political economy of welfare' or a critique of welfare under capitalism. From this perspective the Welfare State is seen as a result of the conflict and tension between capitalism and the working class, that is:

> the working class struggling for changes in their interests, for greater security or for more rights, and the capitalist class attempting to maintain political stability, but also ensuring policies for the maintenance of capitalism. (Williams, 1989ii)

This critique contends that welfarism has two faces, namely: as a 'sop' to the working class to fend off mass discontent and ensure a healthy workforce for the good of capitalism; and as a benevolent provider of material comfort and benefits, hard won as the result of the working-class struggle and the capitulation of capital.

This duality of the Welfare State, both helping and constraining the working class, means that the creation of social policies to effect change is theoretically an impossible task – to do away with the State is to lose the benefits, while endorsing or increasing the role of the State may only serve to increase the control and constraints imposed through welfare.

Williams (1989) describes the explanation of welfare offered by a Marxist perspective as being both materialist and structuralist (as opposed to idealist or individualist), as it identifies the structures of capitalism as the forces which dictate the social relations of society. These social relations, however, are based on a conflict of interests: the interests of workers to improve the material and social conditions of their lives; and the interests of capitalism to maximize profits. The resulting struggle leads to change, such as the development of the Welfare State. This perspective explains the way in which people's lives are constrained by the structure of society, as well as allowing room for an understanding of how people act for themselves in pursuit of materialism. In other words, people do exert some control over their lives and are not total puppets of the wider social forces.

Williams (1989) argues that this perspective gives a much more rounded explanation of welfare than the other theories discussed so far. Individualism (as described within the anti-collectivist view) recognizes the person's actions but not the structure; and idealism (with its origins in Fabianism) sees change as occurring through adoption of superior values, for example equity and equality, but provides no explanation as to why society needs these values, that is, why is society not equal and not equitable to start with.

A fuller discussion of this perspective appears in chapter 11 when class as a basis of power in the policy process is examined.

Feminist critique

It is only relatively recently that the feminist critique of postwar welfarism has started to be recognized as having legitimate concerns with regard to the values and assumptions inherent in public policy. As Pascall (1986) and Williams (1989) both point out, the collectivist Welfare State has to be understood as developing within a capitalist system, which was itself under-pinned by the social relations of patriarchy and, as is seen in the next section, of imperialism. From this perspective the ideologies of sexism and racism have been seen to shape fundamentally and find expression in, not only the entire system of state welfare policies and practices, but also in Social Policy as a discipline.

In brief, early Fabianism embodied ideas about family and motherhood which have since served to control the lives of women within the home and constrain their development outside of the domestic sphere. The predominant Fabian view of the family, the breadwinner father and the dependent wife, as being the basic unit of welfare consumption, has militated against women claiming benefits in their own right and finding work outside the home, and has allowed the Welfare State to be built on the backs of women's unpaid domestic labour and informal care giving (Pascall, 1986; Williams, 1989).

The feminist critique of welfare can itself be subdivided and split into a variety of different approaches, all of which have their own analyses of welfare and its goals and values, and which proscribe their own strategies for social change. Williams (1989) lists these approaches as: libertarian feminism; liberal feminism; welfare feminism; radical feminism; social feminism; and black feminism. These are not explored further here, as chapter 6 is devoted to an exploration of gender and social policy issues and these theoretical approaches will underpin this discussion. The feminist critique of welfarism is of growing importance in helping us to understand the relationship between women, the family and the State.

Anti-racist critique

The race and gender blindness of the mainstream, Fabian-inspired, collectivist approach to understanding and developing social policies has already been indicated in discussions above. Williams (1989) points out that aspects of racism and the black experience of the Welfare State have either been ignored or distorted in both descriptive and analytical accounts of social policy. The development of ideas about, and the evidence for the existence of, an institutionalized racism, that is a system of domination based on race, has tended to change this, although a distinct anti-racist critique has not yet fully emerged from these challenges in the same way as has happened with feminist theories. Much of Williams' (1989) work is involved in trying to construct this critique.

Issues concerning the adequacies of public policy in serving the needs of black and minority ethnic groups in Britain are fully explored in chapter 8.

Having explored briefly the main tenets of the differing approaches to viewing and understanding welfarism and the actions and role of the state in the welfare policy arena, it is necessary to explore the part power plays within the policy process. The following section begins with an explanation of the distribution of economic and political power within society and the State and thereafter, the way power operates will be considered.

The distribution of power and the policy process

The actions of the State and the effectiveness of its policies cannot be assessed independently of an analysis of economic and political power within political systems. Although power itself was not explicity discussed in the exploration of the various theoretical approaches to welfare, there was an implicit suggestion that each perspective located power differently within the relationship between welfare and society. For example, the Marxist critique saw the vested interests of capitalism as a powerful force in the development of welfare policy, while the collectivist approach was seen by feminists and the anti-racist critique to be fundamentally informed by dominant male and white interests.

Within the policy arena, the operation of power is the process by which the interests of one group are recognized and acted upon over and above the interests of another – a process which may well mean unequal and inequitable outcomes within political decision making. Differing theoretical approaches have been developed to explain the distribution of power among competing interest groups both within and without the political structure, of which four will be discussed here, namely: pluralism; elitism; Marxism; and corporatism. These are explored only briefly, guidance being given at the end of the chapter for further reading. The way these approaches link into the broad classification of welfare action outlined above will become apparent.

Pluralist theory

The pluralist approach focuses on interests and groups in society and their relation to government and the development of public policy. Dearlove and Saunders (1991) explain that in the first half of this century, political theory did not place much importance on the role of interest groups within the political system, rather attention tended to centre on the constitution and explanations of voting behaviour as methods of influencing policy making. It was only in the 1960s that pluralism rose to prominence as *the* theory to make sense of British politics, by suggesting that interest-group politics was the way the political system in Britain really functioned.

The foremost exponent of this school of thought is Robert Dahl, who carried out an empirical study of power at local-government level in the town of New Haven, USA, in 1961 (Ham and Hill, 1984). Dahl argued that power in Western industrialized societies is widely, but unequally, distributed among a variety of different pressure or interest groups. No group is without the power to influence decision making in respect of policy, and ultimately no group can be seen to be dominant. If it is sufficiently determined, any group can ensure that its voice is heard at some stage in the policy-making process.

In essence, Ham and Hill (1984) describe pluralism as presenting the political system as resembling a political market-place where what a group achieves depends on its resources and its 'decibel rating'. In other words if the feelings of the group are sufficiently intense and it is prepared to shout loud enough, then political action will follow. Correspondingly, if a group fails to have its interests placed on the political agenda, then this is symptomatic of the group not feeling strongly enough, rather than of a situation of powerlessness. From this perspective, it is interest groups, not individuals, parties or classes who are the crucial policy actors.

Underlining this model is the idea of a State which is neutral and open to external influence, which is constantly taking account of public opinion and shaping policies accordingly. The State is seen as divorced from any one class, race or sex and is not an instrument of the economically powerful. In other words the State is not generating its own policy, rather government and State agencies can in fact be seen as one set of pressure groups among many others (Dearlove and Saunders, 1991).

Much of this pluralist understanding of power, as being diffused and fragmented throughout society, correlates with the mainstream collectivist approach to understanding welfarism. The Welfare State and the policy decisions taken to provide welfare, can thus be seen as resulting from the demand of pressure groups for increased State response to the ills of society. However, just as the collectivist way of viewing welfare began to be attacked in the 1970s, with the development of the New Right, Marxist, feminist and anti-racist critiques, the pluralist account of power, interest groups and democracy also began to be severely criticized from this time.

Dearlove and Saunders (1991) describe exponents of the New Right as condemning the whole interest-group system as being out of control. The New Right point to organized labour and the unions as being overwhelmingly dominant in the world of interests, resulting in an overload of demands on government, the

State and the national purse. Taxes have risen out of control in order to finance the public services demanded by interest groups.

A Marxist perspective argues that pluralist thinking, far from being purely a theoretical view, does in fact have an ideological underpinning. As an ideology, pluralist beliefs are instilled into common sense thinking in such a way as to veil the reality of power and help the legitimization of a system which is grounded fundamentally in inequality and domination (Dearlove and Saunders, 1991). Feminist and anti-racist critiques reject pluralist explanations on the same grounds (Williams, 1989).

Elite theory

Elite theory challenges the view that power is distributed between interests groups as described by pluralists. Rather, as Ham and Hill (1984) explain, power from this perspective is seen as being concentrated in the hands of a minority of the population, that is a political elite. It is argued that this political elite is composed of military leaders, members of the government, leaders of powerful economic enterprises, possibly influential members of the aristocracy, leaders of political parties in opposition, trade-union leaders, businessmen and politically-active intellectuals. Often this elite is unified through common experiences, such as having attended the same schools or universities and having similar career pathways. It is argued that they may well share the same values or even have kinship ties linking into common backgrounds and processes of socialization.

Dunleavy and O'Leary (1987) suggest that from this perspective, with power seen to be concentrated in the hands of the minority elite, the democratic apparatus becomes increasingly fictitious. In other words, plurality does not exist. The key elites, outside of the political arena, make polity and policy decisions for all. From the feminist or anti-racist perspective, conclusions might easily be drawn as to the colour, race and sex of these key elites and the effect this non-representation of women and black people may well have on policy decisions.

C. Wright Mills, in a study of the USA in the 1950s (cited Ham and Hill, 1984) concluded that the overlap and connection between the leaders of institutions such as government, business corporations and the military went some way to create a coherent and resilient power elite. However, Dearlove and Saunders (1984) argue that the evidence of a power elite operating in contemporary Britain seems slim. They suggest that the activity and influence of groups in one area of policy are not often transferable to another, citing, as an example, teachers' unions, which may play a significant role in the educational policy arena but have little input into shaping defence policy. Likewise, military leaders are unlikely to determine the content of the national curriculum.

As with pluralist approaches, the elite explanation of power in State action and policy making has for the most part been abandoned. Marxist theory in particular suggests that the power elite is but a ruling class by any other name. As Ham and Hill (1984) explain, this view contends that institutions may well be run by minority groups, but that these groups come from similar social backgrounds and are therefore exercising power in the interests of a dominant class. At this point elite theory merges into the Marxist explanation of power.

Marxist theory

This approach to understanding the role of power in the political system and the making of policy has already been explored to some extent in the previous section. Marxist theory essentially points to the continued concentration of wealth in a small section of the population, a situation which raises questions about whether this economically-dominant class is able to exercise decisive political power. In other words, a Marxist approach explores the relationship between economic power and political power.

In a classic work, Miliband (1969, cited Ham and Hill, 1984) argues that unlike the pluralist interpretation, the State is by no means a neutral agent. Rather it has an in-built bias towards the interests of the propertied classes. As such it is an instrument for class domination – an approach that has come to be known as 'instrumentalism'. From this point of view all of State action and policy can be understood as having three main objectives: serving the interests of capital accumulation; maintaining social control; and keeping the workforce healthy.

More recent interpretations of Marxism, however, suggest a less deterministic approach to understanding the relationship between the State and society. As described by Williams (1989) the 'political economy of welfare' approach moves away from a purely structuralist view of capitalist society, within which the individual is merely a puppet, moulded and controlled by wider forces, to suggest that human action is also a source of power in creating and influencing State policy making (see earlier discussion).

Corporatist theory

Corporatism emerged in the late 1970s as some sort of uneasy compromise between the competing explanations, in particular Marxist and New Right critiques, of the role of interest groups in the policy process and the distribution of power within the political system (Dearlove and Saunders, 1991).

Corporatists shared with pluralist thinking a belief that interest groups were the basic building blocks of the policy process, even to the point of having more significance than representation through elections and Parliament: however they also accepted the widespread criticisms of pluralism that not all groups had equal influence within this political structure. Their embrace of Marxist explanations stopped short of accepting that it was solely the capitalist business interests that dominated the system, and likewise New Right ideas were rejected for insisting that demands from trade unions for more welfare services were leading to overload on the system and a state of ungovernability.

Rather, corporatists argued that together with the elected government, both union and business interests had considerable influence in the polity and policy process, even to the point of forming a triage of powerful interests. Dearlove and Saunders (1991) suggest that within this state of affairs large organized interests were no longer having to put pressure on the government from the outside. As the State became more involved in management of the economy, so it became more reliant on business and the unions to assist the implementation of economic change. The fact that they were needed by the State meant that union and business interests were actually drawn into the government to give advice and to act as agents through which State policy was implemented.

As such, corporatism rejected the idea that the interest-group system was competitive, accessible to all or equal, arguing instead that it was very much a system of closed competition, leading to policy outcomes that failed to give fair shares to everyone. As Dearlove and Saunders (1984i) explained: 'The state's involvement in managing the economy and in organizing a welfare state enabled certain interests to secure exclusive access and an inside track to the ear of government as well as a permanent relationship to the administrative side of the state machine'.

This theory of tri-partite, corporate-style policy making appears to hold little relevance for the 1990s. With the New Right endorsement of a hands-off economic policy, the rolling back of the State frontiers and the breaking of trade union power in the eighties, the government no longer needs to enter into collaborative arrangements with the unions and business to such an extent. As Dearlove and Saunders (1991) explain, this theory was really a child of its time and although it might well be useful in explaining how government and interest groups might relate, it is probably not applicable to the current situation to any great extent.

Although it is useful for nurses to have a broad understanding of the differing perspectives of how power might be distributed within the political structure, it is also worth considering, at a micro-level, exactly how power operates within the policy process. In other words, how does one interest group exercise power over another, and how does this process become routinized, so that some groups are automatically considered more powerful and their requests more legitimate than others (in exploring the dynamic between doctors and nurses this is an interesting question). This area is the focus of the next section of this chapter.

Power and systems of domination

Ham and Hill (1984) suggest that the debates about the methods used to examine the operation of power and how to define this concept have often received more attention than the larger questions to do with the nature of the overall power structure within society, as described above. In reality, of course, it is difficult to separate the methodological and definitional questions from their wider framework. This is particularly so with regard to pluralism and elitism, as each of these theories gave rise to their own ways of defining how power operates, and how evidence for its existence is to be collected. Writers in this field have developed different dimensions of power.

One-dimensional power

The primary exponent of pluralism, Robert Dahl, arguing against an elitist description of power, for which he said there was little evidence, insisted that in order to determine who held power in any situation, conflict had to be observed and the outcome of actual decisions had to be examined. In this way the individual or group who had power would be revealed. From this perspective individuals whose preferences prevail in conflicts over key political issues are those who exercise power in a political system (Ham and Hill, 1984).

Two-dimensional power

This one-dimensional view of power was criticized by Bachrach and Baratz (1962, cited Dearlove and Saunders, 1984) who developed the idea of a second level of power, operating covertly by suppressing conflicts and preventing them from entering the political process. This was known as 'non-decision making' and is associated with an elitist view of power. According to these two authors, power not only involves the ability to shape decision outcomes, but also the ability to dominate the political process so that some issues never arise and certain decisions never get made with the result that the status quo is never challenged.

From a research point of view, if the process of decision making alone is studied in an attempt to ascertain the source of power, then study is limited to only those issues which have been allowed access to the political system. As Dearlove and Saunders (1984) explain, this ignores crucial questions of power exercised at a much earlier stage where a power elite may have been able to predetermine the agenda for discussion.

Bachrach and Baratz suggested three ways in which a powerful elite may stifle issues and prevent them entering the political system, namely: ignoring political demands so a decision one way or another is not necessary; ensuring awkward political demands are never raised by encouraging disadvantaged or less powerful groups to think that there is no alternative or that change is impossible; and by preventing people from formulating grievances in a coherent way, through control of the media, schooling and shaping of preferences through socialization.

According to Dearlove and Saunders (1984) this theory of power has been very difficult to research and prove empirically, and is today widely regarded as basically unproved and is to all intents and purposes, disregarded. In its place a far more compelling analysis of power has been developed, in which power is seen to be located not so much in individuals or groups of people, as is the case in pluralist and elitist thinking, but in systems of domination.

Three-dimensional power and systems of domination

Power relationships implicit in this third dimension penetrate the very structures of society itself. At this level it extends further than simple, observable conflict, as understood from within a pluralist tradition. Neither can it be fully understood as an elitist concept concerned with the overt operation of power through co-option and non-decision making. Lukes (1974, cited Ham and Hill, 1984) argued that this third level of power involves the shaping of people's preferences so that neither overt or covert conflict exists. In other words, when power operates at this level, conflict is latent.

Lukes' view of power focuses not only on people's actions and inactions, but subscribes to the idea that power is a *system of domination*. In this sense the term domination refers to a power relationship which has become routinized and, as Dearlove and Saunders (1984ii) explain: 'involves sets of social relations in which one party has established routine command over another, such that he or she is rarely challenged'.

Within this relationship rules with unequal outcomes are obeyed as a matter of course and overt conflict fails to surface.

Power at this point becomes generalized and is accepted as a 'normal' part of relations that exist between certain groups in different social settings, spheres of activity or policy making and implementing.

Power operating in the third dimension links into the idea of institutionalized inequalities – inequalities occurring at a systemic level and underpinned by ideologies such as sexism, racism or ageism, for example. Here institutional rules, procedures and practices generate unequal outcomes, regardless of the motives of individuals involved. In other words the system is biased, not individual behaviour (Dearlove and Saunders, 1984).

A system of domination therefore is societally-structured behaviour in accordance with rules, norms or values, backed by formal or informal sanctions of approval or disapproval and inclusion or exclusion. A system of domination goes beyond discouragement from action, fatalism or resignation, in an elitist sense, to the point where it becomes internalized or accepted as part of the natural order of things (Ham and Hill, 1984).

Lukes (1974, cited Dearlove and Saunders, 1984) argues that through this process a false or manipulated consensus may exist whereby people's wants are formed by the society in which they live, and these may not be the same as their *real* interests – an idea taken up by Marxist critique to explain people's inaction in the face of capitalist subordination (see chapter 11). Difficulties obviously exist here in determining exactly what people's real or 'unfalse' consensus may be. As Lukes pointed out, this can only be determined by studying what people would choose when expressing choice free from the constraints of their socialization, a situation which is impossible to achieve.

Much of this micro-level analysis of power was described by Dearlove and Saunders (1984) in their first edition of an *Introduction to British Politics*. By 1991, when their second edition appeared, all reference to a micro-analysis of power in the policy process had been expunged, to be replaced by far more concentration on the workings of the institutions of the British State. In trying to develop a nursing perspective of social policy, this shift of focus is unhelpful and it is the belief of this author that an analysis of power is an appropriate platform from which to understand the policy vacuum that surrounds nursing.

Why is this theory important to nurses?

Many nurses may already be asking where nursing is located within this complex web of theory, and how a knowledge of varying perspectives on welfare and power can enhance their practice. The answers to these questions are diverse and various and depend as much as anything on the political and value stance of individual readers. This section will move on to explore these issues in more detail.

The first important question concerns the value position of nurses and nursing generally in relation to the Welfare State, which is an extremely complex question to answer due to the diversity of the profession. Nurses are not a homogeneous group – there are a multitude of differing types and levels of nurses, from student nurse to nurse manager, as well as a variety of disciplines such as midwives, mental health nurses, health visitors and so on. Each of these has its own set of values and priorities which may well locate it completely differently to other nursing groups within the welfare framework outlined.

One way of sifting through this maze is to ask how you, the reader, would express your view of welfare? Do you see yourself as having a foot in the collectivist camp, believing in State provision of universal services as a way of responding to and resolving social problems, or do you see a radical re-distribution of resources, in a Marxist sense, as the only way of eliminating societal ills such as poverty, squalor and disease? Alternatively, can you feel yourself leaning more towards an anti-collectivist view, whereby you believe that the State interferes too much in people's lives, creating and encouraging dependence and laziness? Should the family take on more responsibility for the care of its members and, instead of relying on the State, buy in from the market those services that are needed over and above family resources? At the end of the day, to what extent does this fundamental philosophy or understanding of welfare actually inform the care that you give?

Additionally, where do you stand in terms of the feminist and anti-racist critiques of welfare? As a nurse you are part and parcel of the Welfare State (this is indirectly so, even if you work within the private or voluntary sector, as explained earlier). You have a prime responsibility as a front-line deliverer of services, and as such determine, on a day-to-day basis, the priorities as to who receives nursing care, what care is given and what the quality of the care is. How much of this care is truly informed by an awareness of the rights of everyone to equal and equitable services? How involved are you in the movement for equal opportunities for oppressed groups and for the development of anti-racist and anti-sexist strategies? More importantly, what lead do you get for this from the profession of nursing as a whole? To what extent does the profession address these issues, not only of sexism and racism but also ageism, homophobia and able-bodyism, and is any of this reflected in the way you deliver care on a minute-to-minute, person-to-person basis? This leads to other questions such as: what are the values espoused publicly by the nursing profession; do these reflect the views of individual nurses; and if not, how has this situation arisen?

Overall, this may seem like a lot of questions, the answers to which are complex and often paradoxical. Take for example the issue of nurses being practitioners of welfare – a fact which presents nurses and nursing, along with other welfare profession-als, with something of a dilemma, facing them as it does with two countervailing pressures. As Williams (1989) explains, on the one hand some individual nurses as well as professional nursing organizations are strong advocates of the movement which is critical of the Welfare State in respect of its discriminatory and subordinating policies and practices. On the other hand, however, nurses are well aware of the social and economic policies of the last twelve years, which have lead to a worsening of poverty and ill-health (Townsend, 1991), a rise in unemployment and, with diminishing access to decent housing, a growing population of homeless people. This situation may well have nurses wondering if it is appropriate to be criticizing welfare, when they should really be defending what remains of universal State provision. Is it possible to juggle this paradox – to defend and criticize at the same time. Williams (1989) suggests it is not only possible but should be addressed with great urgency. Arguing from a predominantly Marxist stance, she promotes a rigorous defence of the concept of State provision, but within this also identifies the need to reconstruct a welfare which combines class, race and gender interests within democratic user-led services.

This view may or may not reflect individual nurses' opinions. What should be universally embraced by nurses, however, is the fact that a broad understanding of the prevailing political views of welfare is of fundamental importance in order to influence proactively the public policy agenda. It is this lack of political insight and the inability to recognize and manipulate particular perspectives of welfare that has contributed to nurses' powerlessness through the ages. This situation is examined in more detail in chapter 12.

An overview of the way power is exercised and the way it operates both overtly, covertly and at the level of being a 'system of domination' is also of profound importance to nurses and nursing. The ability to challenge the marginalization and subordination of the nursing voice within policy decision-making circles as well as in the face of medicine, is dependent upon this knowledge. The power dynamic cannot be tackled unless it is known and understood. Consider the following set of questions. The overt operation of power, by its very nature is easily recognized. How often, though, have you as a nurse been aware of and identified the covert operation of power? Think of examples from your everyday practice or experiences to date in the nursing field. Consider, for instance: the disappearance of the nursing voice within key decision-making groups – a prime example being the loss of nurse managers in the Griffiths reforms of 1984 and the significant lack of nurses with executive powers in the new Trust arrangements; the feeling that it is no use fighting your corner as you will be unable to change the status quo – that is, power has operated without conflict surfacing; the expectation that nurses will simply conform to arrangements made with regard to the running of the health services and the allocation of health resources; and the fact that doctors' decisions have a priority which is often difficult to challenge. A vital question here concerns the tenuous ability of nurses to empower patients/clients if the nurses themselves lack power. It could be argued that power cannot be shared effectively if the equation has no power base to start with.

On the other hand, to what extent are you part of the professional covert operation of power in relation to your clientele/patients? This is a difficult question with which to deal. You may be able to recognize the case of 'non-decision making' when you failed to give your patient or client the full picture about an aspect of nursing care, thus not allowing the individual to raise particular concerns. It is sometimes easier to own up to being the victim of powerful relationships than the perpetrator of sub-ordination within a professional system of domination. As a professional are you aware of the power society automatically gives you – a relationship which has become routinized through the operation of power at the third level, that is, the individual is socialized into a 'respect' for, even awe of, professional groups?

None of these questions can be answered simply. Rather they have been raised to provoke an awareness of the way power operates and to create a greater understanding of the position of nurses and the wider profession in relation to power. It would be inaccurate, however, to portray nurses as being either totally helpless victims of more powerful groups, or as Machiavellian exploiters of professional control. Rather, nurses and nursing swing from one end of this continuum to another. Nurses are fighting back against a historical lack of professional power, as well as examining their practice in terms of enabling their clients or patients to make informed choices about the care given. Further reading on this subject is listed at the end of this chapter.

Conclusion

This chapter began by summarizing some of the content of previous chapters which looked at the constitution of the State. It was seen that the State could be understood both in terms of the *institutions* of which it is composed as well as the *functions* which these institutions perform. These institutions include not only those of the public sector, but also aspects of voluntary and private services as well. Trying to make sense of the way social policy is formulated and implemented, and the role of State action in all of this, led on to an examination of a number of perspectives or theories of welfare. Drawing on the work of Williams (1989) a framework was sketched out which allowed the multiplicity of welfare theories to be classified into five main groups or categories, namely: collectivism; anti-collectivism; Marxist critique; feminist critique; and anti-racist critique. None of these theories hold the complete explanation as to 'what is really going on' in the complex world of political activity. Rather the aim here was to enable the reader to understand the world from a variety of differing perspectives, which is the basis of informed action within the policy arena.

The distribution of economic and political power within society and its systems of government and the way that power operates both overtly and covertly in reaching policy decisions was the next focus of discussion. Although power itself was not explicitly referred to in the exploration of the various theoretical approaches to welfare, there was an implicit suggestion that each perspective located power differently within the relationship between welfare and society. Four main bodies of theory, pluralism, elitism, Marxism and corporatism were examined in order to create a broader understanding of this.

Discussion then switched from the broad canvas of macro-analysis to considering, at a micro-level, exactly how power operates within the policy process. This examination drew on sociological theories about differing dimensions of power, the work of the pluralist, Robert Dahl, who described the overt operation of power, was considered along with the work of Bachrach and Baratz, who, from an elitist perspective, argued that power could also be exercised covertly, through the process of 'non-decision making'. Finally Lukes' description of power in the subconscious third dimension was examined, a view which links into Dearlove and Saunders' idea of 'systems of domination', wherein power becomes routinized and subordination along certain axes, such as class, race, age or gender, becomes a matter of course.

The final section of this chapter raised many questions regarding the position of nursing and nurses in relation to welfare and the distribution of power. None of these questions were able to be answered here, but more clues as to their possible solutions will be found in other chapters, all of which are underpinned by the theme of power and policy and the allocation of values.

Discussion points

1. To whose benefit is the Welfare State being run? Discuss examples drawn from your experience of the NHS.
2. What are the fundamental weaknesses of the Welfare State? Draw on theoretical explanations to illustrate your answer. How could you possibly rectify some of these from your position as a nurse?

Further reading

Dearlove, J. and Saunders, P. (1984) *Introduction to British Politics*, Polity Press, Cambridge
This highly-readable book has a clear, accessible style and offers a comprehensive introduction to the major issues concerning British politics in the 1980s.

Dearlove, J. and Saunders, P. (1991) *Introduction to British Politics*, 2nd edn, Polity Press, Cambridge
The second edition offers as good an account of the British political set-up as the first, but with very different emphases, that is there is far more focus on the sheer might of the institutions of the British State, rather than on a micro-analysis of power.

Dunleavy, P. and O'Leary, B. (1987) *Theories of the State: The Politics of Liberal Democracy*, Macmillan Education Ltd, London
This book provides a carefully-structured introduction to the five broad schools of political, social and economic thought that dominated the discussions of the 1980s, namely: pluralism; the New Right; elite theory; Marxism; and neo-pluralism. It is still pertinent in the 1990s and makes for very interesting reading.

Finch, J. and Groves, D. (eds) (1983) *A Labour of Love: Women, Work and Caring*, Routledge & Kegan Paul, London
A fascinating collection of feminist writing exploring the concept of caring, both in and out of the domestic sphere. Essential reading for nurses.

Green, D. (1987) *The New Right: The Counter Revolution in Political, Economic and Social Thought*, Wheatsheaf Books Ltd, Great Britain
A useful introduction to the various themes and diverse strands in New Right thinking and offering a very accessible style.

Ham, C. and Hill, M. (1984) *The Policy Process in the Modern Capitalist State*, Wheatsheaf Books, Great Britain
This book offers a comprehensive introduction to policy studies and policy analysis. It contains some very useful chapters on the operation of power in decision making and summaries of major political theories. A good mixture of both micro- and macro-analysis.

Pascall, G. (1986) *Social Policy: A Feminist Analysis*, Tavistock Publications, London and New York
This book describes the way in which social policies bridge the gap between domestic work and the public sphere of paid labour. Pascall explains that in order to understand the workings of the Welfare State,

one must first appreciate the way in which it deals with women. Very readable without being simplistic. A good section on health and nursing.

Williams, F. (1989) *Social Policy: A Critical Introduction*. Polity Press, Cambridge
Essential reading for students of social policy. Presented in a clear style, this book provides an excellent introduction to the variety of ideological perspectives on the Welfare State. The author weaves into this the argument for the centality of race, gender and class in welfare theory and practice.

References

Ben-Tovim, G., Gabriel, J., Law, I. and Stredder, K. (1986) *The Local Politics of Race*, Macmillan, London

Dearlove, J. and Saunders, P. (1984) *Introduction to British Politics*, (i) p. 149; (ii) p. 212. Polity Press, Cambridge

Dearlove, J. and Saunders, P. (1991) *Introduction to British Politics*, 2nd edn, Polity Press, Cambridge

Dunleavy, P. and O'Leary, B. (1987) *Theories of the State: The Politics of Liberal Democracy*, Macmillan Education Ltd, London

Finch, J. and Groves, D. (eds) (1983) *A Labour of Love: Women, Work and Caring*, Routledge & Kegan Paul, London

Gilroy, P. (1987) *There Ain't No Black in the Union Jack*, Hutchinson, London

Gough, I. (1979) *The Political Economy of the Welfare State*, Macmillan, London

Green, D. (1987) *The New Right: The Counter Revolution in Political, Economic and Social Thought*, Wheatsheaf Books Ltd, Great Britain

Ham, C. and Hill, M. (1984) *The Policy Process in the Modern Capitalist State*, Wheatsheaf Books Ltd, Great Britain

O'Connor, J. (1973) *The Fiscal Crisis of the State*, St James's Press, New York

Pascall, G. (1986) *Social Policy: A Feminist Analysis*, Tavistock Publications, London

Rex, J. (1983) *Race Relation in Sociological Theory*, Routledge & Kegan Paul, London

Townsend, P. and Davidson, N. (1992) *Inequalities in Health: the Black Report and the Health Divide*, Penguin Books, Harmondsworth

Williams, F. (1989) *Social Policy: A Critical Introduction*, (i) p. 30; (ii) pp. 34–5. Polity Press, Cambridge

4

Health and social policy

Jean Neave

Introduction

The purpose of this chapter is to describe the context in which health policy has been made and to explore some of the reasons for the changes in the delivery of health care which have particularly affected the development of nursing. I begin by analysing the concept of health and demonstrate how a medical model of health has dominated the development of the National Health Service. A short historical review of the National Health Service will discuss the policies surrounding the creation and successive re-organizations of the service. Particular emphasis will be placed on how these reorganizations have affected nursing and the care nurses give to patients. Recent policy changes are then examined within the context of the Conservative Party's ideological roots and commitment to the Welfare State. These changes include the introduction of the internal market, the development of National Health Service Trusts, the rights of the 'consumer' of health care and the encouragement of individualism.

Defining health

Although the word 'health' is used freely in everyday speech, it is a complex concept to define. This lack of conceptual clarity has led to problems in measuring the effectiveness of the National Health Service and social policy provision in general on the health of the population. Health is not a static state and our understanding of

illness and wellness changes over time and place. When the National Health Service was founded in 1948 it was based on a view of health which had dominance at that time. It was thought that there was a limited amount of ill health and, if this was treated, the sickness rate in the population would be reduced and there would be less demand for health care (Connolly, 1978). It is now accepted that this goal was unrealistic, that there is no finite amount of ill health and the Western world's ability to consume health resources is apparently limitless.

Models of health

The model of health and health care which had the greatest influence on the foundation of the National Health Service was the 'medical model'. The concept of health which had emphasized environmental, economic and social causes of ill health in the nineteenth century gave way to a view that the causes of ill health were to be found from the scientific study of disease. It was felt that illness could be cured by the medical profession with their knowledge of pathological processes and the pattern of disease. The importance of medical diagnosis and treatment was emphasized. Health, therefore, was seen to be synonymous with the elimination of medically-defined disease (Ham, 1992). Correspondingly the acute and curative services received priority for funding and the National Health Service became focused on sickness rather than health.

This narrow or negative model of health has increasingly been challenged. In 1948, the constitution of the World Health Organization defined health as 'a state of complete physical, mental and social well-being and not merely the absence of disease and infirmity' (WHO, 1948). This definition of health is much more positive and highlights not only the importance of physical health, but also mental health and social factors. It also acknowledges that health has a subjective element, and that one's views of health will be based on such factors as age, culture, experience and expectations.

However this definition of health has been criticized as too inclusive and idealistic (Harrison *et al.*, 1990; Seedhouse, 1986). Harrison *et al.* (1990) consider that, according to this definition, few policies and few agencies would not be health policies or health agencies. The more holistic views of health which can be derived from this definition have been embraced by nursing and used in the development of nursing models to guide and enhance practice. The importance of nursing and care are highlighted when one moves away from a narrow model of health.

The medical model of health has also been criticized because it does not take into account the context in which health care takes place and the underlying structures, or structural determinants such as housing, the wider economy and so on, which also affect health. The publication of the Black Report (1980) and the Health Divide (Whitehead, 1987) highlighted the importance of social class, occupation, geographical location and economic conditions on health status. Although overall health may have shown some improvement the rate of this has not been equal. The cause of these continuing inequalities are primarily social and economic. In this book we adopt a broad definition of health which encompasses the impact of factors such as poverty, housing environment, education and global issues.

The World Health Organization has continued to lobby for a positive and inclusive approach to health. In the Declaration of Alma Ata (WHO, 1978) the importance of the establishment of a social, economic and legislative environment that provides the requirements for healthy living was highlighted. This declaration, to which the United Kingdom was a signatory, issued a challenge to the world to 'attain health for all by the year 2000' and identified nurses as a powerful force for achieving this aim.

In 1985 the European office of the World Health Organization in 'Targets for Health for All' defined thirty-eight targets for European countries (WHO, 1985). The first two targets specify that:

(i) the actual differences in health status between countries and between groups within countries should be reduced by at least twenty-five per cent by improving the levels of health of disadvantaged nations and groups and
(ii) people should have the basic opportunity to develop and use their health potential to live socially and economically fulfilling lives.

It is for each country to interpret these in the context of its own needs and capabilities.

Measuring health

The lack of agreement on a definition of health has created problems in measuring the outcomes of health policy. Mortality rates are the measures most frequently used to compare improvements and changes in health status of populations, mainly because they are concrete, absolute and routinely collected. Additonally, there is a lack of reliable indicators which measure morbidity (sickness). The Royal Commission on the National Health Service (1979) found it impossible to separate the effects of a universal health service on health from the effects of other wider socio-economic changes; or what would have happened if the National Health Service had not been introduced (Ham, 1992; McKeown, 1979).

Health models in action

The choice of a model of health and the way it is measured has implications for planning policy as the following overview will demonstrate, starting with an exploration of the history of the establishment of the National Health Service in 1948 and subsequent re-organizations. The overview will primarily focus on England. There are variations in detail between England, Wales, Scotland and Northern Ireland. However, the reasons and principles underpinning reorganization in the four countries have been consistent.

The development of the NHS

When the Beveridge Report was published in 1942, it recommended that a national health service should take over provision of medical care from the old insurance systems and that a comprehensive health-care system be introduced to conquer the 'Giant of Sickness'. The coalition government in 1943 accepted the principle of collective responsibility by the State for comprehensive health services and started negotiations with interested parties, particularly the medical profession, local authorities and voluntary groups (Levitt and Wall, 1992). As the first chapter described, health services had developed in an uncoordinated way with the State, particularly local authorities, gradually assuming more responsibility for health care. In the 1920s and 1930s shortcomings in the provision of services were highlighted by pressure groups and the medical profession. The decision taken by the coalition government was largely welcomed by the general public but all was not plain sailing. The final structure of the National Health Service in 1948 was to be the product of considerable bargaining, negotiation and compromise between competing political and professional interests.

The National Health Service Act placed a general duty upon the Minister of Health to:

> promote a comprehensive health service for the improvement of the physical and mental health of the people of England and Wales for the prevention, diagnosis and treatment of illness (HMSO 1946; cited by Allsop, 1984i).

Much of the debate about the form of this service took place in forums other than Parliament. Ham (1992) notes that the resultant policy was more strongly influenced by conflicts between major pressure groups with an interest in health services, for example the medical profession, than the formal parliamentary process. It was agreed that the service should be funded from general taxation rather than by social insurance, which until this time had only covered half the public and involved two-thirds of GPs, and that health care would be free at the point of use.

The National Health Service was based on the principles of collectivism, comprehensiveness, universality and equality (Allsop, 1984). The organizational form which emerged in 1948 was based on a tripartite structure and reflected the three main spheres of medical interest which were hospital services, public health services and general practitioner services.

The 1948 structure

The most radical changes were made to the hospital services which were in effect 'nationalized'. They were administered under the Minister of Health by a two-tier system – Regions and Districts.

England was divided into thirteen regions (fourteen in 1959) and Wales became a region in its own right. The regions were planned around a university with a medical school, except London which was divided into four regions. The main function of the Regional Boards was to plan, provide and supervise services. Within the regions a total of 388 Hospital Management Committees were created which managed large hospitals or groups of hospitals. Teaching hospitals were administered separately by Boards of Governors and retained their elite status.

Local authorities retained some of their responsibilities for environmental and personal health services and were responsible for the provision of community nursing services, maternal and child welfare services, and vaccination and immunization. The direction of these services was under the control of the Medical Officer of Health. Funding came from both central government and the rates, and the Medical Officer of Health had to compete for resources with other local authority departments (Levitt and Wall, 1992).

General practitioner services, dentists, opticians and pharmacists were administered by the 134 Executive Councils who replaced the old insurance committees. GPs provided, under the terms of their contract, twenty-four hour care at their practice premises or at the patient's home, and were paid on a per capita basis. Essentially, however, they continued to practise independently (Allsop, 1984). A similar structure was established in Scotland and Northern Ireland.

Thus the National Health Service was based on the historical development of health-care services and maintained (or even enhanced) the autonomy of the medical profession. Nursing had little effect on the decisions made.

This tripartite structure influenced the early development of the National Health Service. The administrative structure was biased towards the hospital sector which had a significant influence on policy making. However the system of regional planning and the grouping of hospitals helped to eliminate some of the shortages and duplication of resources which had existed before 1948. The amalgamation of local authority and voluntary hospitals also achieved a better use of resources (Levitt and Wall, 1992).

The community services, however, because of the tripartite

structure, developed independently and more slowly. There was also a lack of liaison with hospitals.

From the very beginning of the service there were concerns about the costs of health-care provision. It was decided in 1951 to supplement NHS resources by levying charges for dentures and spectacles, and in 1952 for prescriptions and dental treatment. This reneged on the promise of a service free to all at the point of use and consequently undermined the principle of universality.

Concerns about cost have continued (Leathard, 1990), particularly within the acute sector which grew the most rapidly due to advances in medicine, increased use of technology and the cost of drugs, soaking up a disproportionate amount of available resources. Nursing remained subordinate to medicine although comprising the largest group within the new service. What resulted was a medical rather than a health service, which is still the case today.

The 1974 structure

Reorganization became desirable to remedy the fragmentation resulting from the tripartite structure and to increase the central accountability of the service. Ninety Area Health Authorities were created in England, their boundaries co-terminous with those of the metropolitan and non-metropolitan districts established by the Local Government Act 1972 which came into effect at the same time.

This reorganization had three main objectives, namely:

1. to unify the health services by bringing all services under the direction of the Area Health Authorities. Thus the three branches of the service could work more effectively and efficiently. GPs remained independent contractors under the Executive Councils;
2. to develop Joint Consultative Committees with the restructured local government authorities' Social Services Departments;
3. to develop better management through multidisciplinary teams composed of medical, nursing and administrative staff (Leathard, 1990).

The Area Health Authority took responsibility for general policy and monitoring of services. The District Management

Team, consisting of a nursing officer, an administrator, a treasurer, a medical officer, an elected consultant and a general practitioner, was collectively responsible for keeping district services under review and implementing area policies. The members were also responsible for managing their own spheres of work.

The planning system was based on rationality and was standardized throughout the country. Plans were agreed at district level, then at area level which forwarded them to regional level and to the Department of Health and Social Security. Community Health Councils were appointed at district level to represent the interests of the consumer and to monitor the health services. Most importantly for nursing there was to be no hierarchy in the management structure. Consensus management was to be adopted.

However, there was greater accountability to the Department of Health and Social Security and greater control from the centre to ensure that policy decisions were carried out – for example, ensuring sufficient priority for the 'Cinderella' services (see chapter 9). For the first time nurses had gained, structurally at least, an increased role in decision making (Allsop, 1984).

Criticism of the 1974 reorganization soon mounted, Concerns centred on delays in decision making, the elaborate machinery for consultation, the structural complexity and increased bureaucracy resulting from tiers of management. In addition resentment grew about the increased central control.

The 1979 Royal Commission on the National Health Service recommended that there should only be one tier of authority below region and in 'Patients First' (DoH, 1979) the Conservative government announced the removal of one level of administration and the replacement of Area Health Authorities by smaller District Health Authorities.

In April 1982 the Area Health Authorities were replaced by 201 District Health Authorities. The government did not view this change as a major reorganization. The principle of co-terminousity with local authorities was lost and District Health Authorities became responsible for assessing needs. The decentralization of decision making and the simplification of bureaucratic structures were in line with Conservative philosophy (Leathard, 1990).

The 1984 structure

In 1983 the Conservatives were re-elected with an increased majority and with a manifesto which had committed them to better management of welfare services and more effective planning and use of resources. In the same year an independent inquiry was set up to investigate NHS management practices under the direction of Roy Griffiths, the managing director of Sainsbury's. This inquiry (DHSS, 1983) concluded that the National Health Service suffered from 'institutional stagnation'. Change was difficult to achieve and there was a lack of clarity about objectives. The aim of the Griffiths recommendation was to introduce the concepts and methods of business management (Allsop, 1989). Griffiths proposed that a Health Services Supervisory Board should be established within the DHSS to decide objectives, budgets and NHS strategy. The formation of a NHS Management Board to be responsible for the operational management of the service was proposed. General managers were to be appointed at regional, district and unit level to replace the teams, and clinicians were to be more involved in the management process through resource budgeting.

These proposed changes were introduced quickly. They marked a radical change from the previous style of management with more overt control from the centre. The nursing profession was not successful in securing representation and status in the new management structure and many nurses felt aggrieved that they had lost the right to manage nursing (Leathard, 1990). The Royal College of Nursing waged a vigorous campaign demanding that nurses be represented at the highest levels of decision making so that they could retain accountability for the provision of nursing care. However, this campaign was not successful. Nurses ended up reporting to administrators, who were the most successful professional group in securing management posts. Many former chief nursing officers became responsible for quality assurance or planning, a position that usually lacked executive power.

Following the Griffiths Report (1983), further initiatives were introduced to improve efficiency and effectiveness, including the establishment of extensive information systems. Allsop (1989) states that the introduction of general management can be viewed as a continuing search by the centre for control over the resources and professionals involved in health care. Within this business model prescribed by Griffiths health care can be seen to be as a series of goods provided for consumers by specialists who are managed by expert managers – many of whom were direct appointees of the Secretary of State.

Changing directions

Until recently the Conservative government, which has been in power since 1979, focused on reforming the National Health Service itself, highlighting the need for improved management, greater efficiency and cost containment. The importance of the individual, or consumer, of health care was stressed as was their ability to make informed health choices. The concentration of resources on the National Health Service and the delivery of care reflected a policy choice which focused on an illness service. This has been in preference to intervention at a wider policy level to improve general standards of living, an alternative recommended by those involved with publications such as the Black Report (1980) and the Health Divide (Whitehead, 1987). Public health issues have tended to become marginalized, although pressure group activity for improved public health measures has grown (Allsop, 1989). These priorities in planning are consistent with the medical model of health.

However, from the late 1980s some changes in the direction of government policy can be traced, and the importance of primary care, health promotion and prevention have been highlighted. Thus, in the revised contract for general practitioners with the National Health Service in 1990, financial incentives for screening procedures and immunization targets were introduced. General practitioners were also encouraged to develop health promotion clinics. Moreover, in response to the Acheson Report (1988) all health authorities were required to appoint Directors of Public Health, to take a key role in purchasing services with other members of the new health authorities. These Directors of Public Health are required to provide an annual report on the state of health within the health authority, and are responsible for developing policies on prevention.

The most significant change occurred in 1992 when, following consultation, the Department of Health published a strategy for health in England, 'The Health of the Nation' (DoH, 1992). This strategy is based on 'Health for all by the Year 2000', the challenge issued by the World Health Organization in 1978 at Alma Ata. Thus it could be argued that the government's overall goal is to secure continuing improvement in the general health of the population by adding years to life and life to years. The achievement of success in this aim will centre on such initiatives as healthy surroundings, healthy lifestyles and high-quality health services. This strategy will be discussed in more detail later in the chapter, but what is important to note is that for the first time since the National Health Service was founded, a strategy for health with key targets has been developed.

It was not the intention of the government to make any more significant changes to the National Health Service when in 1987 public controversy about the financial problems, which had led to cuts in services, caught the media headlines. These concerns also included pressure from nurses about their level of pay and working conditions.

In 1988 the Prime Minister announced a review of the National Health Service. The radical proposals, following this review, published in the White Paper, 'Working for Patients' (DoH, 1989) marked the most significant changes in approach to the National Health Service since it was formed in 1948. The main aims of the proposals were to extend patient choice, to delegate responsibility to where the services were provided and to secure the best value for money. At the heart of the reforms was the decision that the purchasing role of District Health Authorities should be split from their provider role of services. The most controversial proposals included the fact that:

1. Hospitals could apply for self-governing status from 1990 as National Health Service Trusts. These Trusts would be managed by boards of directors and would have more autonomy to manage their affairs. They would sell their services to District Health Authorities, GP budget holders and private patients.
2. General Practitioners with larger practices of eleven thousand patients or more would be able to apply to control their own budgets to buy hospital care for patients and to plough back savings into their practices.

3. Regional and District Health Authorities would no longer have to provide all the services themselves.

Policy and ideology

The historical overview of the many changes in the National Health Service presented above has described how the service has evolved since it was established in 1948 and how it is now administered. In the following section I will discuss in more detail some of the changes which the Conservative Party has introduced since 1979 and explore some of their ideological roots. This knowledge of Social Policy and the political process can help in our understanding of why change has occurred and to whose advantage it is. Moreover, this analysis offers nurses the tools to enable them to become increasingly proactive in the management of change and in influencing the policy process.

Recent changes

In the 1980s it became apparent that the National Health Service was experiencing severe financial problems. The money allocated to the service was tightly constrained and, in common with many other countries, the NHS was faced with an increasing demand for health care. Some of this demand was due to demographic changes in the population, namely a growing number of people overall, but in particular an increase in the proportion of older people (see chapter 9). Other reasons included the expanding costs of technology and the increased take up of the services offered. People were also much more aware of health issues and had increased expectations of the service. Despite this perceived crisis, it should be noted here that costs for the administration of the service, even at that time, compared favourably with other countries (Ham, 1992; Leathard, 1990).

The government was unwilling to commit extra resources to the service; 80 per cent of NHS funding comes from general taxation. The government considered that a high level of taxation and increased spending on the Welfare State had increased dependency and sapped individualism (see chapter 3). Ideologically, the government was committed to slimming down the Welfare State overall and reducing public spending. Moreover, there could be more efficient, less bureaucratic and less wasteful ways of providing health care than the National Health Service – for example through internal competition, competitive tendering of services and use of a more mixed economy of welfare provision (Ham, 1992).

It can be argued that many of the changes which have occurred were needed and although not welcomed by all groups, were not in fact political and did cut across ideological boundaries – for example the emphasis on information technology, used to inform decision making and highlight the cost of health care inputs in relation to the measurement of outcomes. However, other changes which have occurred are more controversial and emphasize the differences which have arisen about the nature of the Welfare State.

The internal market

The White Paper, 'Working for Patients' (DoH, 1989) introduced for the first time into the National Health Service the concept of the internal market. This was seen by the government to be a solution for the delivery of care which would inject into the service some of the qualities of competition and choice that one would find in a well-run private enterprise (Ham, 1992). The internal market was consistent with the philosophy of the New Right and the belief that the free market and competition are the most efficient and effective ways to provide goods and services (see chapter 3).

The key players within the internal market, created to deliver care, consist of the purchasers, for example the District Health Authority, GP fundholders, Family Health Service Authorities and the provider units which may include Directly Managed Units, other District Health Authorities, NHS Trusts or the private sector. Money to purchase care has been allocated to each Health Authority on the basis of their population and those units which provide care are paid from these fixed budgets. General practitioners with practices of over eleven thousand patients may also directly manage their budgets and purchase care within the internal market.

By splitting the provider role of the District Health Authorities from their purchasing role, competition has been injected into the system. The well-managed providers will attract more contracts to provide services than those less successful providers who will be under considerable pressure to improve their services. It is claimed that the benefits will be a more responsive and flexible service, and the providers will become more efficient and provide a larger volume of care at a lower cost (Perrin, 1992).

However, there are some major problems with the creation of a market for health care which should be highlighted. The demand for health care is not the same as for other goods and services and does not successfully transfer to the free market – there is not the same balance between supply and demand. Moreover, the internal market for health care is an inadequate example of a free market as the purchaser is not the client/patient but the 'once removed' District Health Authority or GP. The providers do not have the same independence as their counterparts in the commercial sector as their budgets are controlled and they are also constrained by political pressures. The patients who require health care are often vulnerable and inarticulate and do not have the information needed to make decisions about their health requirements. They therefore have to rely upon those who are providing the service and who may have more knowledge of their needs and of the organization of available health care (Allsop, 1992).

Overall it is the healthier and more educated members of society who can benefit most from this change, thus perpetuating the inequalities in health already present in society. The Health Divide (Whitehead, 1987) for example, as well as other studies, showed that the middle classes have gained more from the National Health Service than deprived groups because they know how to use the system.

However, it is the introduction of competition itself into a service which is there to provide health care for those who do not want to be ill, and therefore who are reluctant consumers, which has caused the most debate. On the one hand, there are those who believe that the introduction of wider provision and the use of the private sector will result in a more efficient and responsive service. On the other hand, however, there are those who are concerned that competition could be unproductive. The creation of an internal market could lead to duplication and fragmentation of the service and competition could undermine accessibility, equitable provision and the quality of care over all could suffer (Ham, 1992).

As discussed in chapter 3, these differences depend very much on one's views about the Welfare State and the provision of health care. The solutions proposed also depend on the underlying values and beliefs of the government.

The development of NHS Trusts

To facilitate the provision of an internal market for health care the White Paper, 'Working for Patients' (DoH, 1989) allowed individual hospitals to become self-governing. Originally, it was conceived that it would be the major acute hospitals who would be allowed this option, but under the National Health Service and Community Care Act (1990) other services may also apply for trust status.

The first Trusts came into existence in April 1991 and they have been given a range of powers and freedoms not available to other hospitals and services within the National Health Service, including the DMUs. The White Paper (DoH, 1989) suggests that the Trusts have been released to manage the services for which they were responsible. The new liberty enables them to provide a responsive, market-driven service, determine their own management structures; set their own terms and conditions of service; acquire, own and sell their own assets; retain surpluses; and borrow money, subject to annual limits (Ham, 1992). The Trusts have been promoted as being able to encourage a stronger sense of local ownership and pride, stimulate commitment, harness skills and foster local initiative and greater competition (DoH, 1989).

They are run by small Boards of Directors accountable to the Secretary of State and are very similar to small independent corporations.

Because of these freedoms and the prestige involved in Trust status the number of hospitals and services applying for self-governing status has increased. Despite this apparent popularity of the changes the concerns expressed by the Royal College of Nursing (1989) and others are important and need to be discussed. Trust hospitals do not have to provide the full range of services which other district hospitals have to provide. The emphasis on profitability favours the treatment of patients with acute, self-limiting illness. There is a fear that Trusts might dispense with the treatment of patients with chronic illnesses or conditions and yet it is these illnesses which are the most important health problems today – this is not to ignore the fact that services for older people, the mentally ill and those with learning disabilities did receive some extra funding and priority because of central planning (see chapters 9 and 10). The development of trusts however could hinder comprehensive planning and lead to greater fragmentation of services.

Criticisms of Trust hospitals also centre on their need to remain profitable and to market aggressively; there are profound concerns about the quality of care which can be offered and about the skills of the staff who might provide the care. Most importantly, however, are the concerns about the favoured treatment that Trusts receive from the Department of Health. This has allowed a two-tier system to develop and despite assurances from the Department of Health, fears exist that trusts might eventually be allowed to leave the National Health Service altogether (Ham, 1992).

In the House of Commons Health Committee First Report on Trusts (1993) fear of fragmentation and an inability to co-ordinate or implement NHS policies were highlighted. Additionally, concerns were raised that the independence of Trusts might well contribute to lack of consultation over major health changes. Although their managerial discretion enabled Trusts to make quicker decisions it remained to be seen whether consultation mechanisms were sufficient to achieve an effective level of accountability to patients and the wider public (Potrykus, 1993).

The development of an internal market for health care has resulted in some significant changes for the delivery of health services. The decision to increase competition within strict budgetary controls was a political one. However, as has been pointed out, health care is very different from the provision of other goods and services. The internal market has heightened the awareness of costs for purchasers and providers of health care and, as in all large systems, there have been areas found where more effectiveness and efficiency could be injected. However, the need to contain costs and maintain profitability have had far-reaching effects on nursing and patient care. Between September 1989 and September 1991 almost 8,500 nursing posts were lost from the

National Health Service. Correspondingly, there has been an increase of 7,610 managerial posts and 10,500 administrative and clerical posts (Humphreys, 1993); the increased bureaucracy needed to run the internal market has therefore caused administrative costs to rise.

Many management teams have been involved in carrying out skill mix reviews of their workforce and assessing the balance between qualified and unqualified staff. These reviews have often led to a decrease in qualified nursing staff and an increase in unskilled staff – which recent research shows can have a disastrous effect on the quality of care and health outcomes (Carr-Hill *et al.*, 1992).

At the end of the financial year 1993, some Directly Managed Units and Trusts began to run out of money to treat patients, a situation which led to the suspension of non-urgent surgery. There have also been changes in contracts and services between units so that some units have gained contracts at the expense of others. Meanwhile there are large numbers of patients waiting for treatment (Humphreys, 1993).

The rights of the 'consumer' of health care

The first objective of the White Paper (1989), 'Working for Patients', was to give patients better health care and greater choice of services available. This emphasis on choice and the consumer's ability to influence health care has been at the forefront of the Conservative government's policy for the National Health Service since their election in 1979. As chapter 3 explained, lack of consumer control and choice form part of the main criticisms of the Welfare State by the New Right.

The emergence of the importance of the consumer was highlighted in the title of the government's first consultative paper on the National Health Service in 1979 called 'Patients First' (DHSS, 1979). The Griffiths Report (1983) also championed the rights of the consumer and said that the National Health Service should be much more responsive to patients.

Naomi Pfeffer (1992) maintains that the emphasis on responsiveness also comes from a relatively new management ethos, the 'excellence approach'. This stresses that if organizations are sufficiently responsive to their customers they will survive. Staff are expected to be courteous and to establish a close working arrangement with their consumers. Decentralization is highlighted and large bureaucratic organizations are broken down into smaller user-friendly units. Control is exercised through contractual relationships. Pfeffer (1992) stresses that the delivery of health and social care are now heavily influenced by this approach, citing the examples of the purchaser/provider split, self-governing Trusts and the compulsory competitive tendering. This management style is consistent with a philosophy of welfare provision which wishes to eradicate 'welfare professionalism'.

In 'Working for Patients' (DoH, 1989) consumers were promised more choice as a consequence of the creation of an internal market and increased competition. It was also to be made easier for patients to change their GPs. These rights have now been laid down in the Patients' Charter, which was implemented in April 1992, as part of the Citizens' Charter initiative. Advocates of consumer rights, however, have expressed disappointment with the Charter maintaining that it only lays down standards which are already in place or which should be provided in a well-run service anyway.

Much more anxiety has been expressed about the rights which have been lost for consumers following the recent reforms. These include the removal of local-authority representation on District Health Authorities and the loss by Community Health Councils of the automatic right to full observer status with speaking rights at Health Authority meetings. In addition, Community Health Councils do not have the right to scrutinize the activities of General Practitioner fundholders and have experienced difficulty in being involved in consultation about the content of contracts negotiated between District Health Authorities and service providers (Millar, 1991). The House of Commons Health Committee First Report on National Health Service Trusts (1993) also questioned the extent to which users of the service are consulted. The report highlighted the opportunity to involve local people in the purchasing activities of District Health Authorities but this consultation requires time, resources and commitment (Potrykus, 1993a).

In publishing the Patient's Charter the government has made explicit what is to be expected from the National Health Service and it clearly lays down the complaints procedures and systems of redress. Although these processes are important they have been criticized as being too individualistic and inequitable ways of making the public's voice heard. As such they discriminate against the vulnerable (Pfeffer, 1992). Moreover, the Patient's Charter does not lay down any standards for the long-term care of patients who are chronically ill or who have mental health problems.

Pollitt (1989) has argued that the government's view of consumerism is conceived in narrow terms. There is a focus on amenities, appointment systems and visiting arrangements, for example, and consumer opinion is sought by the use of surveys. Yet the government is suspicious of any attempt to give greater participation in decision making to patients. Pollitt (1989) maintains that although the rhetoric may be that of consumerism it is as yet only marginally modified paternalism.

The Royal College of Nursing in their report 'Health Challenge' (1988) advocated that the voice of the consumer of health care should be formally strengthened in several areas including quality assurance, funding, provision of services and ethical decison making. The nurses' role was seen to be vital in helping consumers in their quest for self empowerment. Additionally, the RCN (1988) recognized that consumers also need to make their views known at the collective level. They advocated that this should not be confined simply to representation through the Community Health Council but rather should extend to involvement at District Health Authority and Family Health Service Authority levels and General Practitioner participation groups. If true empowerment of the consumer is to be achieved this involvement at all decision-making levels is vital.

The delivery and management of health care

The government's stated intention in the Griffiths Report (1983) and 'Working for Patients' (1989) has been to delegate more responsibility to people who work in hospitals, community health and the family health services. The strategy has been to push down decision making to the lowest possible tier so that as many people as possible feel accountable. Commentators however argue that in reality central control in the management of the health service has increased dramatically (Ham, 1992). Examples of this tightening central rein include the instigation of an annual review of individual Regional Health Authorities, initiated by the Department of Health in 1982, with the express aim of determining how each region is implementing national policies. Specific targets are reviewed and objectives and dates for implementation of policies are agreed. Similar reviews then take place between regions, their districts and Family Health Service Authorities. Additionally, 'Working for Patients' (DoH, 1989) strengthened management arrangements within the Department of Health by the creation of the Management Executive. NHS Trusts report directly to the Department of Health and have to submit an annual business plan. The formation of the Family Health Service Authorities can also be seen to be part of an overall strategy for greater control. They have been made accountable to Regional Health Authorities and thus have been brought into the 'mainstream' of NHS management (Ham, 1992).

NHS expenditure is allocated from the Department of Health to regions, based on capitation figures. Some funds, however, are allocated directly by the Department of Health. These have included money for the waiting-list initiative, AIDS research and the NHS reforms.

Central control is also apparent when one considers the appointments which are made by the Department of Health. These include the chairs and non-executive members of Regional Health Authorities, chairs of District Health Authorities, Family Health Service Authorities and National Health Service Trusts. Members of Family Health Service Authorities and some of the non-executive directors of Trusts have also to be approved by the Department of Health.

It is too soon to comment on how much flexibility districts have been allowed in the drawing up of contracts with provider units and, similarly, GP fundholders, to meet the needs of their resident populations. However, the reduction of the National Health Service in the direct provision of care and the development of a mixed market will lead to increasing responsibilities in the field of regulation (Allsop, 1989). This has become apparent in the changes which have had to be made by Social Services Departments in the implementation of a mixed-economy approach to community care.

It can be seen therefore that there are some contradictions between the government's expressed wish to devolve responsibility and the need to keep control. The concept of the enabling State could in reality become the regulatory State.

Individualism

Central to the beliefs of those who favour an anti-collectivist approach to welfare is the view that the Welfare State has taken away from individuals their responsibility to take charge of their lives and to be responsible for their actions. The promotion of individualism and 'rolling back' the boundaries of the Welfare State has been an important feature of Conservative Party policy in all areas of welfare provision.

Much of this thinking can be seen in the various policy initiatives surrounding health education and screening programmes. These methods focus on a 'victim-blaming' approach – that is on changing individual behaviour rather than looking at the underlying reasons which might be more important (Allsop, 1989). Smoking can be seen to be an example of this; can the individual really shoulder all the blame for indulging in a habit that is heavily promoted by massive advertising campaigns?

The government's strategy in the 'Health of the Nation' (1992) has been criticized for adopting the same narrow approach – an approach which emphasizes the health worker's role in educating the public to recognize that individual lifestyle can have profound effects on health. Through this education, the individual is then free to make the correct and informed health choices. This policy approach fails to make an explicit connection between ill health and poverty or poor housing, for example, although it does acknowledge that people in manufacturing occupations generally have higher rates of illness and death than those in non-manual occupations.

Even more worrying, 'Health of the Nation' (DoH, 1992) attributes differences in health status partly to increases in 'risk behaviour' – a strategy that may lead to even more 'victim-blaming'. There are already protocols drawn up by some medical teams who refuse to treat individuals unless they give up their 'risk behaviour' (Today Programme, Radio Four, 11 June, 1993).

Community nursing

The changes in the National Health Service and the delivery of care in the community have also had a major impact on community nursing. Reference will be made in chapter 9 to the changes in community care, implemented in April 1993, regarding the care of older people. These changes are also consistent with the government's desire to promote a mixed economy of welfare, to encourage competition, value for money and to involve the voluntary and private sectors in the delivery of care. Social services departments have been given the lead role and statutory responsibility for assessing needs, designing care arrangements and securing the delivery of services. Nurses, however, are expected to be involved in designing packages of care and may take on the role of lead assessor (Community Care Support Force/RCN 1993). Close collaboration between social services and nurses will be required, especially since local authorities are seen to be responsible for social needs and health authorities for health needs. In reality it is often extremely difficult to separate the two. Although the changes have been broadly welcomed, concern has been expressed about the level of funding and the degree of means testing involved (Brindle, 1993). The changes envisaged in the delivery of care could have profound consequences for the organization of community nursing services in the future and on the numbers of people who are cared for in their own homes.

Community nurses are seen to have an important role in assessing the health needs of their local populations. The accurate assessment of health needs and demands for health care are vital components in the drawing up of contracts with purchasers for the provision of appropriate health services. Nurses also have a crucial role in setting standards for the quality of care which should be provided (Mackenzie, 1993). However, they need support in developing these roles, especially at planning and operational levels.

It is envisaged in the report 'New World, New Opportunities' (NHSME, 1993) that primary health care nursing will become more general practice based, GPs becoming more involved in the commissioning process. However, there are concerns that the public-health role of primary health care nurses, particularly school nurses and health visitors, could be cut back. Department of Health guidelines specify that in the GP's contract about 10 per cent of services commissioned should be allocated to a health visitor's public health role, but already some contracts fail to show this allowance (Potrykus, 1993b). It is very important that this area of work is not reduced if nurses are to have an influence on achieving the health targets set in 'Health of the Nation'.

Conclusion

In this chapter we have shown how the provision and delivery of health care has become increasingly politicized. We have emphasized the importance for nurses of developing an understanding of the policy process and the underlying reasons for the major changes which have taken place in the National Health Service. Many of the changes which have taken place have been concerned with the more efficient and effective management of the service and the containment of expenditure. These issues are not unique to the British health service.

We have also highlighted, in our discussion, where and how solutions have been informed by New Right values, with the resulting emphasis on individualism and consumerism. An internal market has been introduced and competition and a mixed-economy approach to the delivery of care have been encouraged. We have pointed out some of the contradictions and problems which have been generated by these policies. Many of the changes have been consistent and closely allied to changes occurring in other fields of Social Policy. However, it has often appeared that nursing has not been prepared for the changes which have taken place and has reacted too late. There has also been little reference to nursing by the government; a notable example is the White Paper 'Working for Patients' (1989) where nursing was not mentioned. Many of the changes occurring could have been predicted and nurses should have been more prepared to act proactively to influence events.

We have also highlighted the dominance of the medical, curative model on the development of the National Health Service. We have shown that recently there has been a renewal of interest in a broader approach to health care which includes policies for health promotion and health education. These are concerns of nurses, generally, not only those working in community care.

The government's attitude to professional groups working in the Health Service is not encouraging. However, it could be argued that a shift in resources towards primary health care could allow the nursing profession to develop rather than constrain it. However, nursing needs to develop an analytical approach which is prepared not only to respond to events but to influence the direction of health care more positively.

Discussion points

1. How does today's health service differ from that envisaged in 1948?
2. Will market forces deliver a better health service than the centralized financial structure in place prior to the late 1980s?
3. Discuss the implications of dividing health and social care in light of community care legislation.

Further reading

Acheson, D. (1988) *Public Health in England: The Report of the Committee of Inquiry into the Future Development of the Public Health Function*, HMSO, London

Allsop, J. (1984) *Health Policy and the National Health Service*, Longman, London

Allsop, J. (1989) Health. In *The New Politics of Welfare* (ed. M. McCarthy), Macmillan, Basingstoke

Allsop, J. (1992) The voice of the user in health care. In *In the Best of Health?* (eds E. Beck, S. Newman and D. Patterson), Chapman & Hall, London, pp. 149–166.

Black Report (1980) *Inequalities and Health*, DHSS, London

Brindle, D. (1993) Nobody's baby. *The Guardian*, March 10 1993, pp. 12–13

Carr-Hill, R. *et al* (1992) *Skill Mix and the Effectiveness of Nursing Care*, *University of York*, Centre for Health Economics, York

Community Care Support Force/Royal College of Nursing (1993) *Community Care*, HMSO, London

Connolly, P. (1978) Definition of health, *Health Visitor*, 51 (12)

Department of Health (1989) *Working for Patients*, HMSO, London

Department of Health (1992) *The Health of the Nation: A Strategy for Health in England*, HMSO, London

Department of Health and Social Security (1979) *Patients First*, HMSO, London

Department of Health and Social Security (1983) *The NHS Management Inquiry* DA (83) 38 (Chairman, Sir Roy Griffiths) DHSS, London

Ham, C. (1992) *Health Policy in Britain*, 3rd edn, Macmillan, Basingstoke

Harrison, S., Hunter, D. J. and Pollit, C. (1990) *The Dynamics of British Health Policy*, Unwin Hyman, London

House of Commons Health Committee (1993) *NHS Trusts: Interim Conclusions and Proposals for Future Enquires*, HMSO, London

Humphreys, J. (1993) An insecure future. *Nursing Standard*, 7 (20), pp. 26–27

Leathard, A. (1990) *Health Care Provision*, Chapman & Hall, London

Levitt, R. and Wall, A. (1992) *The Reorganized Health Service*, 4th edn, Chapman and Hall, London

Mackenzie, A. (1993) Purchasing excellence. *Community Outlook*, 3 (5), p. 14

McKeown, T. (1979) *The Role of Medicine: Dream, Mirage or Nemesis*, Blackwell, Oxford

Millar, B. (1991) 'I have in my hand a piece of paper . . .', *The Health Service Journal*, 101(5277) p. 12

National Health Service Management Executive (1993) *New Word, New Opportunities*, HMSO, London

Perrin, J. (1992) Administrative and financial management of health care services. In *In the Best of Health?* (eds E. Beck, S. Lonsdale, S. Newman and D. Patterson), pp. 251–272, Chapman & Hall, London

Pfeffer, N. (1992) Strings attached. *The Health Service Journal*, 102 (5296), pp. 22–23

Pollitt, C. (1989) Consuming passions. *The Health Service Journal*, 99 (5178), pp. 1436–1437

Potrykus, C. (1993a) MPs highlight loss of planning. *Health Visitor*, 66 (2), p. 38

Potrykus, C. (1993b) Public health role cut as GP contracts start to bite. *Health Visitor*, 66 (6), pp. 188–189

Royal College of Nursing (1988) *The Health Challenge*, RCN, London

Royal College of Nursing (1989) *RCN Response: 'Working for Patients'*, Royal College of Nursing, London

Royal Commission on the National Health Service (1979) *Report*, (Chair Sir Alec Marrison) CMND 7615, HMSO, London

Seedhouse, D. (1986) *Health: The Foundations for Achievement*, John Wiley, Chichester

Whitehead, M. (1987) *The Health Divide*, Health Education Council, London

World Health Organization (1948) *World Health Organization Constitution*, WHO, Geneva

World Health Organization (1965) *Constitution Basic Documents*, 10th edn, WHO, Geneva

World Health Organization (1978) *Alma Ata 1978 Primary Health Care*, WHO, Geneva

World Health Organization (1985) *Targets for Health for All*, Regional Office for Europe, WHO, Copenhagen

5

Caring and social policy

Sian Maslin-Prothero

Introduction

This chapter discusses caring, beginning with an explanation of what caring means. The main emphasis will be on women as carers, because there continues to be sexual division in caring in both the public and private domains. Women are still primarily responsible for the majority of care that takes place both inside and outside the home. There will be some discussion of how, and in what way, social policies define and impact upon the caring role. Against this background the position of nurses and the way in which they are affected by the ideology underpinning caring will be examined. The framework used throughout is that of 'radical feminism' a theoretical approach that traces the source of women's oppression to the universal system of patriarchy. Throughout there will be links made to many of the other chapters in the book.

Explanations of caring

There has been much written about caring, in both nursing and social policy literature, and there is a need to define what care means. The dictionary definition (Cassell, 1990) contains ideas such as providing for, having affection, respect and liking for and being concerned about. Interestingly the definition also invokes images of being careworn and having sorrow and grief which implies an associated pain and suffering. Caring is thus complex and has a multiplicity of meanings. There is the additional dimension of caring for and caring about (Dalley, 1988); caring for someone is usually associated with tending, whereas caring about is identified with feelings for a person. The assumption is that those who care for someone, should also care about them – particularly if they are women. Bishop and Scudder (1991) suggest that caring has a double meaning in that it can mean both concern for others and taking care of others. Caring is also associated with kin relationships, this is an assumption rather than an absolute.

However, caring need not be a parasitic relationship, but one where an individual sees caring for someone as an extension of themselves, thus being supported and encouraged to grow (Mayeroff, 1971). Caring is a two-way, reciprocal relationship, where each individual has something to contribute to the relationship. An example of this would be two older sisters living together independently in the community and who appear to be coping with little or no support. One of them is admitted to hospital with pneumonia and subsequently the sister remaining at home is noted to be disorientated and confused. On closer assessment she is found to be suffering from dementia. Prior to the admission, each of the sisters supported and compensated for the other's inabilities or difficulties. This scenario illustrates the complexity of the caring relationship. To care for someone is seen as a form of love, a feeling, hence the carer has some kind of fondness for the individual being cared for; this will be returned to when discussing the nursing perspective.

There is also the need to recognize the multidimensional nature of caring and the variety of those cared for who may include the young or old, family, friends, partners, clients, patients – who may be able, disabled or ill.

The majority of caring takes place in the home, known in policy terms as the private domain, and in the literature is often referred to as informal caring. Only a small amount occurs in the public domain, such as hospitals, community homes and hostels – this is referred to as formal caring. Wherever caring is occurring it is usually associated with women, as caring is seen as predominantly women's work. However the National Carers Association dislikes the term 'informal' care because it implies a casual thing and caring for someone in their own home is anything but casual.

Patriarchy and caring

Within this chapter a radical feminist approach has been used to make sense of the assumptions made about responsibilities for care. This approach identifies the source of women's oppression as patriarchy, which has played a key role in the establishment of sexual divisions in both unpaid and paid employment. Walby (1990i) describes patriarchy as 'a system of social structures and practices in which men dominate, oppress and exploit women'.

Not all feminist analysis subscribes to this explanation of the unequal treatment of women. Socialist feminists for example point to the capitalist mode of production and the class system as being equally subordinating. The precise way in which capitalism and patriarchy interconnect to oppress women, however, remains unclear and much feminist discourse concerns these issues (see chapter 6, on women and policy, for a fuller discussion of feminist theory).

Radical feminists, although accepting that there is a relationship between class and subordination, argue that women's status is in fact independent of their social class; women of higher social classes are subordinate to men, just as women from other social classes are subject to male oppression (Pascall, 1986; Millett, 1970 cited in Haralambos and Holborn, 1990). Patriarchal values pervade both the domestic domain (home) and the public sphere (work) and in both locations women are still to be found in a subordinate position to men. Jobs continue to be sex-typed so that women are segregated from men and frequently paid less (Hartmann, 1976; Walby, 1990). Consequently, women are often in the position of being financially dependent on men and are thus unable to break the bonds of their oppression – and so the system of patriarchy is reproduced and maintained.

At its simplest patriarchy gives men both overt and covert power over women; there is an expectation placed upon women to perform tasks – domestic or caring – and women may find themselves in the position of being unable to disagree. For the most part, however, this is not an open conflict between men and women, rather it is seen as being the 'natural order' of things (see chapter 3 for a discussion on this dimension of power). In addition, many men (and women) would be horrified if it were suggested that men actively encourage and support patriarchy – it is more the case that this male hegemony is simply accepted and expected at every level of our societal structure.

Through women's entry into the labour market, however, women's exploitation within the private sphere is lessening, although women continue to be responsible for the co-ordination and running of the home, including caring for the family. In the late 1960s and early 1970s there was much talk about 'the symmetrical family', and a move to share the household tasks, including cleaning, cooking and caring, equally. In the 1990s, however, we continue to see mothers undertaking a triple shift: having to care for the children and partner, do the housework and often work either in a full or part-time job (British Social Attitudes Survey 1992).

Sexual division of labour and caring

Assumptions that women are the main providers of care are well recognized and arguments have been presented to support this. These include both genetics and women's biological ability to have children.

Gene theory

Some socio-biologists suggest that women's genes are both 'submissive and nurturing', whereas men's genes are 'domineering'; therefore they see women's natural inclination as to nurture (Tiger and Fox, 1972). This explanation has been widely rejected by a number of feminists, in particular by Oakley (1972) who points out that sex-differentiated roles are not inevitable and in some societies individuals are equally cared for by men and women.

Biological fact

Women are also perceived as being closer to nature due to their biology and reproductive role, as they are the ones capable of actually giving birth. Although men participate in procreation through providing the sperm to fertilize the ovum, they are still unable to give birth. Upon this biological fact the whole of women's social experience is built.

Chodorow (1978, cited in Graham, 1983) suggests that women also have the power to reproduce themselves through the mother/daughter relationship wherein the sexual division of labour and their role within the private sphere is reinforced and maintained.

The nature/culture debate, of which there has only been a brief discussion here, goes some way to explaining the stereotypes of men and women. However, if men chose to be more involved in the nurturing and parenting of their offspring and other family members, this might result in a change in the stereotypical roles adopted by men and women in both the private and public sphere as well as in the assumptions that accompany these roles.

Because women are seen as being 'natural' carers either due to genetics or their reproductive role, they are also seen as being the main providers in the home, which is seen as an 'expressive' role, whereas men are perceived to be 'instrumental', that is they go out into the public sphere to earn money to support the family. Consequently, we see the sexual division of labour both inside and outside the home, that is both privately and publicly.

Private division of labour

In the home women are seen as carers by the family, care managers and other professionals (Graham, 1991; Finch and Groves, 1983; Graham, 1983; Oliver, 1983). There is an expectation that they should nurture and provide sustenance for the family members through support, feeding, cleaning and healing (Oakley, 1974; Graham, 1991). Caring is demanding, time consuming and has few financial rewards. Caring has been relegated to being both a low-status job, lacking in power and with little control personally or financially.

Assumptions are often made about families' ability to care for their members. For example there is a belief common in nursing that the Asian groups have extensive extended families who will provide care for all family members (Gunaratnam, 1993; see chapter 8). It has been identified that some black communities are unaware of the facilities and support available from the UK's health and social services (Hek, 1990). Some of the issues are being addressed by such publications as 'Talkback' (King's Fund, 1993). This is a bulletin from the King's Fund Centre which informs black carers in the UK about services which may be appropriate and accessible to them.

Despite there being a difference between men and women and their caring roles, there is evidence to suggest that it is a myth that men do not undertake caring activities (Green, 1988; Parker, 1992; Bond, 1992). Following analysis of the 1985 General Household Survey, the results implied that there may be as many as two-and-a-half million male carers, compared to three-and-a-half million female carers in Great Britain – this does not include those caring for children (Parker, 1992; National Carers Survey, 1992). Parker (1992) and others have offered explanations of why there appear to be increasing numbers of men undertaking the caring role, for example, women are less likely to identify that they are caring for someone (other than a child) because they perceive caring to be a normal part of their life. Moreover since the advent of HIV, and because homosexual and bisexual males are vulnerable to sero-conversion, there are more men caring for male partners, or 'buddying' individuals living with HIV.

However, the experience of male carers is different to that of females. For example men are less likely to be found performing personal care such as washing, toileting and bathing and men are more likely than women to receive additional support from health and social services, which varies according to marital status (Hicks, 1988). Men are also more often to be found caring only for wives or partners, whereas women are caring for a variety of different people such as immediate family, in-laws, neighbours and friends (Ungerson, 1987). But the impact of caring can be far greater for men, when compared with women, particularly with regards to employment and careers. Men experience a greater loss in earning than women; however, this can be explained by the fact that on average men's earnings are 25 per cent higher than women in comparable jobs (Equal Opportunities Commission (EOC), 1992). One of men's perceived roles continues to be that of the breadwinner, thus the objective of health and social service workers appears to be to enable men to remain in paid work. There is evidence to suggest that men find it easier to get time off work, or negotiate flexible working patterns, without the fear of being discriminated against in their employment (Care to Work, 1990).

There are networks of carers (of both sexes) operating in the community. However, there is usually one person primarily responsible for the co-ordination of the network, and that is usually a woman (Nissel and Bonnerjea, 1982).

Public division of labour

Outside the home, within the public world of paid work, the expressive role ascribed to women continues to impact upon the work to which they are assigned and to which they have access. In the labour market women are to be found undertaking work which rarely rewards the skills and attributes they bring with them to the workplace. They are usually to be found working in low-status, low-pay jobs; this was highlighted by Davies and Rosser (1986), who noted that women's psychological, social and managerial skills acquired through domesticity were exploited and these women took on responsibilities in the workplace that went unacknowledged and unrewarded by their managers. Managers appear to exploit what women are seen to be good at, namely nursing, nurturing and caring. It would appear that those women who do choose to work outside the home have sanctions imposed on them, because they are seen as deviating from their 'natural' role. The sanctions include low pay, low status, unequal pensions and labour-intensive work. Graham (1983i) summed this up succinctly when she commented 'Women's paid work, is often the market equivalent of the unpaid work [that they do at home]'.

In spite of the increase in the number of women working, there continues to be evidence of occupational segregation, that is those jobs deemed suitable for men and those for women (Bradley, 1989). It could be argued that women are not as economically active as men, because they are encouraged to take time out of the labour market to care for dependents and this accounts for differences in representation.

There appear to be two types of occupational segregation, identified by Hakim in 1979; horizontal segregation whereby men and women work in different occupations, such as the example of nursing for women and engineering for men; and vertical segregation, where men are to be found in higher grades to women within the same job (Hakim, 1979).

Primary and secondary socialization into sex and gender roles is the first explanation for this pattern of segregation. Gender development occurs as a result of interactions from a variety of sources, such as parents, siblings, games, the media and schools. The expectations, aspirations and behaviours instilled by the process of socialization are pervasive and deep-seated, for example, in terms of employment segregation there is evidence that the school curriculum and careers advice has long been underpinned by sexist attitudes and beliefs (Garrett, 1987; Spender, 1982). In the same vein Cockburn's (1987) examination of Youth Training Scheme trainees identified that, in spite of the promise of equal opportunities, girls were still attracted to traditional women's work, such as office work or caring. Cockburn (1987) went on to recommend that boys and men should be encouraged to develop nurturing and tending skills – if stereotypes are socially constructed, they will only be changed by life experience. Some of these are being addressed by the National Curriculum.

Becker's human capital theory is an economic explanation of work inequalities wherein men and women have different commitments to paid work and the home; subsequently, women choose to see the home as their main priority and, as a result, either take time out of paid work (in order to have a family), or do not invest in themselves by obtaining further and relevant qualifications (Becker, 1985 cited in Hakim, 1991; Chiplin and Greig, 1986; Winters, 1992).

But are women pressured to take jobs that they perceive to be feminine, or does sexual stereotyping take place because men and women have different working patterns? It could be argued that because of women's domestic role, they are restricted in the hours that they work, the training they undertake, and subsequently the occupation they choose.

There is the need to recognize that men are not solely responsible for the financial support of families, due in part to male unemployment, the rising numbers of single-parent households and more women in the labour market. With the increase in the number of women raising families on their own, either through necessity or choice, the idea of the family wage being a male prerogative is out of date (Brannen, 1992). However, women's limited access to better jobs does prevent them from earning a 'family' wage. Employers and trade unions have a responsibility to recognize this and enable women to move freely, according to their skills, to jobs which acknowledge and reward their abilities.

It is difficult combining the responsibilities of family and career in Britain, and the government's apparent philosophy is that care of dependants is predominantly the responsibility of the family, with additional support from employers. Neither the government nor some employers see this care as part of their remit, nor do they see that there is a link between equal opportunities policies and enabling careers.

Sex-role stereotypes are often reinforced by managements' perception of women. Some women experience being 'tied' to a particular job because their current managers are willing to be flexible and to change jobs would mean that they would lose this advantage.

In addition some would argue that women's wages actually reflect managers' view of their 'proper' place – in the home (Ungerson, 1983) – as women's rates of pay continue to be below those of men in similar positions, in spite of the Equal Pay Act (EOC, 1992). This, along with many other social policies, actually discourages some women from seeking work outside the home (Brannen, 1987).

Children appear to have a significant effect on the careers of women but not on those of men (Hunt, 1991). There is a belief on the part of managers that women would choose to put their children before their careers, subsequently there tends to be a lack of facilities for those women with children, such as job sharing, flexitime, part-time work and child-care facilities, in spite of initiatives such as Opportunity 2000 (Davies and Rosser, 1986; EOC, 1991; Hunt, 1991; NHS Management Executive, 1991). Those women who have achieved leadership positions, in the NHS, tend to be unmarried and childless (Hardy, 1986).

Legislation fails to tackle power operating at the third level (see chapter 3), for example sex-stereotyping, and encourages (and enshrines) the dual labour market. As such legislation can only be used retrospectively, women are still being channelled into occupations which can be seen as an extension of their domestic roles. Notwithstanding, women do not want to become 'token men' and lose skills that they possess but to have these skills recognized and to be given credit for their knowledge.

In 1989, the EOC identified some themes and objectives they wanted achieved in order to make both women and men effective and responsible employees and effective and responsible family members (EOC, 1989 cited in Ungerson, 1990). Included were such things as: support for carers and parents; out-of-school care and holiday schemes; valuing of part-time workers and equal benefits (same as for full-time workers); and improved training and status for child-minders. But there are other points that need to be included: better maternity and paternity leave and benefits; increase in the numbers of job shares and more flexible working arrangements, all highlighted in the NHS Management Executive handbook (1991).

In addition, there is the need to look at how we socialize children (in the home, school and through the media) and to encourage girls to be strong and assertive, as well as developing boys' sensitivity and caring.

Equal opportunities aim to eliminate sexual, marital and racial discrimination; there have been nearly twenty years of legislation, but how much has been achieved during this time? Soon the demographic changes in the population will have an effect on the recruitment of 18 year olds into the labour market; employers, not only in the NHS, will have to look beyond traditional areas of recruitment, and turn to other forms of labour, that is older women, men, parents and carers. However, the current recession may mean that women are jettisoned from even those jobs they have traditionally held, as described by the reverse army of labour thesis (Bruegel, 1979).

Social policies and caring

Underpinning much welfare provision is the assumption that caring for someone is not true work – a fact reflected in the division of labour at home and at work. This section takes a critical look at social policy and caring. Much of this critique draws on material covered in more detail in those chapters concerned with policy and the family, older people and those with a disability.

As discussed earlier, in Western societies motherhood is socially constructed and it is assumed that young children will be cared for by their mothers. There has been a belief that if children were not cared for by their mothers they would suffer from maternal deprivation, and as a result suffer psychologically (Bowlby, 1953 cited in Pascall, 1986) – a claim now modified to suggest that so long as children have a safe and secure relationship with an adult they should not experience deprivation. The majority of young children live with either one or both parents (Lewis, 1992).

This emphasis on the need for maternal care, however, is still the mainstay of much of our social policy. Public provision of day care for children under the age of five years in Britain is a case in point, especially when compared with other European countries such as France, or the Scandinavian countries. Those facilities that are available for children under five years are for those with special needs, such as physical or learning disabilities, or for families who require additional support because of social problems. There is nursery provision for children over the age of three years but this is usually for half a day, either five mornings or five afternoons a week. This means that a carer needs to be available to drop off the child at nursery, and then be available to pick him/her up again two-and-a-half hours later. This paucity of State care forces many families and carers to rely on informal networks such as family or friends for help and support with caring for small children when they want to engage in paid work.

All welfare benefits are payable to the (male) head of the household with the exception of Child Benefit. This is the only allowance payable to mothers directly for caring for children and is paid on a weekly basis, at a flat rate for each child (£10 for the first child, the £8.10 for subsequent children [April 1993 rates]). This allowance is universally provided, that is it is not means tested and is available for all families, regardless of income. It is however constantly under threat of cut and discontinuation. For several years the rate of benefit, usually linked to cost-of-living rises, was frozen by the Conservative government, and there is still the very real possibility of it becoming means tested. Underlying this policy review is the assumption that the family finance is shared and therefore the need for the State to financially support carers of children, usually women, is obsolete. The male breadwinner will provide as required. In reality however women are responsible for the management of costly expenditures such as food, heating, rent and clothing, but men actually control the money (Graham, 1984). Women and children are often living in an individual state of poverty, even though adequate finances are seemingly entering the household (this 'feminization of poverty' is discussed by Payne, 1991).

The concept of community care has become increasingly popular over recent decades in respect of people with mental health problems, learning disabilities and the old and infirm. Feminist writers increasingly see 'community care' as an abdication of responsibility for care by the State and men; care in the community is increasingly seen as being care by the community, which essentially means care by women. The assumption is that women will care – that is, women are expected to substitute for nursing and social services (Pascall, 1986). Only when individuals are in institutions, such as hospitals, does the State bear the full cost of care – that is the care is both organized and funded by the State.

Institutions, however, are very expensive and the cost of maintaining them continues to escalate. Hospitals are able to treat more conditions than previously, they have more advanced equipment for diagnosing and as a result care is more intensive and more expensive. With the changes brought about by the government's White Paper 'Working for Patients' (DoH, 1989), which emphasizes cost effectiveness and value for money, there is tremendous pressure on hospitals to treat more people, limit the amount of time patients stay in hospital and generally to create a more rapid turnover (Audit Commission, 1992). Consequently more people are being discharged earlier into the community. Unfortunately there is often limited support for those who are discharged home, especially if it is perceived that there is someone at home who could look after them (Payne, 1989). Again the expectation is women will provide the care. On the other hand, as already suggested above, male carers receive more help and support from social and community services (Nissel and Bonnerjea, 1982). Where there is no family, the State sometimes substitutes and provides care, although this is not always the case – consider the plight of the homeless.

A common belief in health and social services is that the family, rather than the State should support dependants – a legacy from classical liberal economics when families were seen as being liable for family members (see chapter 3). It has been postulated that the money saved by carers providing for dependants is equivalent to the total expenditure for both health and social services (Land, 1991), Yet there are different experiences for men and for women. Men are not expected to care for dependants, but it is anticipated that they care about them. Hence, a 'good' son provides for his family, and a 'good' daughter juggles her career, marriage and independence to care for relatives. There has been considerable discussion and debate about '1990s man', who is allegedly more caring and compassionate than his predecessor (Segal, 1987). Does he really exist, or is it another myth dreamt up by the advertisers to sell more products? According to the latest edition of the British Social Attitudes Survey (1992), the thought is there, but in reality women are still undertaking those tasks seen as 'women's work', that is cleaning, caring and cooking. Men continue to have both the power and resources to choose not to be involved in care. Men obtain self worth from their activities and achievements through their work, rarely through caring (Baldwin and Twigg, 1991).

Many of these ideas about caring have been embodied in the considerable changes taking place both in the health and social services over the last decade. Griffiths (1988) in his examination of community services saw family, friends and neighbours as being the cornerstone of care. His review formed the basis of the subsequent White Paper, 'Caring for People' (1989) which was the second part of the NHS and Community Care Act 1990, implemented in April 1993.

Under this new legislation responsibility for financing and assessing requirements for care will be in the hands of local social services departments. Assessment will be undertaken by social service care managers who have a devolved budget to 'buy in' care as suited to the needs of the client – for example residential or nursing-home care, home help, meals on wheels and so on. The overall aim is to encourage a mixed economy of care by using voluntary, private and statutory providers (Audit Commission, 1992) and to secure the most cost-effective package of care, taking into consideration the needs of the cared for and the carers (DoH, 1989). We have yet to see the full implications of this legislation.

Women and work

Paradoxically, in the midst of these myriad policy changes that are assuming women's support, it can no longer be taken for granted that there will be women available to care. Since the Second World War there has been an increase in the number of women working outside the home, particularly married women (Dale and Glover, 1990). The reasons for this increase are multiple and include: the increase in the number of single-parent households and their subsequent need for money; the need for a double income to keep the household out of poverty; women's own wish to recommence or start a new career; the need to recruit more women to the labour force to counteract the falling numbers of available 18 year olds for training and education; and as a means of providing a break for women from the home environment and giving them opportunities for mixing and socializing with other adults (Cohen and Clark, 1986; Graham, 1983; Ungerson, 1983).

The move towards care in the community and the closure of many large institutions, as well as the growing numbers of people over the age of 75, raises questions as to who is going to be responsible both physically and financially for the care of these people in the future.

Increasingly, women are trying to arrange adequate care for their dependants, while they are working, at a cost which is not prohibitive. In some areas, this situation has led to outside agencies adopting the responsibility for non-institutional care, the majority of which is provided by informal caring networks, such as families and voluntary groups. As has been mentioned previously, care in the community is often seen as care by the community – and this is a euphemism for women (Rimmer, 1983).

The new policy changes, combined with the increased involvement of women in the labour market, means that women, in either multiple or single-income households, have a worsening experience of the double burden of paid work outside the home and unpaid work in the home (Arber and Gilbert, 1992), plus having to 'juggle' their responsibilities of work, home and dependants – the triple shift (Pascall, 1986). Women often find themselves restricted with regard to the work they are able to undertake due to the growing responsibilities they have at home. This can lead to the situation of the 'understanding' employer, who appears to provide flexible employment through allowing women to come in late after dropping children at school, or taking a day off when their elderly aunt is too ill to go to a day centre and not be left alone at home. The reality of the situation is that these women are often at an increased disadvantage because they do not get paid when they are not at work, plus they may well suffer additional disadvantages of part-time employment: low pay, lack of pension rights and maternity leave, and no sick pay.

For those families who have disabled children, this responsibility, the triple burden, may continue throughout their child's life. What is to happen as the carers grow older, and are less able to lift or handle an adult who perhaps does not want to get up and dressed, and how much does this impact on the main carer's ability to continue working outside the home?

The failure of the State to provide adequate compensation to those who care often precludes the option not to work. People literally cannot afford to stay at home. Yet, the cost of caring for someone in a hospital is astronomical – not only are there the costs of the building but also maintenance, staff wages, lighting, equipment, drugs and heating. In reality it is unlikely that these costs will be transferred to the community to finance the on-going care there.

A classic example of this poor support was the Invalid Care Allowance, which prior to 1986 was not available to married or cohabiting women caring for someone at home. This was eventually changed by the European Court of Justice. The assumption was that married or cohabiting women's responsibility was to care, it was both natural and normal, and therefore they did not need financial compensation for undertaking this labour of love.

It is evident that the cost of caring is high for women in every sense: physically, emotionally, psychologically, financially and socially (Graham, 1983; Smith, 1992). However there has been little research carried out to identify in detail the costs to carers' health (Brotchie and Hills, 1991). But with the increasing numbers of older and physically and mentally disabled people being cared for in the community, by either family or voluntary agencies, it can be presumed that the physical and emotional work necessary to provide care – lifting, moving, disrupted sleep, lack of additional support – can contribute towards the ill health of the carer.

There has been a tendency for both social workers and nurses to blame those carers who are no longer able to cope with caring for dependent relatives, rather than recognizing the tremendous cost caring makes on those who care for family or friends (Dale and Foster, 1986). These costs are not only financial – through lost earnings, pensions, bills and so on as discussed previously – but also physical, social, psychological (Graham, 1983; 1984; 1985; 1990). It is the nurses' contribution to care which is examined next.

Nursing perspective

Caring at work: the nursing workforce

Ninety per cent of nurses and midwives are female (EOC, (1991). However, historically this was not always the case, contrary to popular belief men have been involved in caring throughout history. Dolan (1993) discusses men undertaking nursing for various religious orders in the third and sixth centuries. During the crusades, there was a need to supply fit soldiers to fight; women were believed to be unsuitable for this kind of work, therefore men provided nursing skills (Bush, 1976 cited in Dolan, 1993). This began to change over the centuries, and since the Crimean War (and the influence of Florence Nightingale) women have become associated with nursing, except in those disciplines of mental health and learning disabilities which continue to recruit significant numbers of men. Nursing is now an example of occupational segregation.

The NHS is the largest employer of women in Western Europe and a large number of these workers are nurses (EOC, 1991). Walby intimated that by entering nursing, women avoided the controlling influence of private patriarchy, that is of father or husband (Walby, 1990). She goes on to argue, however, that doctors are the individuals with power and control in hospital, and that it is invariably men who achieve the more senior medical and general management positions. This could change as over 50 per cent of those entering medical training are female (Allen, 1988). However, medicine is chauvinistic, and this is illustrated by the paucity of female doctors who are consultants, particularly in the prestige specialities such as surgery (EOC, 1991).

Walby suggests that 'lady bountifuls' and individuals like Florence Nightingale have reinforced the idea of women as unpaid carers (Walby, 1990). As Oakley proposed, if Florence Nightingale had taught nurses about assertiveness, rather than obedience, perhaps nurses would be in a more advantageous position now (Oakley, 1984 cited in Bridges, 1990). Jones (1985, cited in Savage, 1987) went as far as to suggest that female nurses actually choose not to become leaders or managers, and that women are where they want to be – at the bedside – and not because of discriminating policies and procedures within the NHS (Davies and Rosser, 1986; Winter, 1992). It appears that there is still a tendency to rationalize rather than identify the real problem – women are discriminated against in the health service because of their gender, and the institutionalization of patriarchy.

In nursing men are over represented in senior jobs, such as education – an example of vertical segregation (as discussed earlier), and they achieve these positions far more quickly than women (Nursing Standard, 1992a; Nuttall, 1983). Spencer and Podmore (1987) recognized that women are seen as natural carers and domestics, and that there are few women in senior positions available to 'sponsor' or support those women who want to develop their career (Spencer and Podmore, 1987; NHS Management Executive, 1991). There are a few female role models at the top in nursing, for example Yvonne Moore (DoH) and Christine Hancock (General Secretary to the Royal College of Nursing). When there are more women in nursing leadership, then perhaps attitudes towards women will begin to change (Hunt, 1991; Nursing Standard, 1992b).

Part-time nurses appear to be disadvantaged in comparison to full-time staff; women are overrepresented in part-time nursing. In a recent study Beechey and Perkins (1987) found that of the 44 per cent of qualified nurses working part-time, only 4 per cent of them were charge nurses. These nurses tended to have lower grades and hence wages, and were employed on a sessional basis, and therefore did not receive holiday benefits.

Part-timers also experienced problems in accessing further development and training, (Beechey and Perkins, 1987; EOC, 1991). Additionally, there appears to be little choice for part-time workers with regard to the shifts they work. The majority tend to work night duty, and at busy times during the day (EOC, 1991); there is the common assumption that this is to their advantage, rather than to the organizations'. In spite of increased calls for flexibility within the NHS, there still appears to be little choice about what hours nurses can work.

Nurses and caring

Nurses claim that caring has a central role to play in nursing. However there is minimal investigation into the nature of these core elements, particularly qualitative research (Morrison and Burnard, 1991). In America at the University of Colorado School of Nursing, nurses have created a Centre of Human Caring. This centre (which has a branch in Inverness) explores the issue of caring through education, research and practice with a view to developing philosophies and theories about caring and thus empowering both women and nurses as carers (Watson, 1991).

Nurses have actively pursued professionalism (Hugman, 1991) and yet continue to be seen as a semi-profession because nurses lack autonomy and control over their work. However, do nurses really want to adopt wholesale the male characteristics (objectivity, control, distance and so on) of other professions, such as doctors and lawyers (Hugman, 1991)? Surely nurses should recognize the unique and infinitely preferable alternative contribution which caring has to make to our profession.

Nursing is the practice by which concern for patients/clients is expressed through providing expert professional care (Bishop and Scudder, 1991). There are others who argue that within the formal and informal care giving, the individual being cared for is in a subordinate position to that of the care giver. Bond (1992) refers to this as political dependence. The views of the care provider are seen as paramount rather than the recipient's.

Kitson (1992) explores these ideas further and identifies three phases in the development of a conceptual framework for caring: caring-as-duty; caring-as-a-therapeutic-relationship; and caring-as-ethical-position. Caring-as-duty is closely associated with women and the perception of women's caring and nurturing role. This was operationalized in nursing as task orientation with the nurse being placed in a subservient position, characterized by dedication and obedience. In the 1960s and 1970s the concept of caring-as-a-therapeutic-relationship was developed from psychotherapeutic philosophy. Once adopted and adapted by nurses, a more individualized approach to care, incorporating qualities such as empathy, trust and respect and a valuing of patients'/clients' views, resulted (Kitson, 1992). The final concept – caring-as-ethical-position – encourages a problem-solving, patient-centred approach, where both the patient and nurse are actively and equally involved in decision making. As Kitson suggests 'Caring practices are seen as grounded in the shared experiences of the nurse and the patient' (1992i). Kitson (1992) argues that the ultimate aim for nurses is to move from a needs-based to a holistic approach to care.

There is a difference between carers and nurses. Nurses have developed the caring practice of nursing. It is something they have chosen to enter. Nurses need to develop their ability not to dominate and take over the care of a 'person' but to assess that 'person' and, as a result of this assessment, to offer support and encourage self care, not dependency. Such an approach aims to empower patients/clients, giving them the freedom to make informed choices.

Conclusion

Caring and the way in which social policies define and impact on the caring role have been the central themes of this chapter. The multidimensional nature of caring and the way the responsibility for this falls predominantly on women in both the public and private domains was examined. In addition the legitimacy of the profession's claim that caring is the foundation of nursing was debated. This argument was linked into the way in which nursing has been affected by the ideology which underpins caring. Through this exploration it became apparent that caring is subordinated to having a lowly status in both the private and public domains.

Nurses are in the perfect position to recognize the strain that carers are under, emotional, physical, psychological and financial, through listening and providing help and support. Too often we add to the burden by failing to recognize these difficulties. In addition, nurses need to become more aware of social policies influencing their own and carers' roles. Thus empowered they can create change through raising their own awareness and becoming actively involved in lobbying governments to make changes to social policies.

Discussion points

1. Is caring in crisis? Discuss in relation to recent changes in the provision of caring in the public sector
2. Is there such a thing as 'women's work'? And if so, why?
3. What are the problems for carers, and how might they be overcome?

Further reading

Equal Opportunities Commission (1991) *Equality Management: Women's Employment in the NHS*, EOC Manchester
This provides an overview of what is going on in the NHS with regard to equal opportunities.

Finch, F. and Groves, D. (eds) (1983) *A Labour of Love: Women, Work and Caring*, Routledge & Kegan Paul, London
An excellent introduction to the issues surrounding women and caring.

Kitson, A. (ed.) (1992) *Nursing: Art and Science*, Chapman & Hall, London
This book is based on a series of seminars at the Institute of Nursing in Oxford. It offers a conceptual framework for nursing, and encourages nurses to be more involved in health policy formulation.

Hugman, R. (1991) *Power in Caring Professions*, Macmillan, London
This book should be essential reading for all those involved in the caring professions. Summarizes the reasons why nurses (including other semi-professionals) lack power.

Pascall, G. (1986) *Social Policy: A Feminist Perspective*, Tavistock, London
An introduction to social policy from a feminist perspective. You cannot understand the workings of the Welfare State without recognizing how it deals with women. This book gives a feminist perspective on social policies and how they can sometimes enable women, or control women.

References

Arber, S. and Gilbert, N. (1992) Re-assessing women's working lives: an introductory essay. In *Women and Working Lives: Divisions and Change* (eds S. Arber and N. Gilbert) Macmillan, London

Audit Commission (1992) *The Community Revolution: Personal Social Services and Community Care*, HMSO, London

Baldwin, S. and Twigg, J. (1991) Women and community care – reflections on a debate. In *Women's Issues in Social Policy*, (eds M. Maclean and D. Groves) Routledge, London, pp. 117–135

Beechey, V. and Perkins, T. (1987) *Women, Part-time Work and the Labour Market*, Polity Press, Oxford

Bishop, A. H. and Scudder, J. R. (1991) *Nursing: The Practice of Caring*, National League for Nursing, New York

Bond, J. (1992) The politics of caregiving: the professionalisation of informal care. *Ageing and Society*, **12**, 5–21

Bradley, H. (1989) *Men's Work, Women's Work*, Polity Press, Oxford

Brannen, J. (1987) The resumption of employment after childbirth: a turning point within a life-course perspective. In *Women and the Life Cycle* (eds P. Allatt, T. Keil, A. Bryman and B. Bytheway) Macmillan, London, pp. 165–177

Brannen, J. (1992) Money, marriage and motherhood: dual earner households after maternity leave. In *Women and Working Lives: Divisions and Change*, (eds S. Arber and N. Gilbert) Macmillan, London, pp. 54–70

Bridges, J. M. (1990) Literature review on the images of the nurse and nursing in the media. *Journal of Advanced Nursing*, **15**, 850–854

Brotchie, J. and Hills, D. (1991) *Equal Shares in Caring*, Socialist Health Association, London

Bruegel, I. (1979) Women as a reserve army of labour: a note on recent British experience. *Feminist Review*, 3, pp. 12–23

Care to Work (1990) *Survey Report 1*, London Opportunities For Women, London

Cassell (1990) *The Cassell Paperback English Dictionary*, Cassell, London

Chiplin, B. and Greig, N. (1986) *Equality of Opportunity for Women in the NHS*, DHSS, London

Cockburn, C. (1987) *Two Tracked Training: Sex Inequalities and the YTS*, Macmillan, London

Cohen, B. and Clark, K. (1986) Childcare and equal opportunities: some policy perspectives. In *Childcare and Equal Opportunities*, (ed. Equal Opportunities Commission) EOC, London, pp. 1–9

Dale, J. and Foster, P. (1986) *Feminists and State Welfare*, Routledge & Kegan Paul, London

Dale, A. and Glover, J. (1990) *An Analysis of Women's Employment Patterns in the UK, France and USA: The Value of Survey Based Comparisons*, Department of Employment, London

Dalley, G. (1988) *Ideologies of Caring*, Macmillan, London

Davies, C. and Rosser, J. (1986) *Processes of Discrimination: A Study of Women Working in the NHS*, DHSS, London

Department of Health (1989) *Caring For People: Community Care in the Next Decade and Beyond*, HMSO, London

Department of Health (1990) *Policy Guidance: Community Care in the Next Decade and Beyond*, HMSO, London

Dolan, B. (1993) Gender and change. In *Project 2000: Reflection and Celebration*, (ed. B. Dolan) Scutari, London, pp. 75–88

Equal Opportunities Commission (1991) *Equality Management: Women's Employment in the NHS*, EOC, Manchester

Equal Opportunities Commission (1992) *Annual Report 1991: The Equality Challenge*, EOC, Manchester

Finch, J. and Groves, D. (eds) (1983) *A Labour of Love: Women, Work and Caring*, Routledge & Kegan Paul, London

Garratt, S. (1987) *Gender*, Tavistock, London

Graham, H. (1983) Caring: a labour of love. In *A Labour of Love: Women, Work and Caring*, (i) p. 27. (eds J. Finch and D. Groves) Routledge & Kegan Paul, London, pp. 13–30

Graham, H. (1984) *Women, Health and the Family*, Harvester, London

Graham, H. (1985) Providers, negotiators, and mediators: women as the hidden carers. In *Women, Health and Healing*, (eds E. Lewin and V. Olsen) Tavistock, London, pp. 25–52

Graham, H. (1990) Behaving well: women's health behaviour in context. In *Women's Health Counts*, (ed. H. Roberts) Routledge, London, pp. 195–219

Graham, H. (1991) The concepts of caring in feminist research: the case of domestic service. *Sociology*, **25**(1), February, 61–78

Green, H. (1988) *Informal Carers*, HMSO, London

Griffiths, R. (1988) *Community Care: An Agenda for Action*, HMSO, London

Gunaratnam, Y. (1993) Breaking the silence: Asian carers in Britain. In *Community Care a Reader*, (eds J. Borrat, J. Pereira, D. Pilgrim and F. Williams) Open University Press & Macmillan, London, pp. 114–123

Hakim, C. (1979) *Occupational Segregation, a Comparative Study of the Degree and Pattern of the Differentiation between Men and Women's Work in Britain, the United States, and Other Countries*, Research Paper, No 9, Department of Employment, London

Hakim, C. (1991) Grateful slave and self-made women: fact or fantasy in women's work orientations. *European Sociological Review*, **7**(2), 101–121

Haralambos, M. and Holborn, M. (1990) *Sociology: Themes and Perspectives*, 3rd edn, Unwin Hyman, London

Hardy, L. (1986) Career politics: the case of career histories of selected leading male and female nurses in England and Scotland. In *Political Issues in Nursing, Past, Present and Future 2*, (ed. R. White), John Wiley, London, pp. 69–82

Hartmann, H. (1976) Capitalism, patriarchy and job segregation by sex. In *Women and the Workplace*, (eds M. Blaxall and B. Regean) University of Chicago Press, Chicago, pp. 137–169

Hek, G. (1990) Old people's uptake of district nursing services. Unpublished MA in Sociological Research in Health Care, University of Warwick, Warwick

Hicks, C. (1988) *Who Cares?: Looking After People at Home*, Virago, London

Hugman, R. (1991) *Power in Caring Professions*, Macmillan, London

Hunt, M. (1991) Who flies the highest? *Nursing Times*, 87 (7), 29–31

King's Fund Centre (1993) *Talkback: Black Carers Forum News*, May, 1 (3)

Kitson, A. (1992) Formalizing concepts related to nursing and caring. In *Nursing: Art and Science*, (i) p. 41. (ed. A. Kitson) Chapman & Hall, London, pp. 25–47

Land, H. (1991) Time to care. In *Women's Issues and Social Policy*, (eds M. Maclean and D. Groves) Routledge, London, pp. 7–19

Lewis, J. (1992) *Women in Britain Since 1945*, Blackwell, Oxford

Maclean, M. and Groves, D. (eds) (1991) *Women's Issues and Social Policy*, Routledge, London

Mayeroff, M. (1991) *On Caring*, Harper & Row, London

McKee, L. and O'Brien, M. (eds) (1982) *The Father Figure*, Tavistock, London

Morrison, P. and Burnard, P. (1991) *Caring and Communicating: The Interpersonal Relationship in Nursing*, Macmillan, London

National Carers Survey (1992) *Opportunities For Women*, 1 Survey Report, Centre Two, London

NHS Management Executive (1991) *Women in the NHS. Good Practice Handbook*, HMSO, London

Nissel, M. and Bonnerjea, L. (1982) *Family Care of the Handicapped Elderly: Who Pays?* Policy Studies Institute, London

Nursing Standard (1992a) 'High Flyers' list for women managers. *Nursing Standard*, 6 (42), 11

Nursing Standard (1992b) Attitude change needed in NHS. *Nursing Standard*, 6 (39), 7

Nuttall, P. (1983) Male takeover or female giveaway? *Nursing Times*, 79 (2), 10–12

Oakley, A. (1972) *Sex, Gender and Society*, Temple Smith, London

Oakley, A. (1974) *The Sociology of Housework*, Martin Robertson, London

Oliver, J. (1983) The caring wife. In *A Labour of Love: Women, Work and Caring*, (eds J. Finch and D. Groves) Routledge & Kegan Paul, London, pp. 72–88

Parker, G. (1992) The myth of the male carer? *Cash and Care*, Summer, Social Policy Research Unit, University of York

Pascall, G. (1986) *Social Policy: A Feminist Perspective*, Tavistock, London

Payne, S. (1989) Problems in the continuity of care. In *Home From Hospital: A Study of Elderly People Leaving Hospital in Bristol*, (eds P. Townsend, T. Davies, S. Payne and T. Willamson) University of Bristol, unpublished paper, pp. 59–76

Payne, S. (1991) *Women, Health and Poverty: An Introduction*, Harvester Wheatsheaf, London

Qureshi, H. and Walker, A. (eds) (1989) *The Caring Relationship: Elderly People and their Families*, Macmillan, London

Rimmer, L. (1983) The economies of work and caring. In *A Labour of Love: Women, Work and Caring*, (eds J. Finch and D. Groves) Routledge & Kegan Paul, London, pp. 131–147

Savage, J. (1987) *Nurses, Gender and Sexuality*, Heinemann, London

Segal, L. (1987) *Is the Future Female? Troubled Thoughts on Contemporary Feminism*, Virago, London

Smith, P. (1992) *The Emotional Labour of Nursing*, Macmillan, London

Social and Community Planning (1992) *British Attitudes Survey: The 1992 Report*, Gower, Aldershot

Spencer, A. and Podmore, D. (eds) (1987) *In a Man's World: Essays on Women in Male Dominated Professions*, Tavistock, London

Spender, D. (1992) *Invisible Women: The Schooling Scandal*, Writers' and Readers' Publishing Company, London

Tiger, L. and Fox, R. (1972) *The Imperial Animal*, Secker & Warburg, London

Ungerson, C. (ed.) (1990) *Gender and Caring: Work and Welfare in Britain and Scandinavia*, Harvester Wheatsheaf, London

Ungerson, C. (1987) *Policy is Personal: Sex, Gender and Informal Care*, Tavistock, London

Ungerson, C. (1983) Why do women care? In *A Labour of Love: Women, Work and Caring*, (eds J. Finch and D. Groves) Routledge & Kegan Paul, London, pp. 31–49

Ungerson, C. (ed.) (1985) *Women and Social Policy: A Reader*, Macmillan, Basingstoke

Walby, S. (1990) *Theorising Patriarchy* (i) p. 20. Basil Blackwell, Oxford

Watson, J. (1991) Preface. In *Caring and Nursing: Explorations in Feminist Perspectives* (eds R. M. Neil and R. Watts) National League for Nursing, New York, pp. ix–x

Winters, J. (1992) Nursing: a boy's own world. *Nursing Standard*, **6** (**46**), 53

6

Women and policy

Pippa Gough and Sian Maslin-Prothero

Introduction

In the following discussions of gender and social policy issues we concentrate explicitly on women's experiences of welfarism, as according to Pascall 'it is impossible to understand the welfare state without understanding how it deals with women' (1986i).

Our examination of policy from this woman-centred perspective concentrates on gender as a basis for a system of domination of women by men. This routinized subordination, as well as the assumptions about women's dependence on men, is reflected not only in the way policy is formulated and implemented but also in the way the discipline of Social Policy is conceptualized and its knowledge base constructed.

Links and overlap with other chapters will become apparent as we rehearse the case for adopting a gender specific approach. For example, much of the discussions about 'caring and policy' as found in chapter 5, as well as the 'family and policy' in chapter 7, raise some of the same issues and cross some of the same theoretical terrain as offered here. We feel however that this repetition serves to enhance the book and make it a coherent whole, rather than to detract from it. Likewise, the explorations of gender as a basis of power is similar to that found in those chapters on class, race and age which demonstrate clearly that there are many sources of power and domination in our society; gender being yet another platform from which power operates.

Much of the analysis here is informed by feminist thinking which, since the early 1980s, has posed an important challenge to the current (male) orthodoxy in Social Policy. The significance of this analysis to the discipline and the way it fits in with other welfare perspectives is discussed at the beginning of this book in chapter 3.

Our woman-centred critique of social policy starts with a historical review of women's role in the family which gives rise to the assumptions that inform welfare policies today. We then consider the theoretical underpinnings of this analysis and examine aspects of women, power and policy. The final part of the chapter focuses on: the nursing workforce and institutional sexism; gender and nursing practice; and finally nurses as oppressors in their role as 'welfare professionals', all of which are issues which resonate in policy terms at several levels.

Since the early 1980s the available literature concerned with women and policy issues has grown dramatically. Much written material now exists which deals with issues ranging from broad theoretical discussions of feminist analyses to specific and detailed inquiry into particular aspects of policy from a women-centred perspective. Further reading is given at the end of the chapter and we advise strongly that this bibliography is used as a resource to put the flesh on what are purely the bare bones of the issues presented here.

The history of women's roles and welfare

The way in which the family and families have changed over the centuries explains the construction of gender roles as we know them today: women being seen as predominantly responsible for the running of the home and men as the primary breadwinner. Broadly speaking, this division of labour has effectively confined women to the private, domestic sphere and men to the public world of paid work. Even where women have crossed the boundary into the public arena they still bear the major responsibility for domestic work (Social and Community Planning, 1992).

In the pre-industrial, agrarian society most work took place predominantly in the home and there was minimal segregation between men and women's roles. In other words all labour took place within the vicinity of the home and the whole family was involved in the production of goods (Bilton *et al.*, 1987).

During industrialization, paid labour moved from the home to factories with the result that men and women's work became more distinct and separate. Women's work became increasingly limited to the confines of the home and the care of dependants while men went 'out' to earn a living. The family not only became effectively segregated from the public world of paid labour but work within the home became heavily demarcated into women's and men's tasks. In addition, other restrictions were placed on women and children, for example through the passing of successive Factories Acts in the 1830s, 1840s and 1850s which limited the areas where they could legally work outside the home (Dearlove and Saunders, 1984).

This slowly evolving state of affairs led to a division between men and women's roles not only at home but also within the public arena. Women's work, for the most part taking place within the home and being strongly associated with domesticity and caring, began to become less visible and to be perceived as low status and of little consequence. Where women were able to break into paid work, these lowly expectations and limited appreciation of their abilities strongly influenced the types of jobs women could access, the wages received and overall career progress. Men's role in the public world of paid labour, on the other hand, became all important and most debate about labour relations and class struggles of later years have tended to concentrate exclusively on this male domain of public work (Pascall, 1986).

In the nineteenth century the advent of the Poor Laws signalled the start of welfarism and increasing State responsibility for those unable to earn a living, namely the sick, the disabled and the poor (mostly women without a husband and no independent means). In conjunction several assumptions began to be made within welfare policy terms in respect of the family form and the roles therein, for example: a family consisted of husband, wife and children; women did not work outside the home; and men were responsible for earning a family wage (Bilton *et al.*, 1987). (See chapter 7 on the family for a fuller exposition of this).

There are three main factors occurring within the family that affect women's position, namely: motherhood; the domestic division of labour; and economic dependency. Women are identified with the home and care of dependants. This is underpinned by the ideology that women are more genetically suited to this role than men – a belief further reinforced by biology, in that only women are capable of giving birth. This biological fact dictates the whole of women's social experience. Thus what is created is a system of dependence, where women are dependent on men financially, work in the home does not receive remuneration and money is the main basis of power, independence, well-being and privilege (Pascall, 1987).

This association of women with the domestic role and their dependency on a working, earning male perpetuates a system of domination based on gender known as patriachy. It is institutionalized throughout the organization of society and is informed and maintained by the ideology of sexism. Children raised within a society based on patriarchal values, and where a male hegemony exists at every level of life, come to view this particular power dynamic as being natural (see the discussion on the third dimension of power in chapter 3). Role models as found in the mother/housewife and father/breadwinner as well as the moulding of aspirations and expectations at school and by the media, reinforce these fundamental beliefs (Pascall, 1986; Bradley, 1989).

Historically much of social policy has been formulated and implemented in line with these patriarchal values. It is only recently that women have started to question some of the beliefs and attitudes that underlie these policies and to demand a more appropriate provision of welfare services.

A woman-centred critique of social policy

Much of this critique is informed by feminist theoretical analyses, which will be examined in more detail later. For the present we will define feminism simply as being 'most obviously about putting women in where they have been left out, about keeping women on the stage rather than relegating them to the wings' (Pascall, 1986ii).

Stanley and Wise (1983) have described this feminist approach as encapsulating a distinctive value position – it is a particular way of viewing social reality, of re-seeing the world through a different lens. This 'new way' of seeing the same reality allows women to make sense of the many contradictions present within life. Reality becomes multidimensional and more complex and so discrepancies are exposed. As such, feminism seeks to challenge existing orthodoxy.

Yet in the acceptance of this 'new reality' questions arise as to why previously only certain pictures of reality had been presented. As Pascall (1986) points out, if feminist analysis is about putting women in where they have been left out, then we want to seriously question those structures that have excluded or obscured women in the first place and understand why it is that the mainstream has failed to describe women's experience adequately.

The simplest answer is that, as explained in chapter 3, the academic disciplines which spawned mainstream interpretations and theories are pervaded by male bias and dominated by patriarchal values. This sexism is evident in the 'methodology, approaches, concepts, language, subject divisions and the hierarchy of importance on academic subject areas' (Pascall, 1986iii) and as such provides us with a male view of social reality which is at odds with the interpretation of society by women.

This feminist challenge extends over the range of existing academic disciplines, but, as Pascall (1986) points out, the critique is particularly relevant to those subject areas where gender hierarchy is marked, for example the social sciences, which is the area of concern here.

The challenges that this woman-centred critique makes to these mainstream approaches now constitute a large and growing body of literature and it is worth examining some of these issues further if a full understanding of the critique is to be achieved.

Why is a woman-centred critique needed?

Stanley and Wise (1983i) sum up the main arguments when they say that much of the mainstream 'quite simply ignores women's presence within vast areas of social reality. But also where women's presence isn't ignored, it is viewed and presented in distorted and sexist ways'.

Oakley's foundational work (1974, cited Stanley and Wise, 1983) in the field of sociology suggests three reasons for this inattention to women. Firstly, sociology from the outset has been moulded by the interests and values of its founding 'fathers'.

Secondly, it remains a male profession – the majority of people within this discipline are men and so the concepts and approaches are bound to be informed by male interests and views of reality. Thirdly, this male bias is nurtured by the 'ideology of gender' which leads people to interpret the world in sexually stereotyped ways. This world view highlights some areas of social reality – those areas which concern men – and leave other areas in the dark, thus eclipsing those areas which concern women.

Stanley and Wise (1983) also point to the distortion of women's experience, which occurs when sex as a variable is not taken into account during large-scale research. This research readily generalizes from the experiences of males studied to all 'people' and sees this as unproblematic. The fact that women's experience is undeniably different is ignored and so misrepresented.

Pascall (1986) identifies the way this sexism in the social sciences is maintained and perpetuated by the language, concepts and methodologies employed in the construction of its knowledge base. She describes the way the ideas of women's dependency are woven into the language used – a language constructed and articulated by men to define women's social reality. The difficulties persist from the everyday use of this language to the detailed construction of concepts of sociological analysis.

The division of the various academic subject areas into psychology, sociology, Social Policy and so on, is also thrown into question. In her study of women's caring work Graham (1983, cited Pascall, 1986) describes how the partitioning off of these subjects militates against accurate and adequate insight into women's daily experiences. An important key to understanding women's lives is an approach that over-arches these boundaries.

These are but a few examples of many similar challenges made by feminists to the existing academic orthodoxy as found in the social sciences in general and in Social Policy in particular. This woman-centred approach goes some way to making sense of the apparent mismatch between women's needs and the policy decisions taken about how to meet them. It helps us to understand why women's demands have failed to materialize in any coherent way within the Welfare State as well as exposing how women's needs – even when they have not been ignored – have been viewed and presented in a distorted fashion (Stanley and Wise, 1983).

Any analysis of policy which follows on from this approach,

therefore, requires an understanding of the fact that these policies are informed by and are part of wider social processes. Pascall (1986) points out that this analysis is complex and feminists continue to grapple with the problems of trying to understand more adequately the specificity of women's oppression. It is these debates in feminist theory that are the focus of the next section.

Debates within feminist theory – patriarchy and capitalism

Within feminist theory there exists a continuing debate on the relationship of patriarchy to capitalism and women's position in relation to both. That is, which is the prime cause of women's oppression? As a result there is no single, fully-integrated feminist theory and therefore any analysis of policy which draws on this theory will necessarily be multifaceted and complex.

Within feminism two divergent schools of thought have developed, each with highly complex political analyses and each defined by differing preoccupations, priorities and policy. These theoretical extremes are characterized broadly as radical feminism and socialist feminism and although they represent opposite ends of a continuum, they are not static and concrete positions but rather they are changing, dynamic and fluid.

Radical feminists see the roots of women's oppression in biological differences and the universal tendency for male domination. Patriarchy within this analysis stresses the common oppression of women without regard to culture, class or racial differences. In other words the biological divide between the sexes supersedes any other divisions in societal structure along the axis of class, race and so on (Weedon, 1986a). Critics of this position are concerned about the tendency of a purely biological explanation and 'the consequent necessity of cultural inferiority' (Pascall, 1986iv).

Socialist feminists, on the other hand, argue that women's position is also directly affected by the mode of production – in a Marxist sense (see chapter 3). Orthodox Marxism asserts that gender and race relations are reducible finally to class oppression and that this analysis of class provides an adequate platform from which to understand gender and race (Weedon, 1986b). Socialist feminism developed from critiques of this orthodox view and aims to go beyond both this analysis and the radical feminist position to develop a theory in which 'gender, class and race are all taken into account as specific but inter-related forms of oppression, none of which is reducible to the others' (Weedon, 1986bi).

It is only recently that socialist feminists have recognized the need to temper their analysis by this consideration of racial interests. As Filomena Chioma Steady points out, although black women do share similar problems with other women, several factors set the black woman apart as having a different order of priorities: 'She is oppressed not simply because of her sex but ostensibly because of her race and for the majority essentially because of her class' (1985i). Any analysis which fails to deal with the intrinsic needs of the black woman in a racial society is not in the interests of black women.

The debate between radical and socialist feminist theory, as to the sources of women's oppression, rages on. Are women subordinated purely as a result of the system of patriarchy or does it have something to do with capitalist values and structures as well? Questions regarding the connections between the productive and reproductive realms, capitalism and patriarchy, have no simple answer. The debate is succinctly summed up by Pascall (1986) who asks: who benefits from the sexual division of labour and women's dependent position; and secondly, what is the nature of the relationship between patriarchy and the relations spawned by capitalism?

Pascall (1986) examines the interconnectedness of these two facets in her analysis of social policy. She argues that an interpretation of policy which concentrates largely on productive relations, that is the capitalist world of paid work and women's place in it, is too narrowly focused and ignores large areas of women's reproductive work and experience in the home. An extension of this analysis into the family, whereby social policy is understood as supporting the family form best suited to the needs of capitalism, does in fact go some way to making the link between the reproductive and productive spheres, but it is still problematic. It subordinates reproductive relations, that is the relationship of the woman to the family, to becoming merely an adjunct of the productive process. Pascall (1986) argues that the family and reproduction, rather than being secondary to productive relations, do in fact have roots of their own. The relationship of the family, and the way reproduction is managed in it, to the State and social policy can be the focus for direct analysis, rather than being dependent for an understanding on their services to capitalist exploitation. This is the tack that is taken in chapter 7, whereby the Welfare State is analysed in relation to the way it is concerned with putting women in caring roles, supporting relations of dependency within families and controlling the work of reproduction.

Women and social policy

Policies relating to the provision of health care, with particular reference to nursing, are part of a wide network of social policies linking the realms of production and reproduction. The results and implications of these social policies for women are not predetermined and it would be inaccurate to present the Welfare State purely in terms of being a structure of control. If this were the case, women's struggle for more services and their fight against cuts would be difficult to explain. Rather social policies can be seen as having two faces. On the one hand they may deliver the resources of capital production to the private realm of reproduction and the family and by so doing may improve and enhance women's lives. For example, access to contraception as well as the provision of free maternity services have drastically cut the rates of maternal morbidity and mortality. Thus women's activity in the provision and politics of accessible family planning and maternity services can be understood as the fight to increase resources for women and women's work (Lewis, 1986; Pascall, 1986).

On the other hand however there is the face of social policy as a means of public control over the relations of reproduction – often seen as the increasing male control of female work. This is particularly noticeable within the fields of male-dominated professions such as medicine, education, social work and, increasingly, nursing, where the traditional caring work of the family, such as health care, crosses from the domestic sphere into the public arena of paid work and becomes 'professionalized'. This control of women's reproductive work is a key feminist issue and is discussed further in chapter 5.

Social policies can also be seen as supporting a patriarchal family form of woman dependant and male breadwinner. This confines women to the private sphere and excludes them from public life. Lewis (1986) describes how assumptions made about appropriate gender roles and the division of labour within the family are embedded and implied within social policy, rather than being explicitly expressed by the policy makers. The fact that these policies view, albeit covertly, the primary role of the woman as wife and mother, militates against economic and actual independence from her husband or partner. The State's support of this role perpetuates the division of labour and the construction of gender. As Graham (1984) pointed out nearly ten years ago, it is the exploitation by the State of women's availability and willingness to care for family members without pay, that keeps women dependent in the family and without power in the public sphere of paid work and economic activity. The enforcement in April 1993 of the community care part of the NHS and Community Care Act (1990), which continues to do precisely what Graham was highlighting a decade earlier, does not augur well for any change in the position of women in policy terms (see chapter 4 on health policy).

Women, decision making and power

The constraints placed on women's participation in the public domain and their resulting difficulties in obtaining economic independence limits women's access to positions of power in those institutions that decide their fate – for example, the State, political parties, commerce and so on. Even with more women now entering the labour market, Pascall argues that women's experience is still one of subjection: 'The majority of women work in low paid jobs at the bottom of hierarchies and under male supervision. Very few women are at the top of hierarchies, even in jobs that are predominantly female' (1986v). Nursing is a prime example of this phenomenon, which we will discuss in greater detail later.

Ruzek (1986), with specific reference to health care systems and health policy, argues that too few women have either the power or the authority to influence the allocation of scarce resources to various types of health services. Moreover women's health may suffer as a result of this. If women are not in these senior positions they are unable to 'judge if services or technologies are safe and effective by feminist standards' (Ruzek, 1986i).

A similar pattern of unequal access also emerges when one looks at the representation of women in the political arena. Although they have long since won the vote, women still lack influence to the same degree as men in trade unions and political parties and are underrepresented at every level of government and in parliament (Cockburn, 1991) – this is despite eleven years of leadership by a female prime minister in Britain. With such a small corner of political power it is not surprising that women's interests gain only minimal ranking on the political agenda.

Moreover, even if women do achieve positions of seniority or power it cannot be assumed that they will remain loyal to women's interests by giving them sufficient priority. Ruzek (1986) argues, again referring specifically to health services, that those few women in senior positions are typically socialized to conform to conventional professional values and behaviours, some of which may fly in the face of the needs and demands of women as receivers of care. Until the fundamental structure of medical and health institutions are changed so as to reflect different values and ideologies, it would be unrealistic to expect these senior women to behave any differently from their male colleagues. Consequently the situation remains where 'women have access primarily to the type of health care that men deem appropriate to allocate to women' (Ruzek, 1986ii).

Even where women do try to conform to the status quo they are still separated out for special treatment. For example, a recent study by Alimo-Metcalfe (1992) noted gender differences in the implementation and impact of appraisal on NHS managers. She found women were treated differently with regards to objectives set, quality of discussion, effect on the appraisee and ratings given for performance. That is, women generally fared worse than men. Women's chances must remain poor if even when they have achieved the position of being a manager they continue to be disadvantaged in comparison to their male counterparts.

This unequal relationship of women to economic and political power and to social policy results in very little heed being paid to women across the board. Pascall (1986) contends that women are subordinate in paid work and in the family and this subordination in both domains is connected. The concern to protect the patriarchal family structure has been central to decisions affecting all areas of women's lives – decisions which are usually made by men, influenced by male values and protect male interests.

Gender, policy and nursing

It has often been argued that nursing would be far more highly valued and rewarded if we lived in a world that did not discriminate against women. Although there is obviously some accuracy in this statement, is it in fact the whole story? Has nursing been undervalued because it is done by women or have women, over time, simply been allocated to those tasks that have attracted less money and less power? Although this is a somewhat circular argument, Strong and Robinson (1988) suggest that the latter is in fact the more plausible explanation:

> for there is a crucial distinction to be made between the usefulness of something and what people would actually pay to get hold of it. Price is determined, not just by need but by the ease with which others can supply it. Nursing was a bit like water; fundamental to life but has, for the most part, in the past been readily available. (1988i).

It is, however, almost impossible to talk about nursing and policy without placing it in the wider framework of women's work. First of all there is the need to consider the part gender plays in determining nurses' subordinate position in the health services arena – which is a reflection of women's place in wider society. This links in with the second strand in this discussion which is the changing position of women in the labour market generally (which has been examined in part, earlier). And finally, there is the relationship between the ideology of women's caring role within the family and women's caring role within the nursing workforce (much of this material is covered in chapter 5 and only the main tenets of the discussion will be presented here). Each of these separate, but inter-twined, strands will now be examined.

Nursing and the division of labour

Within occupations as a whole sexist attitudes fuel the belief that women cannot undertake certain types of work because of their sex and gender. Ultimately this leads to a segregated workforce and nursing is a prime example. In her analysis of the nursing workforce, Kate Robinson (1992) stated that 45 per cent of the total UK workforce is female, but within the nursing workforce the figure rises to roughly 90 per cent – a typical example of what Hakim (1979) termed horizontal segregation, whereby men and women work in different occupations, for example nursing for women and engineering for men.

However, although nursing is predominantly female, women are not distributed evenly throughout this workforce. In England, for example, one in six full-time staff is male while the proportion for part-time staff is one male in seventy-two. Forty-three per cent of the female workforce works part-time – a figure which reflects the importance of part-time female labour in the nursing workforce as a whole (Kate Robinson, 1992).

Traditionally horizontal segregation has been seen between doctors and nurses. The image of nursing is predominantly associated with feminine qualities and is therefore closely associated with womanhood. The stereotypes surrounding nursing and nurses centre on characteristics connected with the feminine, such as care, intuition and sympathy. Nursing is perceived as low-status, low-technology work and this perception is reinforced by the terms used, i.e. nurses are 'trained' for an 'occupation'. In comparison doctors and medicine are associated with stereotypical views of masculinity, autonomy, rationality and achievement – doctors 'cure' while nurses 'care' (Delamothe, 1988). Consequently, although medicine and nursing are closely allied, medicine has traditionally been more attractive to men and nursing recruits have been predominantly women. Although this is changing, as nearly 50 per cent of medical students are now female (Allen, 1988), the majority of senior positions in the medical profession are still occupied by men.

Vertical segregation (Hakim, 1979), where men are to be found in higher grades to women within the same occupations, is also a strong characteristic of the nursing and health service workforce. The distribution of men and women in nursing demonstrates the location of power in terms of gender within the profession. This power not only relates to sex (that is male/female), but also to social and cultural constructions of gender (Hugman, 1991). Ninety per cent of all nurses are female (EOC, 1991) and yet men occupy managerial positions out of all proportion to their representation in the nursing workforce. Much of the reason for this lies within patriarchal values about the status of caring combined with institutionalized sexism which enhances career advancement for men.

There is considerable empirical evidence to support the view that this vertical segregation is occurring. For example, Davies and Rosser (1986) identified the presence of gender discrimination in nurse management, in that men were promoted to the position of nursing officer faster than women. Following initial registration and taking into account post-registration education and career interruption, it took men on average 8.4 years to reach the position of nursing officer in comparison to 17.9 years for women. Post 'Griffiths' the management base of nursing has been considerably weakened consequently there are even fewer women in senior positions.

The changing position of women in the labour market

In the past, the number of women, mostly school leavers, available to enter nursing was considered to be an unending supply. However, in the light of demographic, social and economic forces this situation is now beginning to change. Paradoxically, as more women enter the labour market generally, the supply of cheap female labour to nursing is beginning to diminish. In today's world, because, or even in spite, of equality legislation and changing attitudes to women, greater alternative employment opportunities are becoming increasingly available to female school leavers. Women's aspirations are changing – they no longer have to confine their career ideas to 'female' occupations, namely teaching, nursing and so on. Employers are having to develop new and creative ways of recruiting, retaining and motivating the workforce. Consequently, the anatomy of the nursing workforce is changing – we have yet to see whether the power dynamic is so easily converted.

Buchan (1992) offers a number of policy options for consideration in terms of addressing the issues surrounding the matching of demand and supply within nursing. He argues that a suitable recipe of options is dependent upon individual employer's staffing requirements, their available resources and the conditions of the labour markets in which they are, or potentially could be, operating. Unfortunately, within the environment of financial constraint, market competition and political moves to dismantle professionalism, the use of unqualified support workers instead of qualified nurses is too often proving to be a 'quick-fix' solution to many employers. Ultimately, this will create yet another workforce of subordinate, poorly-rewarded women.

Dolan (1993) argues, somewhat optimistically, that Project 2000 could be the means by which nurses not only become independent, autonomous practitioners but also the catalyst that creates change and provides nurses with power and status, independent of gender.

Women, nursing and caring

Nurses' occupational identity has increasingly and pervasively been explained as that of carers, with caring becoming the linch-pin of many nursing philosophies and education courses (James, 1992). Whether having care identified as a core element of nursing is ultimately helpful to the profession is discussed in chapter 5. Within that chapter considerable emphasis was given to the examination of the social relations through which ideologies of care are produced and reproduced and we have seen how care has become predominantly associated not only with women's domestic, or private, role but also with their role in the public sphere of paid work. This gender division of labour offers important insights into the ways gender affects employment and employees, including the impact on nurses.

James (1992) argues that many of the difficulties nurses are currently having in conveying the essence and importance of qualified nursing stems from this link with care as being 'informal', unwaged and part and parcel of emotional labour. Nurses have brought to the workplace unpaid domestic skills and developed the art and science of nursing from that foundation.

The importance of care as learned expertise is still lost on many employers. There is still an ambivalence attached to 'women's work' and to the need to create a niche for nursing expertise in a division of labour in which nurses have had little to say.

Conclusion

Nurses lack power, reasons for which are related to the fact that nursing is a woman-dominated profession, and traditionally women do not possess power. This lack of power is then reflected in terms of market position, decision making and the ability to influence allocation of health resources in line with nursing values (at both a local and national level). Moreover, Stevens (1983) suggests that nurses lack the sophistication in power and politics to produce change to advance their own interests. In addition nurses have continued to accept this powerless position, and consequently they continue to be underrepresented at a senior level (Delamothe, 1988).

Discussion points

1. In what ways, and why, does job segregation remain so persistent a feature in the NHS?
2. Are gender divisions in employment due to discrimination, or employer choice?
3. In what way might gender equality be improved and enhanced?

Further reading

Brown, J. (1992) Which way for family policy: choice for the 1990s. In (eds N. Manning and R. Pages) *Social Policy Review 4*, Social Policy Association, London, pp. 154–174
The Social Policy Review compilations are well worth browsing through for useful articles on a variety of policy issues – contributors are usually the leading social policy analysts within the field. In this article Brown examines how trends towards lone parenthood, cohabitation, divorce and child poverty have thrown the government's handling of family policy into confusion and the contradiction

between disapproving of women's work and yet relying on women's paid employment to fund child care.

Cockburn, C. (1991) *In the Way of Women*, Macmillan, London
Read this book! If not now, at some stage in your career.

Lawler, J. (1991) *Behind the Screens*, Melbourne, Churchill Livingstone
This excellent and highly-readable book looks at the way nurses manage the bodies and 'dirty work' of others and links it closely to women's traditional roles. This renders nursing as 'invisible' – a situation which has profound implications for nurses attempting to influence the policy agenda in any coherent way.

Maclean, M. and Groves, D. (eds) (1991) *Women's Issues in Social Policy*, Routledge, London
Highlights the invisibility of women within the Welfare State and examines their traditional role as unpaid carers. A book to dip into in order to obtain an overview of gender and social policy issues.

Meehan, E. and Whitting, G. (1989) Gender and public policy: European law and British equal opportunity policies. In *Policy and Politics*, **17**(4), pp. 337–345
The introduction, by Meehan and Witting, provides a succinct overview of these papers which are concerned with the interface between the implications for these relationships post 1992 and the single EC market.

Pascall, G. (1986) *Social Policy: A Feminist Analysis*, Tavistock, London
In terms of 'gender and policy' this book is the definitive guide. Especially good are chapter 1, outlining the feminist critique, chapter 3, examining 'caring' in policy terms and chapter 6 on health and policy.

Robinson, K. (1992) The nursing workforce: aspects of inequality. In (eds J. Robinson, A. Gray and R. Elkan) *Policy Issues in Nursing*, Open University Press, Milton Keynes, pp. 25–37
This whole book makes excellent reading, but Kate's chapter provides a policy analysis of primary nursing, which she argues will exacerbate existing inequalities between men and women, married and single women and generally reinforce sexist attitudes found in society at large.

References

Abbott, P. and Wallace, C. (1990) *An Introduction to Sociology: Feminist Perspectives*, Routledge, London

Alimo-Metcalfe, B. (1992) *Gender Appraisal: Findings from a National Survey of Managers in the British NHS*, unpublished research funded by NHS Training Directorate

Allen, I. (1988) *Doctors and their Careers*, Policy Studies Institute, London

Bradley, H. (1989) *Men's Work, Women's Work*, Polity Press, Oxford

Buchan, J. (1992) Nurse manpower planning: role, rationale and relevance. In *Policy Issues in Nursing* (eds J. Robinson, A. Gray and R. Elkan) Open University Press, Milton Keynes, pp. 38–51

Chioma Steady, F. (1985) *The Black Woman Cross-culturally*, Schenkman Books Inc., Massachusetts

Cockburn, C. (1991) *In the Way of Women: Men's Resistance to Sex Equality in Organizations*, Macmillan, London

Davies, C. and Rosser, J. (1986) *Processes of Discrimination: A Study of Women Working in the NHS*, DHSS, London

Delamothe, T. (1988) Nursing grievances: not a profession, not a career, *British Medical Journal*, **296**, 271–274

Department of Health (1990) *National Health Service and Community Care Act*, HMSO, London

Dolan, B. (ed.) (1993) *Project 2000: Reflection and Celebration*, Scutari, London

Hakim, C. (1979) *Occupational Segregation, a Comparative Study of the Degree and Pattern of the Differentiation between Men and Women's Work in Britain, the United States, and Other Countries*. Research Paper, No 9, Department of Employment, London

Hugman, R. (1991) *Power in Caring Professions*, Macmillan, London

James, N. (1992) Care, work and carework: a synthesis. In *Policy Issues in Nursing* (eds J. Robinson, A. Gray and R. Elkan) Open University Press, Milton Keynes, pp. 96–111

Lewis, J. (1986) Feminism and welfare. In *What is Feminism?* (eds J. Mitchell and A. Oakley) Basil Blackwell Ltd, Oxford, pp. 85–100

Pascall, G. (1986) *Social Policy: A Feminist Analysis*, Tavistock Publications, London

Robinson, K. (1992) The nursing workforce: aspects of inequality. In *Policy Issues in Nursing* (eds J. Robinson, A. Gray and R. Elkan) Open University Press, Milton Keynes, pp. 24–37

Ruzek, S. (1986) Feminist visions of health: an international perspective. In *What is Feminism?* (eds J. Mitchell and A. Oakley) Basil Blackwell Ltd, Oxford, pp. 184–207

Savage, J. (1987) *Nurses, Gender and Sexuality*, Heinemann, London

Stanley, L. and Wise, S. (1983) *Breaking Out: Feminist Consciousness and Feminist Research*, Routledge and Kegan Paul, London

Stevens, K. R. (1983) Power as a positive force. In *Power and Influence:*

A Source Book for Nurses, (ed. K. R. Stevens) John Wiley, New York, pp. 1–20

Strong, P. and Robinson, J. (1988) *New Model Management: Griffiths and the NHS*. Nursing Policy Studies 3, NSPC, University of Warwick

Weedon, C. (1986a) Radical and revolutionary feminism. In *Feminist Theories and Practical Policies: Shifting the Agenda in the 1980s*, (eds F. Ashton and G. Whitting) SAUS Publications, Bristol, pp. 27–42

Weedon, C. (1986b) Socialist feminism. In *Feminist Theories and Practical Policies: Shifting the Agenda in the 1980s*, (eds F. Ashton and G. Whitting) SAUS Publications, Bristol, pp. 43–58

Williams, F. (1989) *Social Policy: A Critical Introduction*, Polity Press, Cambridge

7

The family and social policy

Hannele Weir

Introduction

In this chapter we aim to give an overview of the current 'state of the family' in terms of theory and practical issues and the way these interconnect with professionals such as nurses. There are two themes which run through this chapter. The first is that of relationships between family members themselves and also between the family and society as a whole. The second concerns the 'private' and 'public' nature of the institution of the family and the way these facets interconnect. The purpose is to examine the complexity of issues and attitudes that confront nurses in the context of their daily work. For instance, what are the implications for welfarism of massive change in such an old institution as the family alongside the wider changes in society? Such developments shape fundamentally the way nurses respond when dealing with families. However, the question remains as to whether nurses should be purely reactive in this response or whether they should be taking a more proactive stance with regard to the policy that informs their care.

What is the family

The concept of the family, as generally used, conjures up images which have never really reflected reality. The advertisers' stereotype of the two heterosexual adults with two children, preferably of opposite sexes, is continually reproduced simply because it sells the product. The success of this stereotype for marketing lies in the fact that it reflects the dominant value system within Western, industrialized society. In a similar vein, families in television soap operas are equally as misrepresentative and depict situations which are 'cultural fantasies' (Denzin, 1987 cited Cheal, 1991). Furthermore, in order to give them dramatic value, the portrayal of real issues (as in *Eastenders*) becomes exaggerated and reflects the family in everyday life even less.

Yet these images do act as a vehicle for exposing and making public the private concerns of members of families; an attempted mirror image of 'the family' in trouble, perplexed by the complexities of change which seem to render family relationships uncertain and unenduring. This is not to suggest that family relationships were uncomplicated in the past. Contrary to popular belief there has never been a 'golden age' of the family. Our cosy image of the pre-industrial extended family is not a true historical model and cannot therefore be compared accurately to the modern nuclear family.

A popular conception of the family is one in which it is seen as a private institution based on marriage and, increasingly in modern society, involving the privately felt emotion of 'love' (see for instance Giddens, 1989). Yet marriage also has a public and legal status as well as an undeniable cultural – including religious – and social basis. In other words, the family has a social significance beyond private assumptions and expectations. This is even reflected in the way the word is applied somewhat hesitantly to couples without children. Within this role one of the social expectations of the family has been that of procreation and reproduction. In fact it is this expectation which has arguably led to its downfall. The very ideal of the family as a provider of support, care and comfort and the emphasis on the mutuality of feelings has placed an unbearable pressure upon this institution. This is borne out by the high divorce rates and the fact that most petitions for divorce come from women (Davis and Murch, 1992).

In social theory the concept of the 'family' has moved through various phases. Firstly there are the more structural, functionalist explanations, popular in the 1950s, which emphasize the complementary roles of spouses. This then changed to an understanding of increased intimacy and symmetry in the husbands' and wives' relationships and roles (Young and Wilmott,

1973 cited Cheal, 1991). For instance, that an increasing number of women would choose occupational careers and therefore the occupational commitments of the spouses will become more similar, and that feminism would have an impact on the redistribution of housework. Finally there are the present-day claims and counter-claims that gender roles are still relatively fixed in the domestic sphere, despite the fact that women have entered the labour market in increasing numbers since the 1950s (see for instance Lewis, 1992).

Apart from the private arrangements and relationships within the family, social theorists have also been concerned with the importance of the family to society with the key focus being socialization. Functionalists, for instance, view the family as a pivotal agency for socializing children into the continuities and values of social and cultural life. From this perspective this socialization process is seen as vital to the overall harmony and survival of society. Marxism on the other hand has regarded the family as the ideal socializing agent for a life of work within capitalist society. Initially the child learns within the family the basics of authority and discipline which is later reinforced at school. Thus the child becomes ready for the discipline and patterns of work life as required by the capitalist mode of production.

However, uncertainty has been created in theorizing about the family (Cheal, 1991) and there are a number of problems in terms of practical issues. This is due to less emphasis being placed on marriage generally (less than 50 per cent of children are now born in wedlock) as well as an increasing number of marriages ending in divorce. In addition there is a growing variety of reconstituted families which exist as a consequence of divorced and bereaved people remarrying, and the existence of lone parenthood and same-sex couples adds to this diversity. As Cheal (1991) points out the family can no longer be understood in terms of comparisons between theory and ideology, fact and value, and the separating of scientific fact from myth. Rather the theoretical focus has shifted to individuals and their relationships or position both within the family and society. The family has been destandardized and as such the sense of individuality and personal autonomy has increased. In other words the focus is now less on the macro, structural overview and more on patterns of diversity – a move which reflects the shift into postmodernity (see chapter 11).

In the postmodern age the family is no longer necessarily based on marriage, a situation for which there are three main explanations (Davis and Murch, 1992). Firstly, there has been a reduction in the social pressure to remain married in that divorce no longer bears such a stigma and marriage as a religious sacrament has less meaning to many people. Secondly, marriage as an institution and an economic unit has given way to the notion of 'companionate marriage'. If this bond of companionship does not exist there seems less point in remaining together. In other words people expect more from marriage; Berger and Berger (1983 cited Davis and Murch, 1992i) succinctly note that 'divorce is mainly a back handed compliment to the ideal of modern marriage, as well as testimony to its difficulties'. Finally, there is a lessening of women's dependence on male support.

Increasingly opportunities for women in education and employment and with regard to legal rights have created the possibility of greater independence. Additionally, as Davis and Murch (1992) point out, three particular policy changes have made women less dependent on their husbands: state financed legal advice and representation which enables more women to petition for divorce; availability of social security to women and their children giving an independent income (albeit one that arguably confines them to near poverty); and local authority housing which gives priority to children and their carers.

Many of these social policy arrangements are, however, precarious. The Legal Aid system has been restructured recently and consequently access to legal advice has been restricted. This means that women on low incomes may find it financially impossible to start divorce proceedings. Furthermore, women can no longer claim maintenance from their ex-partners in respect of financial support for themselves. In other words, the law has recognized that women can access their own means of financial support. The diminishing local-authority housing stock has reduced the chances for accommodation, even if priority is given to children and their carers.

Some writers have suggested that in the light of the changes discussed above the concept of 'the family' is no longer meaningful in a postmodernist society (Cheal, 1991). Scanzoni, Polonko, Teachman *et al.* (1989 cited Cheal, 1991) argue that, as cohabitation and lone parenthood become more widespread, the 'cultural reality' of this way of life cannot be defined in terms of a conjugal family, but that such a new image represents a concept of 'primary relationships' denoting not only legal marriages but also other sexual couplings. Trost (1988 cited Cheal, 1991) on the other hand is particularly concerned with a model that would sidestep issues to do with relationships and the prevalence of divorce. His suggestions of a parent–child unit and a spousal unit would reflect, as Cheal (1991) notes, the current social fragmentation and offer alternative models to the nuclear family more suitable to the postmodernist approach, including Denzin's (1987 cited Cheal, 1991) observation that increasing numbers of children are cared for by someone other than a parent.

However, given this reality of change, it is nevertheless not easy to see immediately how the diversity in human behaviour is interpreted in terms of policy making or, conversely, whether policies may be used as a means of directing and controlling people's behaviour.

Social policy and the family

Ginsberg (1992) argues that Britain has a long history of eugenicist and neo-Malthusian traditions which have continued to surface in the postwar period. Eugenicist is used to describe policies which are concerned with the maintenance and improvement of human populations. This is achieved, for example, by giving financial support to 'desirable' parents and discouraging the breeding of 'inferior' populations through fertility control. Neo-Malthusian thinking revolves around ideas that if the working class are allowed to become too prosperous this section of the population will increase to the detriment of the rest of society. At its simplest this means that social policy encourages certain kinds of families to have children in the belief that 'good parenting' predominantly takes place in white, middle-class, two-parent, families.

Roll (1991) considers 'the family' in terms of benefit models and social realities. In this context it matters how the State and its institutions have defined the family simply because of the money that may be available to one type of 'family' but not to another. Some individuals and agencies see the benefit system as discouraging, possibly even undermining 'traditional family values'. Assumptions about the family as well as the types that exist in reality are important because if these assumptions are unrealistic policies may fail. In addition, if claimants can only qualify for welfare benefits by 'fitting the description' and being seen to belong to a certain type of family then social policies are overtly working to control and shape the way individuals live their lives.

The ever-present and increasing concern about levels of public expenditure and responsibility underlie all family policy decisions and complicate the situation further. This is particularly noticeable in the expectations about the responsibilities of family members towards one another. Ever since the 'liable relative' rules were invoked by the Elizabethan Poor Law, these responsibilities continue to be discussed in one form or another. A contemporary example of this is the setting up in 1993 of the Child Support Agency whereby absent fathers are required to provide financial support for their children.

Since the inception of the Welfare State in the UK we have seen how the model family is envisaged by policy makers as being a married couple in a nuclear household, living separately from other relatives, with the man as breadwinner and the woman as housewife. The principles of the Beveridge Plan 1942 were based on a central assumption of full-time male employment as the basis for the distribution of income. This was accompanied by assumptions about women and children as financial dependants. Benefits, funded through National Insurance contributions, replaced earnings for those with an employment record in situations where there was an acceptable reason for not being in a paid job. Breadwinners were seen to be male and for women the entitlement to benefit was conditional on marriage. Those who were unmarried had to depend on their own contributions although there were certain differences between men and women. Women's central role was that of housewife, with no explicit recognition of the costs and social contribution of caring for dependants. Although this has now changed in terms of benefits available under certain conditions, it nevertheless helps us to understand the persistent expectation that women will fulfil a 'caring function'. Under the burden of this assumption, women campaigned for child benefit for nearly half a century with the demand for this to be paid directly to mothers. Furthermore, continued campaigns have been necessary to maintain not only the level and universality of this benefit but also its very existence.

Ginsburg (1992) suggests that the behaviour and decisions demonstrated by both Labour and Conservative governments have continually reflected the struggle between those forces that represent women and poor people and those supporting conventional and patriarchal principles. Consequently the profile of the 'benefit family' (Roll, 1991) today rests also on the assumption about employment and on who should be dependent on whom. The structure of the whole benefit system has changed dramatically from the original Beveridge Plan in that means-tested benefits for those under pension age have grown. In a way this is not surprising given the growth in unemployment in Britain over the last forty years (Mishra, 1990). Since the 1980s the government has emphasized keeping inflation down which means that employment levels are controlled by market forces rather than by any government policy. Generally speaking there has been a limiting of access to benefits, with marriage still being an important route to gaining entitlement to benefits for women. For lone parents Income Support is still means tested on the assumption that an 'important other' is likely to be on the scene. Once two people are seen as a couple the members of this unit cannot qualify independently for support and the income and capital of both is taken into consideration. Income of a spouse or other adult is taken into account if an additional claim is made for him/her – for example in the case of unemployment (Roll, 1991). The wife (in most cases) can keep the first £5.00 of her earnings, after which the man loses on his benefit on the basis of pound per pound. Given this restriction and the fact that women's earnings fall below those for men, it is not surprising that women remain unemployed out of 'choice' when the spouse or partner is unemployed. Moreover, when the costs of clothes for and travel to work are taken into account, women's reluctance to enter into paid work can be understood in economic terms.

The term 'family' has become more flexible within the policy arena and now includes lone parents, married and cohabiting as well as homosexual couples, who, for the purposes of means-tested benefits such as Family Credit, must have a dependent child. In general, children in these families need not be related to the claimant but live in the same household. The situation is thus somewhat paradoxical and confusing. On the one hand it has been argued that policies continue to make assumptions, despite developments in the real world, in order to present and uphold the model family – even to the extent of trying to curb people's behaviour. On the other hand there are also situations where policies have clearly responded to change, for example: the broadening of the term 'family' to include all the variations listed above; the recognition of cohabitation in relation to protection from violence from partners; and the recognition in the Children Act 1989 of unmarried fathers in terms of more rights, subject to agreement with the mother or a court order. Roll (1991) points out that much of this change is far from clear-cut. The fact remains that if marriage as a basis for the family is removed, the definition becomes more complex and involves value judgements about the 'correctness' or 'legitimacy' of a given relationship.

Children and social policy

In this section we outline some of the developments specifically relating to children and responsibilities for their care within families. Once again the definition of 'family' gains a different emphasis in that 'family' is viewed in terms of responsibility for children be it a two-parent or lone-parent unit. The concern for children's well-being also raises questions about the boundaries between the privacy of the family and its public 'function' of caring for the young. Generally speaking children are the responsibility of their parents and their daily care in most cases is down to their mothers. There has been a tendency to ignore the economic difficulties of the mother as the housewife because of the persistent assumption that the male partner is paid a family wage and that resources are equally divided in the family. The freezing of Family Allowance, now Child Benefit, from time to time since 1945 bears testimony to this belief.

Further emphasis on maternal responsibilities has been evident in the State resistance earlier this century to day nursery provision and the closure of existing provision after the Second World War. Lewis (1992) points out that child-care provision and support have been seen in policy terms as a matter of private responsibility. Following the war women were ousted from the labour market to make room for the men being demobilized. Consequently, State day-care provision was seen to be surplus to requirement. 'Populationist' scares in the postwar period put a moral pressure on women to reproduce (see for instance Lewis, 1992) and Family Allowance was actually increased to woo middle-class women out of the labour market and back into the home. This sluggishness to provide child care on the part of the State is still evident today in that publicly provided child care remains low in Britain compared to most other European countries. The number of local authority day-care places currently available is now fewer than in 1945 (Lewis, 1992).

The importance of women's contribution in the labour market has been underlined by the fact that most developments in day-care provision have taken place in the private sector – in companies and business concerns – either in the form of a financial allowance or creche facilities organized by the workplace. Although the government has granted tax relief on child-care expenses it does not mean, as Lewis (1992) points out, that there is any acknowledgement of direct governmental responsibility.

Lone parents have experienced a great paradox in terms of financial survival and support with child care. As Ginsburg (1992) points out Britain has the lowest number of lone mothers in employment when compared to Sweden, the United States and what was West Germany. This exclusion from work may reflect the importance the British State places on mothers being at home with their children for which they receive social assistance as a paltry reward to maintain them and their children (Finer Report, 1974 cited Ginsburg, 1992). It may also indicate lone mother's susceptibility to the poverty trap by accepting low-paid jobs and then losing welfare payments.

The public and government concern about family breakdown, individual's behaviour and choices, is illustrated by the policies of recent years which are explicitly concerned with active discouragement of lone motherhood. A particular example is the recent setting up of the Child Support Agency at a cost of £150 million which invokes the 'liable relative' rules. As explained earlier, the intention is to make absent fathers pay maintenance for children whether or not they have contact with them. The statistics behind this action may in some sense explain the government's determination: £4.3 billion is spent annually in single-parent benefits; one in three lone parents (women) do not receive any maintenance from the father of their child. The Child Support Agency expects 300 thousand absent fathers to pay maintenance and will replace the court's function in assessing and collecting this (Radio 4 interview, 13 April 1993).

But at what point is the government no longer able to avoid responsibility for care and the private sphere become a public concern? That is, when does it become politically expedient for the State to intervene in the affairs of the family and the domestic terrain of child care? The thorny issue of child abuse is a prime example. The incidence of child abuse has increasingly occupied space on the public agenda since the 1960s in the form of concern about physical injuries and neglect inflicted on children by their families or carers. In Britain this anxiety has been further heightened by a number of well-publicized cases of child deaths and by the 'discovery' of the incidence of sexual abuse to children (mainly girls) of different ages. Against this background Johnson (1990) comments that though legislation such as the Children Act 1989 and the Disabled Persons Act 1986 both impose extra duties on local authorities, fear of publicity will potentially mean allocation of a disproportionate share of the resources of social services to their work with children.

However, the Children Act does bring together most of the private and public law about children in need and their families, including children with disabilities (HMSO, 1991). This Act is an ambitious piece of legislation which in many respects is a development in the right direction. The law concerning children has been very confused and piecemeal and this legislation is at least an attempt to rationalize the way children's needs are met. However, it requires considerable resources in terms of suitable workers in social, health and educational services and police departments as well as in terms of a range of other facilities such as day care, family centres, drop-in centres, parent/toddler groups and toy libraries to name but a few.

Some of the central features of the Act concern the general duty of local authorities to safeguard and promote the welfare of the children in their area – a duty which is underpinned by the philosophy of the Act which clearly states that the best place to bring up children is usually in the child's own family. Most effective help for the child is achieved if the local authority works in partnership with the parents, providing the appropriate services. Parental responsibility encompasses rights as well as obligations and even in cases where courts intervene, the duty on both parents remains to 'contribute to their child's upbringing'. The core principles also include the fact that the focus is on the child's welfare and the views of the child are taken into account in the light of his/her age and understanding. Thus the Act places a great deal of emphasis on 'working together' which is in accordance with a growing endorsement in nursing of patient/ client empowerment, promotion of informed choice, self-care and partnership. These are positive developments compared to the authoritarian attitudes and approaches which often created entrenched views within both the professions and the families: parents feeling powerless in the face of professional scrutiny and judgement of their parenting skills and the management of their lives.

Families and professionals: a partnership?

The Children Act, perhaps optimistically, sees families as having the capacity either to cope with their problems or identify and draw upon resources in the community for support. In other words the assumption is made that families will privately 'sort out their problems' but in the face of overwhelming difficulties they will seek assistance. This is not always what happens in practice. Health services, for instance, clearly operate a surveillance system, with child protection in mind, which undermines this 'hands-off' philosophy. Although many parents well understand and tolerate the necessity of such intervention in the interests of the child, this 'policing' often goes further. On occasions this support has also meant filling the gaps in 'deficient' mothering skills – action which once more draws attention to mothers as being of central importance to the continuity of the family and the development of the children. Berger and Berger (1983 cited Lewis, 1992) have argued that as the sophistication and number of those professionals interested in the family has increased, so has the likelihood of parents being judged to be inadequate.

A number of explanations may exist for this situation. Firstly, professionals, of which nurses are the largest group, can be said to be both a product of the Welfare State as well as providers of welfare services – they exist as a result of it but are also an integral part of it. Expansion of the Welfare State and the rise of many professional groups can therefore be seen to go hand in hand. Secondly, this expansion in professional enterprise is also due in part to the development of technologies and techniques of how to observe, measure and treat 'failure' in human beings. Hence developmental psychology, besides extending our knowledge of the developing person, can be used to 'measure' indirectly the effects of the home environment and parenting (for detailed discussion of this issue, see Rose, 1989).

Such issues pose certain difficulties for nurses. Community or domiciliary nursing, particularly health visiting in the context of child care, cannot be viewed as having entirely unproblematic motives. On the one hand health care in Britain is an important part of welfare services while on the other the legacy of community nursing from the last century highlights a long-standing commitment to services to people in their home. It is precisely in this intersection of the public and private world of the recipient families that the nurse has a particular stance as regards expectations of and by families. For instance, the general view of child protection has tended to target working-class families for professional intervention. Why this should be so is to do with issues such as similarity in lifestyle and values between the professional and the family: what is identified as 'normal' does not draw attention or cause suspicion. It is particularly families who are poor or who are headed by lone parents or who for some other reason (other than established cases of child abuse) are 'visible', that come to the notice of the professionals.

A common approach to the prevention of child abuse has been to identify predisposing risk factors which predict which children are most at risk (see for instance Taylor, 1989) and thereafter intervention should be directed at such families. This makes a clear distinction between families for whom it is necessary to provide public support as stated by the Children Act, such as day nursery provision, and those who are able to pay for child care or voluntarily organize it themselves and who by that definition can choose and exercise some control over the type and quality of care. There is no clear evidence that, for instance, the provision of some inner-city local authority facilities are a satisfactory response to the recommendations of the Children Act. Besides, as it is general knowledge that only 'problem' families tend to qualify for day nursery provision, the children can suffer an additional burden of stigma due to their placement.

The approach to provision is quite different in some other countries. Cannan (1992) makes the point that in France the day-care services are part of the basic infrastructure of society, as children are assumed to need services in their own right as future citizens. This also means that the burden of child care is shared between the State and the family.

Family policy and the voluntary sector

The government in the UK is advocating increased voluntary sector involvement alongside renewed emphasis on the family responsibility for caring in terms of any dependent member of a family: children, the elderly and the sick. Both approaches seem designed to minimize government responsibility for supporting families. The success of voluntary action is hard to appraise as, in the absence of other provision, voluntary services are the only resort and very much needed. What can be noted, however, is that it has the consequence of using women as unpaid workers – as it is women, on the whole, who run and support such services. Nevertheless, use of the voluntary sector gives a chance to identify needs and achieve change flexibly and, furthermore, can be a way of limiting the dominance and control of professionals (Johnson, 1990). Finch (1984 cited Johnson, 1990), nonetheless, has pointed out that not everyone can access the help and support offered by voluntary groups. Running self-help groups is essentially a middle-class activity and makes no contribution to those in paid work who cannot, or choose not, to be full-time mothers. Taking part in running a group requires a certain amount of knowledge, confidence and time in dealing with both paperwork and people. Generally speaking, middle-class people are in a better position to meet such challenges.

Yet if we accept what Johnson (1990) sees as the potential of self-help groups, they and other voluntary organizations can demonstrate to professionals new approaches to care and can articulate the needs of service users – provided of course that professionals recognize the value and relevance of such example and advocacy. Given the close relationship between the State and professionals, albeit that it may appear rather oblique, a third party or dimension could be an advantage in representing local views. This is not without problems and would need careful consideration and planning. Nevertheless, in some cases it would reduce the absolute individualization of problems and, by the same token, intervention by professionals would not amount to interference by the State.

But, given that relationships are in a state of flux in the family unit itself as well as between the family and welfare policies, the expectations that the government has of the family in terms of providing its own private, or informal, care are unrealistic and unreasonable. Perhaps note should be taken of the change increasingly apparent in human relationships in late-twentieth century society, in which close relationships are formed on the basis of choice rather than being anchored to kin relations (Giddens, 1992).

Conclusion

The changes in the form of families and relationships generally make assumptions about the supportive functions of the family difficult to sustain. The Welfare State has not achieved the solution of all social problems thought to be possible to remedy. In this sense the continued reliance on and anxiety about the family by government is understandable. The Welfare State and welfare provision are responding to the changes in part but still contain certain expectations about the way families should act and behave. An increasing amount of work in the area of social welfare has centred on the different aspects and implications of policies for, and their effects on, not only the family as a whole but on different members of the family.

What is not obvious is how such reappraisal of relationships is going to affect the future of caring relations. The ambiguity of understanding about what 'safely' can remain private about the family has been demonstrated by professional practices which can unjustly focus on some families but not others. The difficulties and dilemmas for professional practice also relate to the private and public aspects of the family. Much of the work done by nurses is directed at the individual and the partnership-in-care model is predominantly seen in such context – endorsing the promotion of empowerment, choice and autonomy. Yet the challenges are there for more nursing involvement at a community level of action, particularly because it seems that an increasing number of families live within meagre and finite resources. This means that models of care need to include proactive planning of policy and services.

Discussion points

1. Do social security policies and practices make women dependent?
2. Is the nuclear family patriarchal?
3. Is the family a social construction?

Further reading

Cannan, C. (1992) *Changing Families Changing Welfare*, Harvester Wheatsheaf, London
An in-depth study of family centres and professional practice in relation to social workers.

Giddens, A. (1989) *Sociology*, Polity Press, Cambridge
An introductory sociology textbook in accessible language.

Giddens, A. (1992) *Human Societies: An Introductory Reader in Sociology*, Polity Press, Cambridge
Has a wide selection of readings covering many topics.

Hardey, M. and Crow, G. (eds) (1991) *Lone Parenthood*, Harvester Wheatsheaf, London
A collection of articles on various aspects of lone parenthood and problems confronting lone parents.

Johnson, M. (1990) *Reconstructing the Welfare State*, Harvester Wheatsheaf, London
Looks at the developments of welfare policies between 1980 and 1990, including social security, NHS, education and housing with particular emphasis on inner-city policy and community care.

Lewis, J. (1992) *Women in Britain Since 1945*, Blackwell, Oxford
A useful and comprehensive look at women, family and welfare policies from the 1940s to the present day.

Roll, J. (1991) *What is the Family? Benefit Models and Social Realities,* Family Policy Studies Centre, London, Occasional Paper number 13
Examines the social security benefit system in detail.

References

Cannan, C. (1992) *Changing Families Changing Welfare,* Harvester Wheatsheaf, London
Davis, G. and Murch, M. (1992) Why do marriages break down? In *Human Societies: An Introductory Reader in Sociology,* (ed. A. Giddens) Polity Press, Cambridge, p. 177
Giddens, A. (1991) *Modernity and Self-identity,* Polity Press, Cambridge
Giddens, A. (ed.) (1992) *Human Societies: An Introductory Reader in Sociology,* Polity Press, Cambridge
Ginsberg, N. (1992) *Divisions of Welfare,* Sage, London
HMSO (1991) *Working Together: Under the Children Act 1989,* HMSO, London
Johnson, M. (1990) *Reconstructing the Welfare State,* Harvester Wheatsheaf, London
Lewis, J. (1992) *Women in Britain Since 1945,* Blackwell, Oxford
Mishra, R. (1990) *The Welfare State in Capitalist Society,* Harvester Wheatsheaf, London
Roll, J. (1991) *What is the Family? Benefit Models and Social Realities,* Family Policy Studies Centre, London, Occasional Paper number 13
Rose, N. (1989) *Governing the Soul: The Shaping of the Private Self,* Routledge, London

8

Race and policy

Sian Maslin-Prothero

Introduction

Initially, there was considerable discussion between my colleagues and myself concerning whether or not we should include a chapter on race. We could be accused of being racist by actually identifying race as a separate topic. We debated examining culture and ethnicity instead, but felt that this would not enable us to discuss the effects of racism on Britain's black and minority ethnic groups. We do not want to problematize race, nor to marginalize issues surrounding black and minority ethnic groups and policy. Black populations are not a problem, the real problem is racism.

In this chapter we will discuss race and terminology, the complexity of terminology and racial discrimination and prejudice. There will be a brief reflection on the composition and origins of the United Kingdom's (UK) population, and the link with oppression. This will lead on to a discussion of race and social policy, and how this may impact on nurses and nursing practice.

Race and terminology

Having decided that race was a relevant issue to be discussed separately in relation to social policy, we then had to address which terms we should actually use in describing people who are discriminated against on the grounds of race. We wanted to recognize aspects of culture as well as issues concerning skin colour. Through an appropriate use of language we can identify and challenge racism. This issue of language and how it is used has been addressed in greater detail by other authors (Banton, 1988; Mares, Larbie and Baxter, 1985; Williams, 1989).

'Black' is often used as an umbrella term and during the 1960s the term 'black' became a source of pride and unity. It unites those people who have a common experience of discrimination and exploitation, because their skin colour is not white (Mares, Larbie and Baxter, 1985). However, it can and does alienate some ethnic and minority groups. Firstly, it does not distinguish those who are African, Asian, Afro-Caribbean, and so on; secondly, the use of the term 'black' excludes the experience of non-black groups such as Greek-Cypriots and Irish people in this country, who may also encounter racism. However, the use of terms 'black' and 'white' can be useful because they identify the racist polarity that exists in the United Kingdom.

We will briefly define some terms connected with race and racism. 'Racism' refers to racial discrimination and prejudice, and can be either intentional or unintentional. 'Prejudice' is where someone has beliefs about an individual or group, which are not based on fact, but on pre-judging without knowledge or experience. 'Discrimination' is where someone is treated differently from others, and can be due to race, sexual orientation, disability, sex, and so on. There are two forms of discrimination – direct and indirect. Direct discrimination is where someone is treated less favourably, on racial grounds, than someone else (Gregory, 1987). Indirect discrimination is where policies and practices have a discriminatory effect, even though it may be unintentional.

There is a need to recognize that racism is not only directed at individuals because of their skin colour, but also directed at other groups such as the Irish, Jews or gypsies, who may also be white. It is also necessary to recognize that all of us make assumptions about individuals according to their appearance or the names they have. For example, if someone says they are English it may be assumed that they will be white and speak English. We may also tend to presume that a man wearing a turban is a Sikh, or that someone with the surname Cohen who lives in Golders Green is a Jew.

Sometimes these assumptions might be correct, however, frequently, they are incorrect. We make sense of our surroundings by putting things into categories; a stereotype is a standardized classification which is then generalized, and can be inaccurate because it is based on false information and is too rigid. Stereotypes can be associated with anxiety and fear, and where this occurs individuals can develop hostility or hatred towards a certain group (Giddens, 1989).

When the term 'race' is used it is assumed to be relating to appearance, which has connections with difference and subsequently feelings of superiority or inferiority. But humans cannot be separated into biologically different races (Giddens, 1989). Hugman (1991) asserts that 'race' is a social construction, and does not relate to specific features, but is tied up with social, cultural and political differences between groups.

Countries, other than the UK, throughout the world may use different terminology. For example in the United States the term 'people of colour' has been adopted. In the UK the term coloured is unacceptable and seen as offensive, because of its links and association with colonialism. The term 'black' is seen as being acceptable by many people, however there can be a danger of homogenizing black peoples' experiences, and not recognizing the diversity of their histories, cultures and backgrounds. The term we will use in this book is 'black populations' as is used by the King's Fund Centre (1993i):

> We use the term 'Black populations' to refer to people from racial or other minorities in this country [the UK] who may be disadvantaged because of their racial backgrounds. We are aware that there is no single accepted term and that there are people who do not identify themselves as Black but who share a common experience of racism.

The King's Fund is an organization involved in the development of the health service and in policy issues, which aims, as part of its wider programme, to empower and enable black populations in the UK.

Black populations in the UK

From where does the UK's diverse population originate? Many people have a strong feeling of nation, usually associated with the fact that we are a group of islands and not (as yet) directly linked with Europe. If you think about it the UK is a truly European country, with the influx of invaders and monarchs over the centuries to these islands. There has also been considerable migration of people from Ireland, Scotland and Wales. The Irish have emigrated to England over several centuries, with an increase in the eighteenth century due to famines and economic necessity. England is relatively close to Ireland, thus making the journey easy and enabling continued communication with family and friends. However, there has been considerable and continuing hostility towards this group (Giddens, 1989; Husband, 1987).

The Jewish communities came to the UK for both political and economic reasons. They settled in large urban areas such as London, Manchester and Leeds, and used skills they already possessed to earn a living for example in tailoring, tobacco and shoes, as well as developing new skills and knowledge. Again there was hostility towards the Jewish community because they were seen as taking housing and jobs from the existing working class. Both the Trade Unions Council and governments, on occasions, have attempted to restrict Jewish admission to the UK (Husband, 1987).

The arrival of black people in the UK is very closely associated with its being a seafaring nation. Companies sailed all around the world, and there was exchange of goods and people. In addition there was the UK's involvement in slavery and the transportation of slaves; this was closely associated with the British Empire, imperialism and colonialism. The combination of all these factors led to black people being brought to this country and in the majority of cases against their will (for more detailed information read Husband, 1987, or Hooks, 1982).

After the Second World War, black populations were actively encouraged and recruited to work in the UK. There were several reasons for this; the UK was experiencing economic growth and expansion and as a result there was a marked shortage of labour in postwar Britain. Thus there was a need to recruit people to certain occupations where, because of the long hours and poor pay, there was difficulty attracting staff. As a result of the UK's connection with the Empire and colonialism it was decided to recruit from the Commonwealth countries. It was felt by some members of Parliament that they were all British subjects and therefore entitled to settle here (Giddens, 1989), while others felt that these black people could be repatriated to their countries of origin, when their labour was no longer required.

On closer examination those occupations which actively recruited from the black population, in the majority of circumstances, were those offering more menial jobs, thus reinforcing and perpetuating the perception and belief of black people as slaves.

Domination on the basis of race

There are a number of sources of oppression including age, class, gender, sexual orientation and race. This oppression is manifested in many ways, and we will be focusing on race: prejudice; discrimination; and racism.

Racial discrimination is the oppression of a group or groups of people who are treated unfairly or unfavourably, because they are perceived to be different (in terms of religion, colour of skin or cultural beliefs). In comparison, prejudice is an opinion based on inadequate or inaccurate information, leading to intolerance or hostility towards a group.

Overt racism is where an individual is discriminated against consciously and explicitly because they belong to an identifiable group, such as being black, or because their name is unusual. This may be manifested as verbal racial abuse or other racial attacks. In comparison, institutional racism is not conscious. Institutional racism is built into the structure of an organization, through its policies and procedures; an example could be the NHS where it fails to take into consideration inequalities in power that exist between white and black employees and patients. Covert racism is not explicit, but is hidden; however, it could be conscious. These will be discussed in more detail when examining race, policy and the nursing perspectives (Mares, Larbie and Baxter, 1985).

One of the difficulties is proving that covert racism has occurred or where it has taken place. The Race Relations Act (HMSO, 1976) requires evidence of discrimination, and any investigation that takes place will be after the incident, for example a job application and interview. Discrimination is often hidden, and therefore requires vigorous techniques to pinpoint, expose and subsequently prove that it took place.

Power plays a major part in oppression. Racist power is usually the power of white people over black people. White people see themselves as standard and the norm, whereas black people are seen as the 'other' (Hugman, 1991). This attitude has developed prior to and was compounded through imperialism and colonialism, where white groups believed that they had 'discovered' and subsequently dominated black people. White people incorrectly assumed a racial superiority, not only did they think they were different to black people, but also that black people were inferior. There is, of course, no foundation for this belief. So often we express our concerns about other countries and their explicit and overt racism, such as South Africa and apartheid, or the former Yugoslavia and the ethnic cleansing of Muslims by Serbs. Yet we fail to acknowledge or address the overt and covert racism occurring in the UK.

What we see is an underrepresentation of black people in many professions (Akinsanya, 1988; Rafferty, 1993). In addition many individuals from the black populations are excluded from entry into the higher levels of many professions. The provision of the majority of services in Britain are directed towards the white population and therefore fail to take into consideration the black population's needs and requirements. This is reinforced by the fact that there are very few people from the black population in positions of power, where decisions and policy are being made.

What cannot be ignored is the link between power and the oppression of certain groups because of their race, gender, disability, sexual orientation or class. Black, working-class women may well experience a triple oppression due to racism, patriarchy and capitalism (see chapters 3 and 6 for discussion of these in greater detail).

Race and social policy

It has already been identified how difficult it is to recognize, prove and expose racism. In this section we will address policies pertinent to the UK's black populations, and how these populations can be rendered invisible, or their needs distorted through other peoples' interpretation.

As discussed earlier, the UK has had black populations living here for centuries. It is difficult to ascertain how many different groups there are, and the numbers in these groups, for a number of reasons. Firstly, the terminology for groups is many and varied, such as white, Asian, Afro-Caribbean etc; the monitoring methods are different from organization to organization, creating a lack of consistency. Secondly, any form of monitoring is often treated with suspicion – for what is the information going to be used? Finally any information collected invariably fails to recognize those members of black populations born in the UK, over 50 per cent, which is in fact the majority of the black populations (Social Trends, 1992). In policy terms it can be difficult ascertaining what the needs of minority ethnic groups are because they can be so diverse.

There is sometimes a tendency to view the black population as a homogenous group, under the false belief that they all undergo the same or similar experiences. As has already been identified, this group in fact contains a large number of diverse people, all with very different values and beliefs. There is a need to recognize this, and to appreciate all people's individuality. Sometimes there is an inclination to over-simplify and generalize the black population's experience, which can itself lead to the creation and reinforcement of inaccurate stereotypes.

There are three commonly held interpretations on race, and how black populations should be living within a society. In policy terms these are important because they inform decisions made. Assimilation is a belief that black populations should adapt into the way of life of the country in which they are living, that is abandon any customs or practices they may have (New Internationalist, 1985). This probably has been the majority view of policy makers in Britain (Giddens, 1989). Multiculturalism espouses the belief that black populations have a right to come to the UK (New Internationalist, 1985) and that prejudice and discrimination can be removed, and the experience of all people enhanced by recognizing individuality of groups and sharing information, such things as culture and language. Finally, the antiracist view recognizes that black populations moved to countries because their labour was required by the economy (New Internationalist, 1985). This view identifies that racism is to do with power, and the way to remove prejudice is to have more people from black populations in positions of power and influence. Only through integration will prejudice and racism be dismantled (Giddens, 1989).

Simply raising awareness through the promotion of communication and understanding of different cultures fails to address the real issues. That is, that factors such as substandard housing, low income, unemployment, poor diet, the effects and fear of crime, limited educational opportunities and racism can and does have a significant effect on the individual's life experience (Helman, 1990; McTaggart, 1993; Pearson, 1986; Williams, 1989; Wolk, 1993).

Race and health services

Both the Black Report (1980) and the Health Divide (1987) highlighted that social class and ill health are linked. Individuals from the black population are more likely to be found in the lower social economic classes because of their limited access to occupations. Consequently black populations are likely to experience greater morbidity and mortality. However, there is a paucity of information, as mentioned earlier, regarding the black population's health due to the way the statistics are collected and interpreted (Grimsley and Bhat, 1988). It is very difficult to obtain reliable statistics because there is little or no racial breakdown in health statistics.

Some studies focus on country of birth (Marmot, Adelstein and Bulusu, 1984) and fail to recognize those individuals who were born in the UK, and whose families have lived here for centuries. Therefore information relating to second and third generation families is unavailable for evaluation. It is necessary and essential that there is some standardization of criteria: birth place, social class, and some means of identifying different minority ethnic groups, for example African, Irish, Jewish, Chinese, Afro-Caribbean, and so on.

Marmot, Adelstein and Bulusu (1984), examining the mortality rates of immigrants, identified that they did have a higher mortality rate. Other studies have noted greater perinatal and infant mortality rates, however there is a need to make them more relevant by the inclusion of the black populations actually born in the UK.

Of the little research that has been undertaken relating to the black population's health, most has centred on the more 'exotic' diseases such as rickets, tuberculosis and sickle cell. These diseases are more common among black populations, but it has been suggested that white researchers have chosen to focus on these areas because it interests them, rather than black populations identifying them as specific areas of concern (Donovan, 1986; Pearson, 1986; Torkington, 1987a; Williams, 1989). A phone-in service was provided for the black population by a local radio station regarding health education (Webb, 1982). These calls were monitored over a six-month period, and it was found that the most common issues discussed by callers were: asthma, hay fever, breathlessness, family planning, infertility, psychosexual problems and diabetes. That is, similar concerns to the white population.

But areas such as sickle cell anaemia and thalassaemia can be useful for illustrating how black populations are discriminated against through policy decisions, that is racial discrimination at its most covert.

Sickle cell anaemia is an inherited disorder which affects the red blood cells, which become sickle-shaped and are easily destroyed. The haemoglobin is less efficient, and subsequently the body obtains less oxygen; this can cause severe pain. Sickle cell anaemia is predominantly found among Caribbean (1 in 200) and West African (1 in 100) births (Thomas-Hope, 1992). Thalassaemia minor and major is also a form of anaemia which is genetically transmitted and occurs among people from North Africa, southern Europe and the Indian sub-continent (Mares, Larbie and Baxter, 1985; McNaught, 1987). Although sickle cell anaemia and thalassaemia have been a focus for research and the life expectancy of those with the disease has been improved, there is still no routine screening for these diseases in the UK.

Only a few health authorities choose to screen routinely to identify these anaemias, it is not available to all black populations. However, all babies born in Britain are routinely screened on the seventh day following birth for phenylketonuria; this is an extremely rare disorder, with an incidence of 10–12 per 100,000 births (Thomas-Hope, 1992) and only encountered by white people (Grimsley and Bhat, 1988; Smart, 1987).

Black communities in Britain have campaigned and raised

awareness of sickle cell anaemia and thalassaemia and the treatment available (Bryan, Dadzie and Scarfe, 1985; McNaught, 1987). Yet there is no routine screening available for those individuals who could either be carriers of sickle cell or who actually have the disease; or adequate resources for those who require treatment.

Another example of the invisibility of the UK's black population is where the Asian population is particularly affected by rickets and osteomalacia. These result in defections of the skeletal system and are caused by a lack of vitamin D in the diet and an inadequate exposure to sunlight. During the 1980s the Department of Health and Social Security (DHSS) ran a campaign specifically directed at the Asian community. It focused on diet consumed and the importance of exposing skin to sunlight; as sunlight can manufacture vitamin D in the skin.

The incidence of these diseases among white people has been reduced; they also endured rickets and osteomalacia (until recently), but due to the fortification of margarine with vitamin D since 1940, the incidence of these diseases among whites has fallen. Approximately 40 per cent of the recommended daily requirement of vitamin D is derived from this source (Torkington, 1987a). However, the Asian community prefer to use butter. The Asian community have requested that other foods used regularly by the community be fortified with vitamin D, such as butter, milk and chapati flour, but to date the British government has refused (Torkington, 1987a; Grimsley and Bhat, 1988).

Another aspect of the rickets campaign was to encourage the Asian community to expose their skin to sunlight. This directive fails to consider that because of cultural or religious restrictions, it would be unacceptable for some women to sunbathe or expose their skin in any way. It also assumes that everyone has access to a private garden or facilities which would enable them to sunbathe. In addition, it fails to consider the fear of racist attacks which confine many families inside their homes (Donovan, 1986).

Finally, we cannot ignore the numbers from the black population being diagnosed as mentally ill. Again because of the way statistics are compiled, it is difficult to obtain accurate representation (Grimsley and Bhat, 1988). However there is no doubt that the black population is overrepresented as being mentally ill, and being detained in mental health institutions

(Bandung File, 1987, cited by Torkington, 1991; Nursing Standard, 1992). There have been a number of attempts to explain this phenomenon such as: migration can cause mental illness; those who migrate were already predisposed to mental illness; the culture of black populations within a white culture is responsible for their mental illness; the burden of racism, that is the white hegemony (and racism) of male psychiatrists and misdiagnosis on the part of doctors (for further reading see Gabriel, 1989; Grimsley and Bhat, 1988; Torkington, 1991).

Once an individual is diagnosed as mentally ill, there is no way of removing the stigma associated with mental illness. It must not be forgotten that psychiatry has been used (and continues to be used) as a form of social control. That is those who will not conform to society's norms are seen as deviant and have to be reprimanded. Psychiatry has thus beome a way of controlling rebellious people.

There is a need to recognize the policy implications. 'Conscious' members of the black population are underrepresented in positions of power because they are seen as challenging the system and wanting to create change. The UK's black populations do not want token blacks at the top, they want and need individuals who know and understand the needs of the black communities, and can implement policies which are valid to these communities.

Health policies: who decides and who provides?

Individuals from black populations do have specific health needs. McNaught (1987) identifies four factors which could affect their health needs: common illnesses and conditions; genetically-determined health conditions; racial discrimination; and problems of access to health services. The needs of black populations are similar to others, but these four factors combined with social, political and economic forces contribute to their experiencing discriminatory practices.

We are not trying to identify the differences between black and white populations, but instead recognize how racism contributes to the black population's ill health. There is often a tendency to see culture as an obstacle, rather than addressing the real problem which is a lack of power on the part of the black populations.

There is a need to identify for example why the black populations are overrepresented in mental health institutions.

The most obvious situation is where practices are consciously or unconsciously informed by the belief that one group are sunerior to another, and discrimination occurs because of this belie institutional racism of health-care workers can contribute to the black population's negative experience of the McNaught (1987) identified the following as areas members of the black population encounter discrimin patient reception and handling; clinical consultation; pat consent to procedures; nursing care; and health surveillanc an diagnosis.

This can be illustrated by black women's experience. almost impossible to avoid the NHS if you are a woman becauʌᴄ ʋ the medicalization of reproduction. Most women have to endure certain services – family planning, antenatal care, family health – however, black women not only experience sexism but racism as well (Williams, 1989). Among the white population the pregnancy of a white woman is usually greeted as something positive; in comparison, the pregnancy of a black woman can be viewed by the white population as yet another black child, the reproduction of **more** black people (Williams, 1989).

Whereas feminists from the white population have fought for the right to choose and have an abortion if they are pregnant; black women have experienced the opposite. Black women have found their fertility being controlled by white, middle-class health workers, and there is a common stereotype of black women being highly promiscuous, and unreliable when it comes to using contraception (Gabriel, 1989; Hooks, 1982). Subsequently they find themselves being offered abortions, being administered Depo-Provera (an injectable contraception) and sterilizations without informed consent (Bryan, Dadzie and Scarfe, 1985; Doyal, 1985).

Helman (1990) identifies the importance of recognizing how the culture of the health worker can affect their relationship with a patient, such as the misinterpretation of cultural or religious behaviours. This can be illustrated by the treatment of individuals with sickle cell disease (Smart, 1987), not only were the hospital staff racist in their practice, but they did not believe these patients when they said they were in pain. This could be explained by the fact that sickle cell disease is not experienced by the white population, therefore they are unable, or choose not to, understand how the sufferer is feeling.

Another point which needs to be considered here is the power relationship between patient and professional. Once an individual consults a professional, there can be a switch in power from the patient to the professional (Pearson, 1986); this power can then be used to undermine the patient. For the black populations there is the additional dimension of class, and for women sexism (Torkington, 1987b). Much is written about the differences between black and white populations without addressing the black populations lack of power (Williams, 1989).

In addition, the black populations are underrepresented in the higher echelons of any service (Akinsanya, 1988; Baxter, 1988; Cockburn, 1991; Doyal, Hunt and Mellor, 1981; Pearson, 1987). Multiculturalists would argue that there is a need to raise the awareness of staff through training. This is important and valid, however there needs to be representation of black populations in positions where decisions and policies are made. Policy changes and monitoring are the ways in which more appropriate services can be formulated and change created in a more direct way.

Policy makers, professionals and researchers are predominantly white, middle-class males – these are the individuals recommending, formulating and implementing policy for the rest of the population. There is a tendency to oversimplify and stereotype the needs of the black populations, failing to recognize the part poor housing, unemployment and social class can play in individuals' life experiences (Payne, 1991). This can be changed by the involvement of black populations in the planning and implementation of services. Where they have been involved they have been able to make positive changes, such as the Organisation for Sickle Cell Anaemia Research (OSCAR).

There is a need for a change in authority from the professionals to the people; but to do this these groups need to know how organizations are run and how decisions are made. The black population is not looking for tokenism, but 'conscious' people who will challenge the system and create change (Torkington, 1991). Information is power and therefore it is important that information is disseminated to the black population, and that this information is accurate and culturally appropriate.

NHS and Community Care Act 1990

Over the last couple of decades there has been a philosophy to make health care more accessible for all. In addition there has been an increase in costs of care for the elderly and people with mental illness and learning disabilities. With demographic changes such as the increase in the number of older people, there is an increasing emphasis on the health and social services to provide care (Audit Commission, 1986; Griffiths, 1988; HMSO, 1989; HMSO, 1990).

The NHS and Community Care Act 1990 aims to promote and develop domiciliary, day and respite care, through the assessment and provision of appropriate services for carers and cared for in the community (HMSO, 1990). The King's Fund Centre, in conjunction with the Institute of Public Health, University of Surrey, has established an information exchange service – known as Share – specifically for the black population (Bahl, 1991). In addition the King's Fund Centre has been involved with several health-care purchasing authorities to develop mechanisms by which black populations can have a greater say in the services provided (Mohammed, 1992). For example, Coventry Health Authority actually went into the community and collected information about the black populations' requirements via meetings, community centres and local shops (Jones, 1992). From the information gathered contracts were compiled including specifications identified by the black populations.

There are other organizations, such as the National Council for Voluntary Organizations (NCVO), which also provide information on legislative changes and give advice on drawing up of contracts with health and social services (NCVO, 1991).

Race and the nursing perspective

In this section we will examine the representation of the black populations in the nursing profession; and how nursing care is underpinned by racist beliefs.

Black populations have played a major role in the development of the NHS. During the 1950s and 1960s local selection committees set up in Commonwealth countries actively recruited people to undertake work in transport, factories and health services; as previously mentioned at the beginning of this chapter (Bryan, Dadzie and Scarfe, 1985; Baxter, 1988; Husband, 1987; King's Fund, 1990). The UK's population were reluctant to undertake these occupations because they were not seen as attractive (for a more in depth discussion read Maslin-Prothero, 1992b).

Black populations are well represented in the NHS as cleaners, caterers and nurses (Doyal, Hunt and Mellor, 1981). However they are more usually to be found in lower grades. Many of those entering the nursing profession in the postwar period were directed towards enrolled nursing and to what were perceived as the less prestigious areas of the nursing profession: care of the elderly, mental health and learning disabilities (Baxter, 1988). They were often not even informed about registered nursing. The EOC suggest that as a result stereotypes were formed and it was believed that these nurses wished to remain at 'the bedside' because they possessed good basic nursing skills, could control aggressive patients and lacked written and spoken English (Equal Opportunities Commission (EOC), 1991), and thus were prevented from progressing in nursing.

The Commission for Racial Equality (CRE) (1983) have suggested that some managers in the NHS believe that the fact that there are so many black nurses indicates that the health service is not a racist institution. There are large numbers of staff from the black populations in the health service, but it is difficult accurately to identify where they are in the service because the NHS does not routinely monitor or publish statistics relating to race. Without monitoring it is impossible to ensure adequate representation.

The monitoring of black populations in organizations has been supported by numerous people (Akinsanya, 1988; Cockburn, 1991; King's Fund, 1990). Not only would it identify where black populations are in the organization, but also ensure that strategies such as positive action targets were being achieved. However there is often opposition to ethnic monitoring because of: misunderstanding and suspicion as to why the data is being collected; fear of how the statistics will be used, such as reverse discrimination; or a general opposition to equal opportunities.

There is evidence of both horizontal and vertical segregation for the black populations in nursing, particularly if they are female.

Horizontal segregation is where an individual experiences difficulties getting promoted to a position commensurate with their qualifications; vertical segregation is where there are two separate labour markets. The primary labour market refers to the more prestigious occupations and this is more usually occupied by men; the secondary sector is the more mundane jobs, and is not as well paid – women are more likely to be found undertaking this sort of work.

Thus individuals from the black populations are more likely to be found in the less prestigious areas of any organization, with little opportunity of promotion (Doyal, 1981). There are a number of reasons why this should be occurring. Firstly, it could be explained by overt and covert racism of those recruiting and selecting staff. Secondly there are more black females in nursing than males, and therefore they are also experiencing discrimination on the grounds of sex (as well as racism). Finally, there is the stereotypical belief identified earlier that these nurses are where they want to be, at the bedside, and that they do not want to be promoted.

It is sometimes hard to believe that there has been legislation for over twenty-five years which states that it is illegal to discriminate against someone because of the colour of their skin (Race Relations Act, 1976); on the grounds of sex (whether they are female or male – Sex Discrimination Act, 1975); or that people should be paid the same if they are undertaking the same work (Equal Pay Act). It has been stated that the Equal Pay Act, Sex Discrimination Act and Race Relations Act have done very little to improve the lot of the black populations, women or those who are low-paid employees and that they should either be discarded or those bodies responsible for the monitoring of them (the CRE and the EOC), be given more authority and hence power.

Recruitment and selection

There have been requests from the registrar at the United Kingdom Central Council for Nursing, Midwifery and Health Visiting (UKCC) for colleges of nursing to widen the entry gate, and actively recruit a more diverse group into the profession (Ralph, 1991; Ralph, 1992), a group that reflects the needs of the

UK's population. However, at the same time there has been a move towards a diploma-level course, which may disadvantage those who have little or no experience of academic work. For example, those who might have left school prior to taking GCSEs, and therefore do not have the necessary academic qualifications, or those who were disadvantaged at school due to discrimination on the grounds of colour of skin, sex or social class.

The registrar emphasized that those applicants from the black population should not be disadvantaged. Yet there is evidence that the numbers of individuals from the black population applying for nurse education leading to registration are falling (Baxter, 1988). This is in spite of the increase in the number of black 18 year olds in the population. Baxter (1988) suggests two possible explanations for the fact that potential recruits from the black population are discouraged: either they have been discriminated against when applying for nurse education; or family members or friends who already work for the health services have experienced discrimination from colleagues at work, and have discouraged them from entering the profession.

This has been compounded by the discontinuation of enrolled nursing courses; an avenue available for those individuals who did not have the required qualifications has effectively been closed. The entry gate to registered nursing has already been widened, but there is also the need for nurse educationalists to go out into the community and actively recruit from the black population. Programmes are being devised which are more affirmative. In addition, access courses are being provided for those individuals who may not have the necessary qualifications.

If nursing is to reflect the UK's diverse population and provide appropriate care, we must address issues regarding race and equality of opportunity in recruitment and selection procedures. If the black populations are not represented in nursing, and especially in positions of power where decisions are made, the needs of the black population are not ultimately going to be addressed and met.

Another point which needs to be addressed is the nursing curriculum, and how this tackles issues of racism. Essentially the nursing curriculum continues to be based on white values and beliefs, and fails to recognize the requirements of the black populations (Gough, Maslin-Prothero and Masterson, 1993).

Subsequently the care provided by nurses in British hospitals is quite often culturally inappropriate. How many nurses know how to recognize cyanosis in someone with a dark skin? Or the use of 'flesh coloured' plasters.

Conclusion

We have examined some of the issues surrounding race and social policy and identified that, because of racism, people from black populations continue to experience discrimination when it comes to provision of services. We are not arguing for segregation and the provision of separate services for the black population. Rather, we wish to see that nurse education and nursing services recognize that there has been a failure to provide appropriate services to Britain's black community. How often is a poor uptake of a service associated with the fact that it fails to provide what the community actually wants? This can only be achieved by the black population's involvement in the planning and provision of a service, and by constantly challenging and addressing racism wherever it occurs.

Discussion points

1. What initiatives might be undertaken to improve the black populations' experience of health and social services?
2. Discuss the black populations' experience of working for health and social services?
3. Has equality legislation enhanced the experience of black populations?

Further reading

Baxter, C. (1988) *The Black Nurse: An Endangered Species*, National Extension College, Cambridge
This study summarizes the experiences of a group of black nurses in the health service. It identifies the discrimination experienced by black nurses and how racism discourages black people from entering the nursing profession.

Equal Opportunities Commission (1991) *Equality Management: Women's Employment in the NHS*, EOC, Manchester
This is a summary of the EOC's investigation of equal opportunities in the NHS, and the lack of commitment to equal opportunities in the NHS.

King Edward's Hospital Fund For London (1990) *Racial Equality: The Nursing Profession*, Equal Opportunity Task Force Occasional Paper Number 6, King's Fund, London
This paper reviews the literature and gives some examples of health authorities who have implemented ethnic monitoring. It shows us how we can move towards greater equality.

Mares, P., Larbie, J. and Baxter, C. (1985) *Trainer's Handbook for Multiracial Health Care*, National Extension College, Cambridge
Essential reading for all health-care workers and those involved in education. Not only is there information, but also exercises which can be used to challenge stereotypes.

Maslin-Prothero, S. E. (1992) Minority ethnic women and nursing. *Nursing Standard*, 7 (8), pp. 25–28
This article looks at why so many nurses from black populations are to be found in the NHS and offers possible explanations.

References

Akinsanya, J. A. (1988) Ethnic minority nurses, midwives and health visitors: what role for them in the NHS? *New Community*, **XIV**, 5, pp. 444–450

Audit Commission (1986) *Making a Reality of Community Care*, HMSO, London

Bahl, V. (1991) Ethnic minority health care. *Health Trends*, **23**, 3

Banton, M. (1988) *Racial Consciousness*, Longman, London

Baxter, C. (1988) *The Black Nurse: An Endangered Species*, National Extension College, Cambridge

Bryan, B., Dadzie, S. and Scarfe, S. (1985) *The Heart of the Race: Black Women's Lives in Britain*, Virago Press, London

Central Statistical Office (1992) *Social Trends 22*, HMSO, London

Commission For Racial Equality (1983) *Ethnic Minority Hospital Staff*, CRE, London

Commission For Racial Equality (1992) *Race Relations Code of Practice in Primary Health Care Services*, CRE, London

Connelly, N. (1988) *Care in the Multiracial Community*, Policy Studies Institute, London

Connelly, N. (1989) *Race and Change in Social Services Department*, Policy Studies Institute, London

DoH (1989) *Caring for People: Community Care in the Next Decade*, HMSO, London

Donovan, J. (1986) Black people's health: a different approach. In *Health, Race and Ethnicity*, (eds T. Rathwell and D. Phillips) Croom Helm, London, pp. 117–136

Doyal, L., Hunt, G. and Mellor, J. (1981) Your life in their hands: migrant workers in the NHS. *Critical Social Policy*, 1, pp. 54–71

Equal Opportunities Commission (1991) *Equality Management: Women's Employment in the NHS*, EOC, Manchester

Fenton, S. (1985) *Race Health and Welfare. Afro-Caribbean and South Asian People in Central Bristol: Health and Social Services*, University of Bristol, Bristol

Gabriel, S. (1989) *The Colonial Legacy and its Impact on Black Psychology in the Western World*, unpublished paper

Giddens, A. (1989) *Sociology*, Polity Press, Cambridge

Gough, P., Maslin-Prothero, S. and Masterson, A. (1993) A reflection on issues for practice. In *Project 2000: Reflection and Celebration*, (ed. B. Dolan) Scutari, London, pp. 89–105

Graham, H. (1991) The concepts of caring in feminist research: the case of domestic service. *Sociology*, 25, 1, February, 61–78

Gregory, J. (1987) *Sex, Race and the Law*, Sage Publications, London

Griffiths, R. (1988) *Community Care: Agenda for Action. A Report for the Secretary of State for Social Services*, HMSO, London

Grimsley, M. and Bhat, A. (1988) Health. In *Britain's Black Population*, 2nd edn, (eds A. Bhat, R. Carr-Hill and S. Ohri) Gower, Aldershot, pp. 177–207

Hek, G. (1990) Old black people's uptake of district nursing services. unpublished Masters Thesis, University of Warwick, Warwick

Helman, C. (1990) Cultural factors in health and illness. In *Health Care for Asians* (eds B. R. McAvoy and L. J. Donaldson) Oxford University Press, Oxford, pp. 17–27

Hooks, B. (1982) *Ain't I a Woman: Black Women and Feminism*, Pluto Press, London

Husband, C. (ed.) (1987) *'Race' in Britain: Continuity and Change*, 2nd edn, Hutchinson, London

Johnson, M. (1986) Inner city residents, ethnic minorities and primary health care in the West Midlands. In *Health, Race and Ethnicity* (eds T. Rathwell and D. Phillips) Croom Helm, London, pp. 192–212

Jones, H. (1992) Sensitive purchasing. *Share Newsletter*, December, 4, 4

King Edward's Hospital Fund For London (1989) *Equal Opportunities Employment Policies in the NHS: Ethnic Monitoring*, King's Fund, London

King Edward's Hospital Fund For London (1990) *Racial Equality: The Nursing Profession*, Equal Opportunities Task Force Occasional Paper Number 6, King's Fund, London

King's Fund Centre (1993) A note on views and terminology from share. *Share Newsletter*, April, 5, p. 12

McAvoy, B. and Raza, R. (1988) Asian women: (i) Contraceptive knowledge, attitudes and usage. (ii) Contraceptive services and cervical cytology. *Health Trends*, **20**, 11–17

McAvoy, B. (1988) Women's health. In *Health Care for Asians* (eds B. McAvoy and L. J. Donaldson) Oxford University Press, Oxford, pp. 150–171

McAvoy, B. and Sayeed, A. (1990) Communication. In *Health Care for Asians* (eds B. McAvoy and L. J. Donaldson) Oxford University Press, Oxford, pp. 57–71

McNaught, A. (1987) *Health Action and Ethnic Minorities*, Bedford Square Press, London

McNaught, A. (1988) *Race and Health Policy*, Croom Helm, London

McNaught, A. (1990) Organization and delivery of care. In *Health Care for Asians*, (eds B. McAvoy and L. J. Donaldson) Oxford University Press, Oxford, pp. 31–39

Macquistern, S. (1986) *All Things Being Equal?*, South Derbyshire Health Authority

McTaggart, M. (1993) Does society care about black kids? *The Observer*, 6 May, p. 61

MacVicar, J. (1990) Obstetrics. In *Health Care for Asians* (eds B. McAvoy and L. J. Donaldson) Oxford University Press, Oxford, pp. 172–191

Mama, A. (1986) Black women and the economic crisis. In *Waged Work: A Reader* (ed. Feminist Review) Virago, London, pp. 186–202

Mares, P., Larbie, J. and Baxter, C. (1985) *Trainer's Handbook for Multiracial Health Care*, National Extension College, Cambridge

Marmot, M. G., Adelstein, A. M. and Bulusu, L. (1984) Immigrant mortality in England and Wales 1970–1978. *Studies on Medical and Population Subjects No 47*, HMSO, London

Maslin-Prothero, S. E. (1992) Minority ethnic women and nursing. *Nursing Standard*, **7**(8), 25–28

Mohammed, S. (1992) Improving services to black populations through contracts. *Share Newsletter*, December, **4**, 3

National Council for Voluntary Organizations (1991) *Contracts for Care:*

Issues for Black and other Ethnic Minority Voluntary Groups, NCVO, London

New Internationalist (1985) Three views on race. *New Internationalist*, **1**, March, 19

NHS Regional Manpower Planners' Group (1988) *2001: The Black Hole: An Examination of Labour Market Trends in Relation to the NHS*, HMSO, London

Pascall, G. (1986) *Social Policy: A Feminist Perspective*, Tavistock Publications, London

Patel, N. (1990) *A 'Race' Against Time? Social Services Provision to Black Elders*, Runnymede Trust, London

Payne, S. (1991) *Women, Health and Poverty: An Introduction*, Harvester Wheatsheaf, London

Pearson, M. (1985) *Equal Opportunities in the NHS – A Handbook*, National Extension College, Cambridge

Pearson, M. (1986) The politics of ethnic minority health studies. In *Health, Race and Ethnicity*, (eds T. Rathwell, and D. Phillips) Croom Helm, London, pp. 100–116

Pearson, M. (1987) Racism: the great divide. *Nursing Times*, **84**(24), 24–26

Rafferty, A. M. (1993) *Leading Questions: A Discussion Paper on the Issues of Nurse Leadership*, King's Fund Centre, London

Rashid, A. (1990) Asian doctors and nurses in the NHS. In *Health Care for Asians* (eds B. McAvoy and L. J. Donaldson) Oxford University Press, Oxford, pp. 40–56

Rathwell, T. and Phillips, D. (1986) Ethnicity and health: an agenda for progressive action. In *Health, Race and Ethnicity* (eds T. Rathwell and D. Phillips) Croom Helm, London, pp. 1–20

Saggar, S. (1991) *Race and Public Policy*, Gower, Aldershot

Smart, D. (1987) Sickle cell anaemia – women speak out. In *Women's Health: A Spare Rib Reader* (ed. S. O'Sullivan) Pandora Press, London, pp. 88–92

Smith, P. (1987) Mary Seacole. In *Gender and Expertise* (ed. M. McNeil) Free Association Press, London, pp. 218–224

Tandon, K. (1987) Lumps and bumps . . . racism and sexism. In *Women's Health: A Spare Rib Reader* (ed. S. O'Sullivan) Pandora Press, London, pp. 109–112

Thomas-Hope, E. M. (1992) International migration and health: sickle cell and thalassaemia health care in the United Kingdom. *GeoJournal*, **26**(1), 75–79

Torkington, P. (1987a) Blaming black women – rickets and racism. In *Women's Health: A Spare Rib Reader* (ed. S. O'Sullivan) Pandora Press, London, pp. 82–85

Torkington, P. (1987b) The racist and sexist delivery of the NHS – the experience of black women. In *Women's Health: A Spare Rib Reader* (ed. S. O'Sullivan) Pandora Press, London, pp. 77–82

Torkington, P. (1991) *Black Health – A Political Issue*, Catholic Association for Racial Justice, London

Townsend, P. and Davidson, N. (eds) (1988) The Black report. In *Inequalities in Health*, Penguin, London

Whitehead, M. (1988) The health divide. In *Inequalities in Health*, Penguin, London

Williams, F. (1989) *Social Policy: A Critical Introduction*, Polity Press, Oxford

Wolk, S. (1993) Private lives and public spirits. *The Observer (Housing Report)*, 6 May, p. 9

9

Older people

Jean Neave

Introduction

We decided to include a chapter specifically about older people not because we wanted to categorize or 'welfarize' them but because, as the largest 'consumers' of health care, we wanted to prioritize their particular needs. It is particularly important to be aware of the social policy context in which their care takes place and this chapter will demonstrate how the delivery of health care is influenced by political beliefs and attitudes.

We begin by describing the demographic features of our older population and their health needs, highlighting that social policy has been slow to respond to the challenge of an ageing population. Much of this is underpinned by the dominant ideology that the increasing numbers of older people in British society represent a financial and health-care burden. Taking a historical overview we will explore the changing role of the State with regard to the care of older people.

The prevalence of ageism and the political economy of welfare perspective will be given as explanations for the marginalization of older people in British society, particularly the needs of older women. Finally, the way in which nursing is responding to the needs of older people and suggestions for alternative approaches are examined.

Throughout the chapter we have standardized our terminology choosing to use the phrase 'older people' which has less negative connotations than the term 'elderly'. It also moves away from the idea of older people being a homogenous group.

Demographic features

British society is characterized by an increasing number and a larger proportion of older people. This phenomenon is also a feature of other industrialized societies and is regarded as a sign of a society's economic and social development. The population of older people, usually defined as those over pensionable age, which is, at present, 65 years for a man and 60 years for a woman, has risen steadily this century and at a faster rate than the rest of the population.

Year	Numbers (in millions)
1901	2.4
1951	6.9
1991	10.6
2031 (*projected*)	14.6

CSO, 1993

The percentage of older people in 1991 was slightly less than 16 per cent. Although the absolute numbers of the very elderly, those aged 80 years and over, are small, they are also increasing even more rapidly than other groups.

Year	Per cent	Numbers
1951	1.4	0.7 million
1981	2.8	1.6 million
1991	3.7	2.2 million
2031 (*projected*)	5.6	3.4 million

CSO, 1992

The projected numbers of octogenarians are expected to rise in the late 1990s but less steeply than recently. The numbers of people aged 60 to 64 years are projected to decline because of lower birth rates in the 1920s and 1930s (Audit Commission, 1992).

These changes to the population have happened within the experience of many older people and have occurred so rapidly that individuals and social policy and practice have yet to fully adapt to the changes in the structure of the population. It was quite feasible, until recently, for individuals to discount that they would ever become old (Laslett, 1984).

Discussions about the increasing number of older people are often couched in alarmist rhetoric depicting older people as passive passengers waiting in the departure lounge of life. Such discussions are not new: before the Second World War and in the 1950s concern was also expressed about the number of older people in British society. The implication is that old age is a burden on the economy, with age being given a correlational dependency rating. Discussion focuses on crude age-dependency ratios based on the number of people aged 0 to 19 years and 60/65 years plus divided by the population aged 20 to 59/64. Thus chronological age alone defines whether a person is to be treated as dependent or not. Non-participation in paid employment however does not necessarily imply dependency. Many older people are active in the informal labour market and in voluntary work as well as making important contributions as carers and within the family (Falkingham, 1989).

It is possible to discern more positive attitudes to growing older and retirement in British society. There is a growing interest in the 'third age' which is seen to be a time to realize goals which could not be achieved when younger. Laslett (1987) suggests that interest in the 'third age' commonly appears when average expectation of life begins to be high enough to allow this to happen and there is a larger proportion of the population experiencing longevity. This is now happening in the United Kingdom. In 1901 a man at birth had an expectation of life of approximately 45 years and a woman 49 years. In 1991 the expectation of life for a man was approximately 73 years and a woman 78 years (CSI, 1993). It is important to use our knowledge of trends which might occur to plan for the changes in health care which may be required to care for the predicted number of older people.

Older people and health care

It is important to emphasize before discussing the use made by older people of health care services that the majority of older people are fit and live in their own homes. The General Household

Survey showed that 36 per cent of the over 80s reported no long-standing illness in the past year (OPCS, 1989). However, the Disability Survey (Martin, 1988) revealed that there is an age-related increase in the use of health and social services and that the proportion of people aged over 80 years with very severe disability is more than twice that of people aged 70 to 79 years.

Although only 10 per cent of older people actually need hospital or residential care at any one time (Levitt and Wall, 1992), it has been estimated that, in comparison with the rest of the population, they make seven to eight times more demand on health and social services (Leathard, 1990). Those over 75 years, for example, are ten times more likely to see their GP during the year than the rest of the population (Levitt and Wall, 1992). This is becoming increasingly so as GPs reap the financial reward of age-related financial assessments. Between 1980 to 1988 Wells (1992) has estimated that the proportion of annual prescriptions attributable to older people rose from 36 per cent to 41 per cent. Using figures from the Hospital In-patient Enquiry statistics, he found that between 1980 and 1985 the length of stay in hospital for people aged 75 to 84 years declined from thirty-one to twenty-two days and the length of stay for those aged 85 years and over declined from 49 to 33 days. However, there were more admissions of older people to hospital, so that there was an overall increase of 9 per cent in the use of hospital in-patient services, compared with a 2 per cent reduction for other patients.

The average length of stay for older patients on geriatric wards also fell in the same period from seventy-seven to forty-four days. Some of this decrease is due to the growth in the number of older people in private nursing homes and a decrease in the number of NHS continuing-care beds. In a survey carried out by Panorama in 1992, it was revealed that thirty-two health authorities had reduced continuing-care beds over the past two years and seventeen were planning to contract out care to the independent sector (cited by Gaze, 1992). Other surveys in the same article confirmed this trend. The reasons for this are discussed in chapter 3 on the National Health Service (NHS), but it has profound consequences for older people who expected, when the NHS was founded, to receive care from the cradle to the grave (Gaze, 1992). Highly confused patients are more likely to be found in NHS facilities such as psycho-geriatric or geriatric wards or NHS

Nursing Homes (Audit Commission, 1992). Older patients are also nursed on acute wards and 43 per cent of acute hospital beds are occupied by people over 65 (Audit Commission, 1992).

It has been predicted that there will continue to be a high demand for acute hospital care where intervention can improve the quality of life, for example hip replacement, cardiac pacemakers, corneal transplants (Allsop, 1984). However, nurses have become increasingly concerned about the severely reduced in-patient stays and inappropriate discharges. Dependent older patients discharged from acute care present a high risk of requiring institutional care because the extra services they may need when they return home have not been organized (Audit Commission, 1992). They are perceived to be 'bed blockers' and, although their immediate needs are met, they are often treated less favourably than younger patients.

Two explanations for discriminatory treatment towards older people, which occurs not only in health care but more generally, will now be given. These explanations seek to demonstrate why older people are marginalized and have less power than other groups in society.

Ageism

The term 'ageism' was first used within the study of ageing, known as gerontology, by Butler in 1969. It has predominantly pejorative connotations such as those associated with sexism or racism, for example. It describes negative discrimination on the grounds of age, and can apply to any age group, but in Britain it is most usually practised against old people (Cornwell, 1989). Ageism implies that older people are different from other members of society and less worthy. Old age is seen as a master status trait, in other words 'old' becomes the major identifying characteristic of the individual. Thus, older people, often so described when they reach retirement age, are treated as part of a 'homogeneous' group sharing exactly the same characteristics, although the difference in their ages may span over four decades (Thomas, 1988).

Although the term ageism is new, negative attitudes to ageing are not. As a recent Church of England report (1990i) states:

The Old and New Testaments, while reflecting positive attitudes to ageing, contain cries of despair and sorrow at growing old. There is celebration of old age in literature and visual art, but also fear and many examples of old people being ignored and scorned.

Old age is regarded not as a normal process of development, but as an illness, and Victor (1987) has pointed out that gerontologists may have contributed to the creation of negative stereotypes of old age because several early studies of ageing were based on residents of institutions. Binstock (1985) in describing the situation in the USA has stated that ageism has arisen at a time when older people are seen as an economic burden in society, presenting dilemmas for the allocation of health care, when there is competition between younger and older workers because of high unemployment and politics of conflict between age groups. Moreover, Binstock (1985i) contends that the 'long-time dream that biomedical discoveries might dramatically extend the human life span now seems to loom as a nightmare because its fulfilment might exacerbate these perceived economic, social and political problems'.

However, we are only just beginning to interpret and understand old age (Phillipson, 1982). Most older people look to the National Health Service for assistance in maintaining their health status and caring for their ill health. However, Cornwell (1989i) found that within the NHS negative attitudes to older people were prevalent and that 'services are based on deep seated stereotypes of what old people are like rather than what they need or want'.

Thus adjectives such as stupid, decrepit, feeble or unusually eccentric, wise or sweet-natured might be used to describe them, but in any event they are patronized. Ageist attitudes are not only expressed on an individual level, but also in styles of professional practice and structurally within the management of the NHS. She found that the professional paradigm – the set of concepts, theories, beliefs and ideas that construct the way that health professionals perceive old people and conceptualize their needs for services – is ageist, because it is negative and because it provides a basis for discrimination. Within this paradigm, old people are seen as dependent, and deeply conservative and fatalistic. As nurses, when older people say when their health is good, do we interpret this with a pinch of salt and assume that this perception is evidence of their fatalism and low expectations?

Stereotyping in addition assumes an extra importance because it influences the way the defined group perceives itself. If an older person accepts that they have less worth than younger members of society, and are a burden, they do not articulate their needs and ageism persists. Moreover, they are often less able, because of frailty, to press for change.

The Marxist explanation

This exploration focuses on the organization of production and the primacy of work. In a society which is organized and based on the importance of work and being a productive member of society, older people who are retired are not perceived as useful to the economy. Capitalism has a distinct set of priorities which almost always relegate social and individual needs below the search for profits and the maintenance of defence and law and order. Moreover, when capitalism is in crisis older people are more likely to be made redundant or forced into retirement. Older people may find themselves left behind in areas of decline with poor services whereas younger workers move to more prosperous areas. Pension provision, especially the State pension, will also be inadequate because of the need to maintain profits. Thus, the needs of older people are not important when once their usefulness to Capital has expired (Phillipson, 1982).

The way that ageism and capitalism interlink remains unclear. For example, has ageism only arisen with capitalism, or has it always existed as a separate ideology that can be found in non-industrial societies? Parallels to this can be drawn to theoretical discussions of patriarchy and imperialism (see chapters 6 and 8).

The development of health and nursing care for older people

The development of health care for older people reflects their low status in British society and their difficulty in making their voices heard over other competing groups for resources. An overview of the development of health care also highlights the tensions in the NHS between the acute sector and the less glamorous long-stay specialities, between cure and care, and between hospital and community services (see chapter 2).

Chapter 1 highlighted how the chronic sick, a label which would include many older people, were cared for in workhouses. The Poor Law Amendment Act 1834 stipulated that the parish workhouses should provide wards where people could be treated when they become ill. By 1848 the demands for institutional care had become so great that wards were full of sick paupers, many of whom were old, with no families to support them, or with no independent means, and therefore they could not be cared for in their own homes. The voluntary hospitals were not interested in caring for individuals who were chronically sick and, although links were made between the voluntary hospitals and workhouses, those who were acutely ill or could contribute to their care were increasingly cared for by the voluntary hospitals. However, workhouses outnumbered voluntary hospitals; in 1861 there were estimated to be fifty thousand sick paupers in the workhouses compared to eleven thousand patients in voluntary hospitals.

Some improvements occurred after the Metropolitan Poor Law Act 1867 and the Poor Law Amendment Act 1868 were enacted as these Acts permitted Poor Law Infirmaries to be built for the care of the sick poor. However, older people were still predominantly cared for in the workhouses. In Edwardian Britain about one in ten of older women were inmates of the workhouse and for those in their 80s around one in three were paupers (Walker, 1987).

The responsibilities of the Poor Law guardians were finally transferred to local authorities in 1929, under the Local Government Act. The Poor Law infirmaries were now placed under the control of medical officers of health who had assumed control of public health services in 1872 and were influential in highlighting the need for an improved health service (Ham, 1992). Some local authorities used their new powers to build new hospitals, but others continued to use the workhouses and hospital provision for older people was very patchy. The nursing care older people received was often minimal and the work of nurses caring for long-stay older patients was perceived to be of low status. Ill health was seen to be synonymous with the ageing process.

Medical care, primarily based on a disease model of health, was usually non-interventionist for patients aged 60 years and over. Older people were not covered by national health insurance (Wilkin and Hughes, 1986).

Thus, when the NHS was established in 1948, sick older people were predominantly nursed in the public hospitals and received very little active nursing. After admission for treatment of acute illness, therefore, they often became bedfast and did not return home.

Following the establishment of the NHS, services for the acutely ill tended to improve more rapidly. The inherited inequalities in the provision of services for the chronic sick were not challenged as vigorously as they could have been, as the recipients of the service were the least able to articulate their demands. Attention was focused on the maintenance of services rather than innovation and change. Financial allocation for services was based on past services and therefore incrementalist in nature.

However, specialist care of older people, which had been pioneered in the late 1930s by Dr Marjorie Warren at the West Middlesex Hospital, slowly spread. Wilkin and Hughes (1986) maintain that the NHS's most important contribution to the care of older people has been to facilitate the development of geriatric medicine. Pioneers in the field realized that active investigation and treatment of older people could enhance their quality of life, and geriatric units were gradually set up. When older patients were admitted to these units for treatment of acute illness, active rehabilitation was also provided and the holistic needs of patients were identified. Social and environmental aspects of older people's lives were also considered and multidisciplinary teamwork established with nurses very much involved in contributing to a higher standard of care. Progress however was slow. There was opposition from other hospital doctors, but the specialist units were able to demonstrate their worth with a marked increase in discharge rates and improvements in care (Wilkin and Hughes, 1986).

Fourteen years after the establishment of the NHS the first Hospital Plan for England and Wales was published, in response to the need for a more systematic approach to the allocation of NHS resources. This was seen to be preferable to incrementalism based on precedence. The plan drew attention to the poor state of hospitals in England and Wales: 45 per cent of them were built before 1891 and 21 per cent before 1861. A series of estimates of the appropriate ratios of beds to population in most specialities was laid down. Despite some growth in specialist units, many older people who required long-term care were still nursed in old workhouse hospitals. The need for specific plans for older patients was recommended and it was stipulated that every district general hospital should have an active geriatric unit where older patients could be assessed (Levitt and Wall, 1992).

The changes envisaged in the plan were again slow to materialize, due to this lack of power and difficulties in transferring resources. However, the problems of older patients in psychiatric and geriatric care were highlighted by a pressure group called Aid for the Elderly in Government Institutions. In 1967 they published a book called 'Sans Everything – a Case to Answer' which made allegations of low standards and ill treatment (Robb, 1967). The Minister of Health requested regional hospital boards to investigate, whereby they reported in 1968 that the accusations were unfounded. However, this was followed by evidence of cruelty at a long-stay hospital for people with learning disabilities when the Ely Report was published in 1969. Richard Crossman used this report to give priority to long-stay patients and to allocate funds for them (Ham, 1992).

In his second Green Paper, Crossman, in 1970, announced his intention to develop the so called 'Cinderella services', that is services for older people, those with mental health problems and people with mental and physical disabilities (Allsop, 1984). The momentum provided by Crossman and subsequent enquiries into unfavourable conditions and treatment at other long-stay hospitals did create pressure on the Department of Health which continued to give priority to the 'Cinderella groups'. In 1976 the consultative document Priorities for Health and Social Services in England stated that priority was to be given to long-stay services. The planned growth rate for services for older people was approximately 3 per cent compared to around 2 per cent for health and social services as a whole and between 1975–6 and 1979–80 the average expenditure on services for older people rose by just over 2 per cent compared to 1 per cent for acute services (Klein, 1989). However, despite this shift in resources, the NHS budget for acute in-patient and out-patient services was £3.726 million in 1982–3 compared to £725 million for geriatric services (Wilkin and Hughes, 1986).

More and more, however, the direction for services for older people became focused on community care. Within the hospital sector the geriatricians and the consultants for the 'Cinderella services' were in a weak bargaining position and in a lower place in the hierarchy compared to consultants in the acute sector. Improvements in care for older patients hardly even kept up with demographic pressures. Although the Department of Health could issue consultative documents and white papers on changes in policy measures to monitor and evaluate services, changes in care were not well developed. Additionally, at local level it was difficult to increase services to the priority groups at the expense of stronger groups (Ham, 1992).

Community services

The Report of the Guilleband Committee in 1956 had advocated domiciliary care of older people, not only as a humanitarian measure in enabling older people to maintain their independence, but also because it was believed that such care would be more economical (Wilkin and Hughes, 1986). Earlier in this chapter it was emphasized that the majority of older people live in their own homes and, in the 1960s and 1970s the importance of developing community nursing and social services to enable people to remain at home, to prevent admission to hospitals or to shorten hospital stays was increasingly highlighted. The specialist geriatric units also promoted the importance of effective community backup if they were to achieve their aim of active rehabilitation of older people and a return to their own homes. However, the policy of developing community care was also difficult to implement as it was vaguely conceived and the real issues of meeting need were not specified (Allsop, 1984). Therefore, in the Priorities for Health and Social Services Consultative Document 1976 and the Way Forward 1977, the government stressed the importance of building up primary care and community health services at a faster rate.

One of the objectives of the 1974 reorganization (see chapter 4) had been to facilitate local level collaboration between health authorities and local authorities, and in 1976 special financing arrangements, joint finance, were introduced. Joint finance enabled money to be spent on increasing the support services for older people in the community, such as the employment of more home helps (Ham, 1992).

The importance of support services for older people was reiterated by the consultative document 'A Happier Old Age' (1978). The government emphasized that older people should be encouraged to remain in their own homes for as long as possible, with appropriate support services (Levitt and Wall, 1992). District nurses were seen to be especially important in giving nursing care and advice, as well as social services such as home helps, meals on wheels and day centres. The majority of visits made by district nurses are to older clients.

The Conservative government in 1981 published a White Paper, 'Growing Older', which highlighted their policies and priorities for health and social services. There was a shift in emphasis in this White Paper which has continued and reflects how services for older people have developed since 1981. 'Growing Older' (1981i) summarized the existing policies for older people. It stressed the need for statutory services to support the care provided by families, neighbours and friends which was the keystone: 'Care in the community must increasingly mean care by the Community'.

The importance of the community health services, hospital services and family practitioner services was noted, but care in the community which was the policy highlighted in the 1960s and 1970s as a humanitarian movement away from the long-stay institutions, was increasingly conceived to be care by families, friends and neighbours (Allsop, 1984).

In reality, there was not much evidence of a shift of financial resources to community care in the period under discussion. Between 1976–7 and 1982–3 the gross expenditure on district nursing rose by just over 4 per cent and health visiting by approximately 4 per cent, but in 1982–3 the budget for these services was only £349 million compared to £3,726 million for acute in-patient and out-patient services. Moreover, as chapter 5 on caring has demonstrated, the burden placed on families, particularly women, financially, socially and physically can cause profound stress. The relative cost advantage of community care often depends on not putting a financial value on the contribution of unpaid carers. When these carers are not available community care might only appear cheaper because the level of provision could be considered inadequate.

A major change, however, was made in 1982 to meet the long-term care needs of older people who could no longer live at home. In order to encourage a more mixed economy of welfare (see chapter 3) and to encourage partnership between the private and public sectors, the Conservative government increased social security payments for older people who require residential homes or nursing-home care. This change had significant consequences on the provision of long-stay hospital care and on the numbers of older people admitted to private institutional care. This change has become known as the 'perverse incentive'.

The Audit Commission in 1986 reported that the bill for social security payments increased from £39 million in 1982 to £489 million in 1986. In the same report they demonstrated that there had still been little progress in implementing community care and that provision of services was slow and uneven. Insufficient support had been given to older people living in the community who required services such as home helps or meals on wheels. The Audit Commission advocated that there should be more accountability for services and that ultimate responsibility should be clarified.

The government responded by asking Sir Roy Griffiths to make the review of community care which had been recommended by the Audit Commission. His report, 'Community Care: Agenda for Action', was published in 1988. He accepted the findings of the Audit Commission and proposed changes to secure clearer patterns of responsibility at all levels. He had found that community care was 'everybody's distant relative, but no-body's baby'. He proposed that:

(a) there should be a Minister for Community Care responsible for specifying objectives and providing resources consistent with those objectives;
(b) Social Services Departments should be responsible at local level for identifying community care needs, planning and organizing provision;
(c) Care Managers should be responsible for assessing the needs of clients and carers and arranging care packages to meet their needs.

The government accepted most of Griffiths' recommendations, although a Minister for Community Care was rejected, and their response was made in the White paper, 'Caring for People' (1989), which generally was broadly welcomed (Wistow and Henwood, 1991). The legislative changes necessary were incorporated into the National Health Service and Community Care Act 1990 but, unlike the NHS, social services departments delayed implementation until April 1993 due to resource constraints.

It is too early to comment on the success of the changes. However, the White paper is 'a watershed document' (Wistow and Henwood, 1991). There are similarities to the NHS reforms as social services departments are no longer to be exclusive providers of care but are expected to arrange and purchase services from the voluntary and private sectors. The care element of social security support to older people in residential and nursing homes has been transferred to social services budgets and social workers now have the responsibility to assess the care needs of older people and to purchase the most appropriate form of care. The government intends by removing the 'perverse incentive' to curtail the social security bill for people in residential care.

If the changes work there should be an appreciable improvement in the quality of life for older people. The government wishes to give more choice to older people about where and how they live and to assist and support carers. Nurses will be involved in the multidisciplinary assessment of clients and in providing care at home. Highly-dependent patients will need a full assessment and 'care package' arranged before they leave hospital. However, grave doubts remain about the implementation of these changes and the level of resources. The direction of care for older people has moved from no State involvement through a fully collectivist response with the development of the NHS and social services and ultimately to a response based on individualism and the values of the New Right (see chapter 3).

Older women

It is too early to comment on how the changes in NHS and Community Care provision might affect the lives of older people. However, the changes which are proposed could have the earliest and greatest impact on older women who need extra support when they become frail.

As indicated earlier, women live longer than men and they are more likely, as they become older, to live alone. People who live alone make more use of community care (Audit Commission, 1992). Moreover, women are much more likely to be living in poverty than men. Forty per cent of the population living at or below income support level are old and older women are more than twice as likely as men to be dependent on income support. For people aged over 80 years the ratio becomes even greater as women then are five times more likely than men to require income support. Lone women, those who are single, widowed, separated and divorced, are particularly disadvantaged. Compared to lone men they are more than seven times as likely to be receiving income support (Walker, 1987).

The large numbers of women who require income support are a reflection of their social and economic status. Individuals as they become older carry into retirement the inequalities which they have experienced when younger. Many women, especially those with families or dependants, have had a very different work experience to that of men. They are more likely to have had discontinuous or part-time employment patterns because of their family and caring responsibilities. Women are also employed in occupations which are predominantly female based and this job segregation has resulted in lower rates of pay for women (Lonsdale, 1987). Women, therefore, have much more difficulty than men in building up a full contribution record for their State retirement pension and are less likely to have contributed to an occupational pension or to have built up savings.

The value of the State retirement pension has fallen since 1980 when the link between pensions and wage levels was broken (Alcock, 1990). The New Right philosophy of encouraging individuals to be responsible for their own pensions and creating tax incentives to encourage the take-up of private pension plans will not ultimately benefit many women. They are not seen to be 'attractive' to the pension industry because of their employment patterns and their lower rates of pay.

Thus, women could be particularly vulnerable as services become more selective and the State provides a minimal level of support. There may not be much choice available to women living on income support or without families and the quality and type of services they will obtain may be inferior to those they had expected when welfare policies were based on collectivist principles. However, there has been little real debate or organized challenge to the radical changes in social policy. Promoting choice and independence, increased accountability and more involvement of the voluntary and private sectors sound attractive but these values do not take into account the real needs of many older people. Additionally they ignore the divisions in society which prevent some people from exercising choice because they have not had the opportunity to do so. Older women in particular are marginalized and lack power (see chapter 6).

The existence of ageist attitudes and retirement from work are two explanations which have been given for the lack of power and influence which older people can exert in the political arena. Although there are pressure groups, these have to compete with others which command greater resources. Older people are not a homogeneous group. Their interests reflect their position in society and at present they do not have a formal political organization. However, as the numbers of older people increase this could change and they could become more effective and powerful in influencing policy decisions. An example of this is the success of groups such as the Gray Panthers in North America, and the Sheffield Pensioners' Action Group in Britain.

Nursing and older people

It has been emphasized that nursing makes a large contribution to the care of older people either in hospital, in nursing homes or in the community. Nurses actively work with older people to improve their quality of life and have been articulate in promoting the need for specialist units to provide assessment, active rehabilitation and high quality continuing care. They have also highlighted the need for preventive care and early detection of ill health and many community nurses are involved in screening programmes.

For the past thirty years the Royal College of Nursing has had a separate association for the care of older people which represents nurses who specialize in the care of older people and also highlights issues surrounding this care.

The Royal College of Nursing Adviser estimates that there are 75,000 nurses working with older patients and that nurses' attitudes to older people in society have improved dramatically in the past twenty years (Laurent, 1990). The association campaigned vigorously, but unsuccessfully, for a specific branch programme for the care of older people when Project 2000 was formed. The Care of Elderly Association works closely with pressure groups such as Age Concern to keep the needs of older people in the forefront of the policy agenda. They are concerned about the effects of the NHS reforms on older patients, especially shorter stays, and whether the number of designated specialist units for older patients will decrease (Gaze, 1992).

There are 'care of elderly' units which have pioneered sensitive, personalized and high quality care and nursing initiatives from these units have permeated into other spheres of nursing activity (Wright, 1986; Pearson, 1988). A growing number of specialist units have been awarded grants by the King's Fund Nursing Development Programme and are Nursing Development Units (Allen, 1991). The expansion of the private sector, especially nursing homes, has provided an opportunity for nurses to develop nursing practice in this area of work. There is more evidence of nurses from both sectors working in collaboration with each other and recognition that there will be a number of older patients for whom alternatives to continuing care will not be feasible.

However, the changes of responsibility between the NHS and the private sector need to be monitored and managed and nurses have highlighted the need for this (Gaze, 1992).

Conclusion

In this chapter we have examined the needs of older people for health and nursing care. It was not our intention to problematize them, but as people become older, although the majority will manage well without help or a little assistance from family or friends, there are others who, because of frailty or disability, will need nursing and health care.

The parameters within which the care will be provided depend on political ideology and social policy. Care of older people has changed from increasing intervention by the State to policies which are much more selective. These policies view the role of the State as that of 'enabler' providing services for those who cannot provide for themselves, and only at a minimal level. The private and voluntary sectors are expected, with statutory agencies, to provide services within the competition of the market. Above all, however, it is individuals who are expected to look after themselves and prepare for the future and families are expected to support frailer or disabled people. This, however, can conflict with the number of women in employment. Above all, it can cause real problems to those who do not have families, particularly women, and those who have not been able to build up sufficient savings to exert real choice, and/or do not have the health, knowledge or resources (see chapter 5 and 6).

It is by understanding the framework within which health care is planned and organized that nurses can respond more effectively to the needs of clients. There will be many, such as older people themselves, who are pleased with the changes that have been made but nurses, by having knowledge of the policy process, will be able to lobby more effectively for vulnerable patients in their care.

Discussion points

1. Do social policies reinforce dependence in old age?
2. Discuss the reasons why older women are more disadvantaged in old age.
3. What are the implications for health and social services of the demographic changes taking place in the UK population?

References

Allen, D. (1991) Elderly Care Ideas. *Nursing Standard*, 5 (30), 20–21

Allsop, J. (1984) *Health Policy and the National Health Service*, Longman, London

Audit Commission (1986) *Making a Reality of Community Care*, HMSO, London

Audit Commission (1992) *The Community Revolution: Personal Social Services and Community Care*, HMSO, London

Baldock, J. and Evers, A. (1991) Citizenship and frail old people: changing patterns of provision in Europe. In *Social Policy Review 1990–1991* (ed. N. Manning) Longman, Harlow

Binstock, R. (1985) *The Oldest Old: A Fresh Perspective on Compassionate Ageism Revisited*, (i) p. 421. Millbank Memorial Fund Quarterly Health and Social Security 63 (2)

Board for Social Responsibility (1990) *Ageing*, (i) p. 56. Church House Publishing, London

Central Statistical Office (1992) *Social Trends 22*, HMSO, London

Central Statistical Office (1993) *Social Trends 23*, HMSO, London

Cornwell, J. (1989) *The Consumers' View: Elderly People and Community Health Services*, King's Fund Centre, London

DHSS (1970) *The Future Structure of the National Health Service*, HMSO, London

Ely Report (1969) *Report of the Committee of Enquiry into Allegations of Ill Treatment of Patients and Other Irregularities at the Ely Hospital, Cardiff*, Cmnd 3975, HMSO, London

Falkingham, J. (1989) Dependency and ageing in Britain: a re-examination of the evidence. *Journal of Social Policy*, 18 (2), 211–234

Fennell, G. *et al.* (1988) *The Sociology of Old Age*, Open University Press, Milton Keynes

Gaze, H. (1992) Discontinuing care? *Nursing Times*, 88 (10), 16–17

Griffiths, R. (1988) *Community Care: Agenda for Action. A Report for the Secretary of State for Social Services*, HMSO, London

Ham, C. (1992) *Health Policy in Britain*, 3rd edn, Macmillan, Basingstoke

Klein, R. (1989) *The Politics of the NHS*, 2nd edn, Longman, London

Laslett, P. (1987) The emergence of the third age. *Ageing and Society*, 7, 133–160

Leathard, A. (1990) *Health Care Provision*, Chapman & Hall, London

Levitt, R. and Wall, A. (1992) *The Reorganized National Health Service*, 4th edn, Chapman & Hall, London

Lonsdale, S. (1987) Patterns of paid work. In *Women and Poverty in Britain*, (eds C. Glendinning and J. Millar) Wheatsheaf Books, Brighton

Martin, J. *et al.* (1988) *The Prevalence of Disability among Adults*, (OPCS) HMSO, London

OPCS (1989) *General Household Survey*, HMSO, London

Phillipson, C. (1982) *Capitalism and the Construction of Old Age*, Macmillan, London

Robb, B. (ed.) (1967) *Sans Everything – A Case to Answer*, Nelson, London

Thomas, L. (1988) Images of ageing. In *Nursing the Older Patient* (ed. S. Wright) Harper & Row, London

Thomas, L. (1992) The age business. *Nursing Standard*, **6**(25), 20–22

Victor, C. (1987) *Old Age in Modern Society*, Croom Helm, Beckenham

Walker, A. (1987) The poor relation: poverty among old women. In *Women and Poverty in Britain*, (eds C. Glendinning and J. Millar) Wheatsheaf Books, Brighton

Wells, N. (1992) Responses to changes in demography and patterns of disease. In *In the Best of Health?* (eds E. Beck, *et al.*) Chapman & Hall, London

Wilkin, D. and Hughes, B. (1986) The elderly and the health services. In *Ageing and Social Policy* (eds C. Phillipson and A. Walker) Gower, Aldershot

Wistow, G. and Henwood, M. (1991) Caring for people: elegant model or flawed design. In *Social Policy Review 1990–1991* (ed. N. Manning) Longman, Harlow

10

Disability

Abigail Masterson

Introduction

Oliver (1990) opens his book on the politics of disablement with the acknowledgement that disability and the experiences of disabled people have been given scant attention in academic circles other than medicine and psychology, and argues for a social theory of disability to be developed as a priority. He goes on to link this marginalization in academia with the marginalization of disabled people in society as a whole. Consequently we felt it was crucial to include a chapter on disability and social policy in this book.

There is a great deal of controversy both in the literature and in the press over the use of the word 'disabled'. Some have argued that it is a stigmatizing and stereotypical term used to describe people who have nothing in common except that they do not function in the same way as people who are able-bodied or 'normal' (Lonsdale, 1990). Frequently it is suggested that 'people with disabilities' should be the preferred term as it acknowledges the value of the person with the disability being seen as secondary. Oliver (1990), however, as a person with a disability himself, argues convincingly for the use of the term 'disabled people' as he asserts that the experience of disabled people is that their disability is an essential part of self rather than something secondary and that the term disabled people is an accurate description of an oppressed social minority. Consequently the term disabled people will be used throughout this chapter.

Defining disability

The prevalence of 'disability' in any society depends at least in part on the way it has been defined and measured. Definitions of disability, as we have seen with other definitions of social problems, are related to the economic structures, social structures and values of any society (Lonsdale, 1990; Oliver, 1990). The distribution of disability varies globally and regionally. In developing societies disability stems in the main from infectious diseases, poverty, ignorance and the failure of existing health services to reach those at risk. In industrialized societies many such factors are declining and being replaced by those caused by the ageing of the population, accidents and the advancement of medical technology. This difference in distribution of disability is related to social and economic forces as they influence not only the proportion of people at risk of being disabled but also the recognition and visibility of disability.

Definitions have been important historically in the UK as a means of distinguishing between those who are legitimately unable to work and perhaps meriting help as opposed to those who are unwilling to work and so are seen as undeserving. Nevertheless there still tends to be an inconsistent use of terminology. It is important therefore to identify who we are referring to when we talk about disabled people. Do we mean people with physical or mental disabilities or both? Does our definition include people with non-visible disabilities such as epilepsy?

Harris (1971 cited Oliver, 1990) classified disability into three categories: impairment, disability and handicap. This work was extended further by Wood in 1981 and adopted for international use by the World Health Organization. An impairment is seen as any disturbance in parts or systems of the body which is present at birth or arises from disease or injury. Disability is seen as things that people cannot do as a consequence of such impairment while handicap is the social or economic disadvantages that result from impairment and disability (Lonsdale, 1990). Locker (1983) observes that handicap may result from a linear progression through impairment and disability or may be a direct consequence of an impairment which is not disabling, such as a facial disfigurement or having to eat a special diet.

Disability, as it is dependent on social meanings and social values, is also socially and culturally relative. What is seen as a disability in one society at one time in history may not be perceived in the same way by another society or at another time. Martha's Vineyard, an island off the New England coastline, had a much higher proportion of deaf people than usual as a result of intermarriage, coupled with the presence of a dominant deafness gene. Deaf people nevertheless made a full contribution to community life as everyone knew sign language and the society was 'functionally bilingual' (Groce, 1985 cited Oliver, 1990). Similarly it is well known that in many of the cotton and jute mills in Scotland communication was often in sign language because the noise of the machinery made oral communication difficult and, indeed, induced industrial deafness – hence the saying 'deaf as a weaver'.

Disability is thus a social construct dependent on meanings and values attributed by individuals and society. Consequently people with similar physical measures of disability may experience different degrees of incapacitation and interference with daily life. For example the loss of a finger will have a different significance to a professional pianist than to a primary school teacher. The consequence of inability to climb a flight of stairs will depend on where a person lives. Similarly someone who enjoys sewing for leisure may find blindness more of a disability than someone who loves listening to music (Locker, 1983; Brown and Payne, 1991). The timing of the onset of disability is also relevant. A person born with a disability will have a different experience from someone who becomes disabled at a later stage as a result of illness or injury (Brown and Payne, 1991). Oliver (1990) suggests that anyone who experiences social restriction, either environmental or through the attitudes of the rest of society, is disabled – a definition that we will adopt in this book.

Oliver (1990) and Finkelstein (1993) identify some major criticisms of disability classifications such as Wood's (1981). They argue that these classifications remain too close to medical or disease labels; that they continue to reify the notion of normality and desire for it; and they ignore the environment, keeping the focus of difficulty on the individual rather than society. Consequently disabled people are seen as passive objects of intervention, management, treatment and rehabilitation leading to a perpetuation of discrimination and inappropriate use of resources (Davis, 1986 cited Oliver, 1990).

Theories of disability

Oliver (1990) and others have identified several implicit and explicit theories of disability. The first of these is disability as a punishment from the gods or the result of witchcraft (Evans-Pritchard, 1937). A person experiencing a cerebro-vascular accident might thus be seen as having been either struck down by God or as a victim of 'the evil eye'. Here religious or magical beliefs define disability and dictate its treatment. Consequently the theory implied by a certain kind of religious or related belief would not support scientific approaches in diagnosis and treatment. In addition disability would not necessarily be viewed negatively, it could equally be seen as a sign of being specially chosen or possessed by God or gods and thus lead to enhanced status. Or disability could be seen as a punishment with which it would be impious to tamper.

A second theory is attributed to the work of Turner (1967) and the concept of 'liminality'. From this perspective, disabled people are seen as neither sick nor well but somehow living in a state of social suspension. However this theory is perhaps merely a description of the way in which many societies, such as Western industrialized societies, respond to disabled people, separating and marginalizing them from the mainstream of social life.

Oliver (1990) suggests the 'surplus population thesis' as another theory. According to this theory societies where survival is a constant struggle may, or perhaps even should, dispose of any weak or dependent members who threaten society's very survival. A surplus population theory would support the killing of disabled children at birth and the expulsion of any adult who became disabled and thus unable to make a full economic contribution. Infanticide in the developing world could be explained in this way. Conversely in India and Brazil children may be deliberately 'disabled' if their families' economic survival depends on begging, as more sympathy and thus more money may be available if the begger is disabled.

Bio-medical explanations view disability in terms of individual pathology which can be diagnosed and treated, as for example in the prescription of phenytoin or surgical intervention to control epileptic seizures. Thus disabled people are seen to need medical care in hospitals and cures are sought for disabling conditions such as multiple sclerosis and Alzheimer's disease (Oliver, 1990).

Psychological theories with regard to people with learning disabilities and mental health problems have tended to focus on defects and differences from 'normal' rather than recognizing the more considerable similarities with the norm (Ryan and Thomas, 1987). Those who concerned themselves with the care of the mentally disabled in the UK, whether full-time professionals or not, have had changing views on the aims of that care. Care was initially based on a philosophy of compassion and philanthropy and then on a philosophy of protection of both the mentally disabled person and society. Finally, because of the dominance of the medical model and the requirements of capitalism, care became motivated by scientific optimism regarding cure (Oliver, 1990).

Oliver (1990) highlights 'personal tragedy theory' as the dominant theory currently prevailing in Britain. From this perspective disability is seen as a personal tragedy for individuals so 'afflicted'. Disabled people are seen as charity cases deserving pity with no attention being paid to the role of economic and social structures in the causation and creation of this disability.

Social oppression theory is offered by Oliver (1990) and other writers in the field as an alternative and we believe more useful theoretical explanation than those outlined above. The idea that disability was a particular and deliberate form of social oppression was first articulated by the Union of the Physically Impaired Against Segregation in 1975 and has been used successfully by disabled people to analyse their own experiences of disability (Oliver, 1990; Daunt, 1991). Social oppression theory argues that disabled people are in an inferior position to others in society purely because of their disability and that ideologies are used by the able-bodied to perpetrate and justify this unnatural and avoidable hierarchy to their own ends. There is certainly much empirical evidence that would appear to support this perspective. People with disabilities are almost universally in inferior positions in terms of housing, employment, finance, transport and education (Townsend and Davidson, 1992). Capitalist societies depend on competition to allocate rewards and benefits and disabled people are less able to compete successfully for their fair share. Moreover this oppression is also multidimensional in that more than half the disabled people in Britain suffer the extra burden of sexual and or racial oppression (Abberley, 1987 cited Oliver, 1990).

None of these theories and explanations are mutually exclusive, especially as in many people they may be attitudes and implicit theories rather than carefully thought out theories, although one perspective may dominate at any given time. For example, in modern industrialized societies, although the orthodox explanation given for the birth of a disabled child will be medical or scientific this does not mean that parents will not view this event as a punishment for some previous sin even if they are well aware of and accept intellectually the official theory (Oliver, 1990). The personal tragedy view, despite being prominent in industrialized societies like the UK at present, is not by any means universal.

Disability is culturally produced and socially structured in relation to the mode of production and the core or central values of the society (Oliver, 1990). Disability need not therefore have negative consequences, particularly if an alternative theory such as social oppression theory were generally adopted. Abberley (1989) argues that such a theory is akin to feminist perspectives (see chapter 6), emphasizing and asserting real differences but combating false and oppressive explanations of the origin and nature of those differences.

The prevalence of disability

It is difficult then to define the concept of disability adequately and therefore difficult to estimate the numbers of people affected. Several sources of information are used as a basis for policy making and planning. In the UK there are several official registers for certain groups of disabled people, for example those registered with local authorities, those who are listed as disabled with the Department of Employment, those receiving various disability pensions and so on. These records do not paint a complete picture because not everyone who we might perceive as disabled is necessarily in receipt of state-provided pensions or services and because people have mixed views about defining themselves as disabled (Daunt, 1991).

Social Trends (1992), using General Household Survey (GHS)

data for 1989–1990, estimated that 365 people in every thousand aged over 16 years had a long-standing physical illness or disability and that the prevalence was highest in unskilled manual groups. The GHS measure is based on people's own assessment of their health.

Prevalence of mental disability is even more difficult to ascertain. In 1986 there were about 34 thousand beds in mental-handicap hospitals and 60 thousand mental-illness beds. In addition many more people in both groups had contact with out-patient services. In 1989–1990 in England, there were 59 thousand beds available in the NHS mental-health services but the number of people with mental-health problems who stay in hospitals for long periods has been falling since the 1970s (Social Trends, 1992). In addition, the majority of people with a mental illness or disability have always been cared for at home, many invisibly without any type of formal support.

A survey of physical and mental disability, using a ten-point scale of severity, carried out by the Office of Population Censuses and Surveys between 1985 and 1988, suggested that there were more than six million disabled adults (16 years and over), that is approximately 14 per cent of the total adult population, of these two million, 700 thousand had a severe disability (Daunt, 1991). More women than men were disabled and the prevalence and number of disabilities increased with age. Many of the disabilities reported in older people were related to the loss of hearing, sight and mobility and it has been argued that such broad categories of disability do not adequately distinguish disability from what might be considered the natural increasing frailty of old age (Brown and Payne, 1991; Dalley, 1991). Nearly 10 per cent of adults were found to have a locomotive disability and 5.5 per cent of reducing their ability to care for themselves. The rates for white people were higher than those for Asians and the rates for West Indians were higher still (Daunt, 1991). Although the reasons for these racial differences are difficult to account for absolutely, they may well be due to the relative age of these populations in the UK, the effects of poverty, occupation and so on. (See chapter 8 for a fuller discussion on the complex relationships between race and health.) Most disabled people lived in the community with only 7 per cent in some form of residential care (Dalley, 1991).

Consequently, although there is certainly a lack of precision in the data available, disabled people are clearly not a homogenous or easily defined group. Nevertheless it is now generally acknowledged that at least 10 per cent of all people experience a significant degree of physical or mental disability (Daunt, 1991) and it seems that although the health of the population as a whole has continued to improve, trends in the expectation of life without disability have not improved (Townsend and Davidson, 1992).

The experience of disability

Locker (1983), citing Blaxter's (1976) work, suggests that the experience of disability is the problems that it creates for the disabled person and their significant others. The problems actually experienced, he argues, may not be that different from those experienced by non-disabled people, such as unemployment for example, but the person's physical and mental resources for dealing with them are greatly reduced. Also the experience will not be the same for all who are disabled in similar ways but will depend on the availability of money, a supportive environment, aids, appliances and so on.

Since Victorian times disabled people have been portrayed either as superheroes overcoming a terrible burden, pathetic victims or a combination of the two (Oliver, 1991). Rarely are there representations of people with disabilities being ordinary people and doing ordinary things (Cumberbatch and Negrine, 1992). Nonetheless this is being seen increasingly by pressure groups, professionals and an educated public as unhelpful both in terms of providing role models for people with disabilities and in challenging society's prejudices and stereotypical views. Yet many of the traditional voluntary organizations have deliberately used the view of the pitiful, dependent disabled person as a means of raising funds. The current debate about the 'little Stephen' logo (a stylized depiction of a boy with a learning disability), used until very recently by the Royal Society for Mentally Handicapped Adults and Children (MENCAP), and the long-lasting deliberations over the appropriateness even of the name of this charity, highlight some of the dilemmas involved.

Ryan and Thomas (1987) emphasize the lack of research on the 'lived experience' of having a learning disability. How having a learning disability affects the person's concept of self and how individuals cope with the experience has been almost totally neglected in phychological research. Ryan and Thomas suggest that this omission is more than an oversight, because work of this type would force society to acknowledge the needs that the learning-disabled share with so-called 'normal' people and would undermine their banishment to the margins of society. They argue that there needs to be: 'a recognition of difference amongst people that allows for special needs and unusual behaviour, but which doesn't thereby disqualify anyone from full acceptance as a human being' (Ryan and Thomas, 1987i).

In contrast to the situation of women and minority ethnic groups (see chapters 6 and 8), the principle of equality for disabled people has never been enshrined in law. Perhaps this indicates the degree of importance attached by successive British governments to notions of equal opportunities for disabled people (Barnes, 1991). Locker (1983) asserts that there is no doubt that disabled people are a severely disadvantaged minority within Britsih society. Lonsdale (1990) agrees, arguing that disablement frequently means being unable to take part in social and economic activities that others take for granted as well as having to endure negative social attitudes. Nonetheless she adds that living with a disability can also mean gaining greater insight and personal growth through encountering a wider range of experiences, a sense of achievement and fulfilment through overcoming enormous challenges, and a sense of solidarity with other oppressed people.

The notion that adaptation and adjustment to their disability is desirable for individuals is a concept that is prevalent in current health-care practice. This popularity of adaptation as a legitimate goal and function of intervention is shown in nursing by the success of nursing models such as Roy's (1974). Roy's model encourages nurses to promote patient/client adaptation to stressors such as disability by strengthening the individuals own coping strategies or helping them to develop new ones. Successful nursing intervention relates to the degree of positive adaptation the patient/client achieves. Oliver (1990) challenges the focus of such approaches arguing that society should be forced to adjust rather than the disabled individuals themselves.

Numerous studies have shown that in terms of income, employment, housing and access to facilities in the community, disabled people are much worse off than their non-disabled counterparts (Locker, 1983; Dalley, 1991; Townsend and Davidson, 1992). Disability is thus a significant factor in poverty, which itself is a major cause of disability (Doyal, 1983 cited Oliver, 1990).

Disability has two main financial effects: it can result in loss of earned income for disabled persons themselves or their carers or both and disability invariably leads to extra expense for equipment, help, heating, medicaments such as dressings, medicines and so on.

There is little literature on the ways in which gender might affect the experience of disability. Most investigations, in common with other social issues, has been concerned with the male experience and male concerns. Physical appearance Lonsdale (1990) suggests has long been regarded as having particular significance to women. Women are encouraged to conform to an image based on certain sexual, physical and behavioural stereotypes that do not allow for disability. Body image is usually considered important to self-esteem. The effect of disability on self-esteem is complex and some studies suggest that self-esteem can be increased through the sense of mastery gained through overcoming limitations associated with disability (Lonsdale, 1990).

Sexuality is also associated with physical appearance and assumptions are often made that disabled women will not have sexual feelings nor be in a relationship that includes sex and childbirth. Women are commonly expected to fulfil a number of social roles such as lover, mother, homemaker, carer and worker (see chapter 6). Disabled women on the other hand are perceived frequently as inadequate for both economically productive roles and caring roles thus compounding their oppression, stigmatization and financial disadvantage (Fine and Asch, 1985 cited Oliver, 1990; Lonsdale, 1990). For men, on the other hand, there may be a certain element of heroism associated with disability. For example, the pinned-up uniform sleeve or eye patch may be associated with 'honour' and 'gallantry'.

Even in other areas like treatment or provision of aids there appears to be a sexual divide. Oliver (1990) offers as an example the management of bladder incontinence. Whereas for men there is a range of devices such as urinary sheaths to help the management of this distressing problem, there is conversely very little choice for women other than catheterization or pad and pants. Such discrimination is usually justified on grounds of biological difference but may in fact have more to do with gender and the ability to access and use power (see chapter 6 for a fuller discussion of the relationship between power and gender).

There is a similar lack of information on the ways in which race affects disability. Oliver (1990) quotes an American study which highlighted that black populations fared worse in being able to obtain disability benefits than white people. The record of voluntary organizations in dealing with issues of race is also poor. It appears reasonable to expect therefore that language difficulties and institutionalized racism (see chapter 8) will adversely effect access to services and support.

Oliver (1990) asserts that not only is oppression practised by dominant groups but also it occurs among the oppressed themselves. He offers as an example of this phenomenon the work of some feminist writers such as Dalley (1988) who have portrayed disabled people as chronically dependent burdens in their analysis of the effects of community care policies on women. Similarly some feminists pushing for residential care as a way of alleviating women's caring responsibilities ignore the fact that residential care itself frequently oppresses disabled people.

Disability and social policy

Disability is in a sense defined by social policy. Disability is whatever social policy says it is (Oliver, 1990). Disability therefore implies a problem or disadvantage that seeks compensatory or ameliorative action by society whether through a public or private agency.

The wealth of the country and the resulting size of the economic surplus available for redistribution has an effect on the policies produced. Societies with little or no surplus may be forced to leave individuals to cope for themselves or may even deliberately put them to death. Relatively wealthy countries like the UK have elaborate mechanisms for redistributing wealth between advantaged and disadvantaged groups but who actually gets what will be influenced by the ideology or competing ideologies underpinning politics and so the redistribution process.

Oliver's (1990) thesis that social policy has historically created rather than reduced disability will now be explored. In the UK social policy appears to have been greatly informed and influenced by the personal tragedy theory of disability (Oliver, 1990). Policy has been designed with the notion of compensating people for the tragedies that have befallen them and doing things to or on behalf of disabled people rather than enabling them to do things for themselves. That is, disability has been seen as a problem of individual disadvantage to be alleviated or remedied through the creation and application of appropriate social policies, but there is a growing feeling within the disability movement that social policy should instead be concerned with changing society to meet disabled people's needs (Dalley, 1991).

Oliver (1990) suggests that the values encapsulated in disability policy have been somewhat neglected by policy analysts to date. Oliver explains this neglect through the fact that in the past disability policies have not been developed in their own right but they have tended to be a by-product of other policies with different origins and purposes designed primarily to deal with other social issues such as poverty, health and social welfare.

Disabled people were first treated as a group with special needs by individual philanthropists and voluntary organizations and it is only during this century that specific statutory services have been developed. For example, some educational provision was made for disabled children once the universal state-supported system showed the need. Rehabilitation services developed following the two world wars when significant numbers of young men in particular required employment and the chance of an active productive life (Brown and Payne, 1991; Daunt, 1991). More recently, specific disability policies have been developed such as the Chronically Sick and Disabled Persons Act (1970) and the Disabled Persons (Services, Consultation and Representation) Act (1986).

The Chronically Sick and Disabled Persons Act (1970), the product of a private member's bill, heralded two major policy developments. Firstly, welfare services for disabled people became part of local authority social service departments, which aimed to provide localized services which were more community based. Secondly, local authorities took a more active role in terms of assessment of need (Brown and Payne, 1991). However, there was much confusion about need and demand for services and in most areas there have not been sufficient resources to meet expectations. The Disabled Persons Act (1986), interestingly also a private member's bill, sought to give more substance to disabled people's rights by giving them the right to have their needs fully assessed by local authorities. Unfortunately, however, there was again no mandatory obligation to provide the necessary services (Dalley, 1991).

New Right ideology in the 1980s emphasized the undesirability of the so-called 'dependency culture'. It argued that welfare states have created whole groups or classes of individuals who have become totally dependent on the State for everything. Thatcherism thus sought to reduce dependence on the State and change the perception of individuals as being passive victims of circumstance. Thatcherist policy therefore aimed to reduce the size and scope of State benefits, shifting the focus of provision away from the State to self-help and the voluntary and independent sectors. Voluntary agencies have long made a large contribution in this area. Many organizations such as the Royal National Institute for the Blind and MENCAP provide services on a national basis and there are a multitude of regional and local organizations.

Dependency implies inability to do things for oneself and reliance on others to carry out some or all of the activities of daily living. Independence or non-reliance on others is seen currently as the ideal. Even so, the language of the two White Papers forming the basis for the NHS and Community Care Act (1990) still contain explicit notions of dependency and helpfulness even in their titles 'Working for Patients' and 'Caring for People' (Department of Health, 1989). This aside, Oliver (1990) argues that no one is completely independent, because we all live in a state of mutual interdependence. Consequently he asserts that the dependence/independence dichotomy is false and that it is not dependence *per se* that marks out people with disabilities as being different but the degree and type of that dependence, which is in turn socially created by a disabling and disablist society.

Disabled people are likely to be excluded from the workforce because of stereotypes and prejudice surrounding their perceived inabilities and are therefore forced to be dependent – a state for which they are blamed, at the very least indirectly. Oliver (1990) argues that the quotas favoured in equal opportunities policies worsen this scenario by treating people with disabilities as a special case reinforcing the idea that there is something different and perhaps inferior about them. He supports the better solution of Erlanger and Roth (1985) changing the focus of intervention to the social organization of work and other aspects of life in order to allow people with disabilities to become more employable as part of the mainstream. If, for example, companies were given grants to enable them to design machinery and tools that would be usable by more people, rather than forcing them to employ a quota of certain groups, the prevailing notion of dependency could be transformed.

The theories of social policy which are most influential in a society play a significant role in the social creation of dependency and disability. Social policy operationalizes social beliefs about disability in the institutions created and maintained and the goals they are expected to achieve. This results in a disablist framework within which services are provided and professional practice is carried out.

Oliver (1990) argues that the current political responses to disability and the Welfare State are damaging to disabled people. The traditional left-wing belief that Welfare State expenditure should be increased leads to a reinforcement of socially constructed dependency and inappropriate service provision. Yet the New Right ideal, reducing State involvement in provision, regulation and subsidy, condemns disabled people to isolation and loneliness in the community.

Disabled people are potentially a powerful political force. Oliver (1990) cites Fry's (1987) evidence that not only did 9 per cent of those over 18 years old see themselves as having a disability, but 27 per cent had a relative who was disabled. But disabled people have low rates of political participation. Many are not even on the electoral register. Others, through the nature of their disablility, such as deafness or blindness, are denied access to much of the information necessary to enable an informed political choice and others are put off by the problems of physical access to polling stations and the like (Barnes, 1991).

There are also very few political activists and national

politicians who have a disability. David Blunkett and Jack Ashley, both Labour politicians, are perhaps the best known. The physical slant of political life, meeting places, party headquarters and so on are inaccessible. There are many barriers to campaigning, door-to-door canvassing and so on.

Disabled people since the 1950s, in common with other oppressed groups, have attacked the stereotypical bias in language that helps maintain oppression and have begun to attack disablist vocabulary such as cripple, spastic and mongol, fostering a growing group consciousness and identity (Oliver, 1990). Nonetheless disabled people are not a homogenous group. They differ in social class, age, sex, family circumstances and clinical conditions (Oliver, 1990). This has acted as a brake on the development of an enduring sense of solidarity therefore reducing potential political power (Daunt, 1991).

People's disability may develop after their political affiliations have been formed. Medical and social approaches to disability encourage further divisions. Thus tax allowances are given to blind people but not to others, mobility allowances are only for those who cannot walk and higher benefits are given to those injured through work than to those with a congenital disability. Oliver (1990) suggests this is not pure coincidence but part of a divide-and-rule tactic on behalf of the State to keep disabled people powerless and marginalized. Other, and perhaps more plausible explanations, could be that these differences are merely due to the lack of a co-ordinated disability policy, more successful political pressure being exerted by one group than another, or the belief that work is good and therefore injuries sustained in this way are more deserving of compensation.

Disability pressure groups generally have not been able to exert much positive political change, although some have achieved more successes than others either because their clients are seen as being more appealing or because they are more skilled at putting their case. Some of this is explained by: their weak structural position; their relationship to the State – as registered charities they are barred from any direct and overt political activity; their non-representativeness in terms of the needs and wishes of those with disabilities, because until recently most were organizations for rather than of disabled people; and their acceptance of the 'normalizing' approach – that is aiming to make disabled people as normal as possible rather than celebrating and working with their differences (Oliver, 1990; Barnes, 1991).

It appears that only the wholesale adoption of the alternative theory of disability which views disability as 'social oppression' together with an emphasis on individual rights rather than individual needs might lead to new kinds of social policies. Such alternative policies would be designed to reduce oppression and social restriction rather than emphasizing and attempting to compensate for ideas of tragedy and burden.

Disability and welfare

Earlier in this chapter we said that the definitions and experiences of disability vary from society to society, within societies and over time in response to a range of economic and social factors. We will now examine changes in health and social service provision for disabled people.

In chapter 1 we noted the absence of specific policies and provision for people with disabilities until well into the nineteenth century. Finkelstein (1980, cited Oliver 1990) suggests that when Britain was predominantly an agrarian society disabled people were still able to participate in the process of production. They were regarded as unfortunate but not segregated from the rest of society.

With industrialization many more disabled people were excluded from production as the discipline and speed required by factory work were difficult for them to adapt to. Also the relative decline in domestic or home-based work opportunities for women made it more difficult for disabled people to be cared for at home. Consequently disabled people were increasingly regarded as a problem and began to be segregated in institutions and out of the mainstream of social life.

Finkelstein forecasts a third phase in the development of societies where technology will allow disabled people to live a full life again. Oliver (1990) dismisses such ideas as being overly simplistic as they neglect other important factors such as beliefs, values and attitudes associated with disability. However, even in a competitive capitalist society, if technology could create sufficient economic surplus this would surely allow scope for positive changes in such beliefs, values and attitudes.

It is only during the past twenty years that the social security system has recognized disability as a particular subject for consideration (Barnes, 1991). In the past, disabled people claimed ordinary unemployment or retirement benefits with specific schemes only available for those who became disabled through employment or in the armed services. By 1990 twenty-two different sorts and parts of benefits were on offer (Dalley, 1991). Nevertheless the majority of disabled people are still reliant on general means-tested benefits which do not reflect the extra costs associated with having a disability rather than tailor-made disability benefits. Inequalities between the entitlement of different groups have been perpetuated. Disability pressure groups have argued unsuccessfully for a comprehensive disability benefit to replace the existing confusing muddle of arrangements, promote equity and eliminate poverty (Dalley, 1991; Barnes, 1991).

Existing welfare services have not been developed on the basis of a coherent understanding of the origins and consequences of disability but have emerged in a piecemeal fashion in response to historical contingency and political pressure (Locker, 1983). Although such services are of enormous benefit to disabled people who would be far worse off without them, they are grossly inadequate to secure the full participation of disabled people in all aspects of life (Barnes, 1991). As with other services they reflect and are limited by social attitudes and values.

The historical context of disability

As we saw in chapter 1, in the nineteenth century those who ran the State used institutions to impose order and discipline on the workforce and attempted, particularly through the 1834 Poor Law Amendment Act, to determine deserving and undeserving recipients of support. This led, Oliver (1990) argues to disability becoming a thing of shame. Once certain groups were drafted into the disabled category it was difficult for them to escape. Disabled people became socialized into their role which in turn was legitimized by the medical and welfare authorities. Even today disabled people, in order to qualify for benefits, must accept a categorization which may diminish their self-image, change the way others perceive them and distort their aspirations and chances in life (Daunt, 1991; Dalley, 1991).

From the late 1950s there has been a strong de-institutionalization movement. This movement has gone with changing beliefs about the appropriateness of institutional care and concerns about the cost of such care. Consequently many people previously cared for in institutions have been returned to the community, The community in this case usually means the family or smaller residential units. Much of the debate has centred on the general undesirability of large institutions but their suggested replacements, such as small group homes, still involve disabled people living with each other in 'ghettos'. As Ryan and Thomas (1987) point out, there is no evidence that disabled people actually want to live with each other and there is no indication that disabled people find it any less distressing than anyone else to live with people who are, for example, incontinent or disruptive.

Medicine and disability

It is usually health care professionals who attach the label 'disabled' to an individual. This so-called medicalization of disability is connected to the growth in power of the medical profession. The development of the germ theory of illness and disease allowed the profession the right to define, classify and treat a whole range of conditions and problems that previously would have been regarded as moral or social in origin (Ryan and Thomas, 1987; Oliver, 1990). The person with a permanent disability of any kind came to be perceived as a patient who needed lifelong treatment, care and protection (Daunt, 1991).

Some of this medical intervention is understandable and appropriate, as in diagnosis, stabilization and rehabilitation. However, there are other large areas of control that appear much less relevant and desirable. Doctors and nurses determine the allocation of many financial benefits, assess potential for work and select educational provision. Consequently health care professionals control not only the form of treatment but also the form of life (Lonsdale, 1990; Oliver, 1990).

The main objective of many health care professionals, and doctors in particular, is to treat disabled individuals with a view to curing their disability, and returning them to a state of 'normality'. The closer they are to 'normal' functioning, the more they are thought capable of living a balanced and independent life. The further away from 'normal', the more medical intervention they are perceived to need (Finkelstein, 1993). In the case of disabled children, for example, medical need is frequently seen to take priority over educational need. Children are taken out of class for doctor's appointments or physiotherapy and the school nurse is seen as a more important figure than the teacher, with inevitable results on 'patients'' educational performance and status (Bart, 1984 cited Oliver, 1990).

The 'medical approach' thus ignores the experience of illness and disease for individuals, pays insufficient attention to the myriad of cultural factors involved and neglects issues of prevention as the focus is on curing the problem rather than preventing it occurring. It does not accurately measure the extent to which a person can or cannot perform certain functions. It tends to be physically rather than mentally orientated. It ignores the social context. To categorize people by their medical condition masks the other aspects of their social existence (Ryan and Thomas, 1987). Consequently the dominance of the medical view leads to a partial and inhibiting view of the person with a disability. This problem may be gradually reduced as, under the NHS and Community Care Act (1990), social workers and local authorities are now taking the leading role in assessment and service provision.

Disability and the health service

Within health services disability has had a very low status. Recruitment of staff has frequently been low in both quantity and quality, with trainees often being rejects or drop-outs from other areas. Recruiting and retaining good staff has been a persistent problem (Ryan and Thomas, 1987). The resources allocated to disability services have reflected this low status. Ryan and Thomas (1987) note that even the cost of food per patient is much lower in hospitals for those with learning disabilities than in other hospitals.

In the latter part of the twentieth century it has become increasingly apparent that there are few medical cures for disability and so the medical hold over disability has been increasingly challenged (Ryan and Thomas, 1987; Oliver, 1990). Ryan and Thomas (1987) observe that the medical profession has been responsible for knowingly administering services that have resulted in a deplorable quality of life for disabled people through institutionalization, stigmatization and segregation. And to a certain extent we could argue the same for the nursing profession. The Ashworth inquiry in 1992 highlighted an appalling standard of nursing care and victimization of clients by nurses in a high-security mental health hospital. In response to such accusations, health-care professionals generally have increasingly focused on rehabilitation and 'normalization'.

Oliver (1990) argues that the emphasis on 'normality' has allowed society to continue to treat disabled people as a marginal group. Consequently the responsibility for the restrictions that disabled people face are loaded on to the individuals themselves rather than seen as being socially constructed and therefore the responsibility of society to do away with. Alternatively, if able-bodied society were to accept disabled people as equals, having equal rights with the able-bodied, the priority in debate would shift to society itself, away from the desirability or otherwise of abortion, screening and euthanasia.

The creation of dependency

Dependency is created in many ways through the delivery of health services. The kinds of services that are available, institutionalized regimes and the failure in most cases to involve disabled people themselves in the creation and running of these services all serve to increase dependency (Oliver, 1990). Many of the people in Locker's (1983) study found that services did not seem to facilitate or promote independent living but appeared to lead them into more dependence on formal care. Power and control are in the hands of the professional staff rather than their clients. Community services, too, offer little choice and control to disabled people, even control over the type of aids and equipment available or control over the times that professionals can visit to help with preparing meals and personal care, such as washing and dressing. Often even the range of services offered has more to do with professional boundaries than the needs and wishes of disabled people.

Professionals are also used increasingly as 'gatekeepers' to services and resources. Locker (1983) found that for disabled people 'getting into the system' was a haphazard process which was more often the result of informal rather than formal referral systems. Knowledge and information about benefits and services were just as likely to be provided by friends and acquaintances as by professionals. The recent reorganization of health and social care by the NHS and Community Care Act (1990) has led to named professionals being responsible, on behalf of local authorities, for designing total care packages for individuals. This, together with the blurring of professional role boundaries between for example nursing and social care, may improve the situation.

Under the Act 'purchasers' are expected to assess continuously the total health needs of their local communities when buying in services and the 'purchaser/provider split' is intended to give users more say in service provision and design. The associated devolvement of decision making should make it easier for disabled people and their carers to lobby purchasing authorities with regard to their particular needs and desires. It is too early to say whether such notions of empowerment and consumer centredness as are contained in the Patient's Charter (DoH, 1992) will remain empty rhetoric or herald significant change.

Within Locker's (1983) study the welfare bureaucracies were also found to be inefficient, inaccessible, inflexible and unresponsive to need. They appeared to be governed by rules and regulations which were arbitrary or irrational and either prevented access to the resources required or caused unacceptable delays. Equally worrying in its consequences was the inevitable finding that the skills and resources needed to manage the problems created by the welfare bureaucracies were not evenly distributed. Some people were far more adept at getting providers to respond to their needs while many simply gave up trying. Locker (1983i) found that current service provision favoured those in least need at the expense of those in highest need: 'the philosophy of "rewarding the able-bodied" implicit in welfare provision did seem to bias the services in favour of the relatively strong'.

This situation is paralled in the policy-making process where the most vocal and effective pressure groups are often responded to whether or not they are the most disadvantaged (see chapter 2 for a more detailed discussion).

Benefits in kind create dependency and limit choice. Benefits in cash have their own shortcomings but at least allow disabled people to retain some self-determination and dignity (Shearer, 1981 cited Locker, 1983). Disabled people, despite apppearing on the surface to have many similar problems, do in fact have highly individual needs. Consequently one system is unlikely ever to be flexible enough to suit all. Therefore benefits paid in cash may allow disabled people to design and contract their own services according to their personal priorities. The incredible success and popularity amongst disabled people of the Independent Living Fund seems to bear this out (Berthoud, 1991).

In summary then the bio-medical thinking which has been the dominant perspective in both health and social services has supported the status quo. The disability of the individual rather than the deficiencies of the environment and society have been emphasized.

Nursing and disability

Politicians and commentators working within the New Right ideology have suggested that welfare institutions themselves create dependency of groups and individuals. In nursing too the idea that dependency is intrinsically undesirable has been achieving increasing credence (Orem, 1991).

Work like Miller's (1985) suggests that methods long favoured by nurses for organizing care delivery, like task allocation, have led to increasing dependency in certain patient/client groups. Oliver (1990) suggests that when professionals like nurses talk of independence they are actually talking about something different from the independence aims of disabled people. He argues that professionals define independence in terms of self-care activities such as washing, dressing and toileting without assistance whereas disabled people are more likely to see independence as the ability to make their own decisions about their lives, rather than doing things alone or without help.

Ryan and Thomas (1987) cite Tyne's (1978) finding that the degree of control and autonomy that staff have contributes to the flexibility of the care offered. Arguably then recent service developments such as clinical budgeting and flattened nursing hierarchies should bode well for a more individualized service delivery.

Do nurses have a legitimate role in disability services? The Briggs Report of 1974 and the Jay Report in 1979 recommended cessation of hospital care for those with learning disabilities and preference for social-work training over nursing training (Ryan and Thomas, 1987). This aim was also adopted by some of the voluntary organizations and pressure groups. Disabled people too have become increasingly critical of the role of professionals in their lives (Barton, 1989).

Currently much concern is being expressed about the future of learning disability nursing as a branch programme within Project 2000 and indeed as a worthwhile concept. In March 1993 the Department of Health held a consensus conference (a gathering of experts to debate alternatives through presenting papers in an open forum to reach consensus on the optimum direction of future policy and development) where it was suggested that the learning disabilities branch be subsumed into the mental health branch, with specific preparation in learning disabilities nursing occurring only post registration (Nursing Times, 1993). Nurses and nursing have been accused of responding defensively to such demands, seeing them only as a threat to the profession rather than exploring the other issues involved (Ryan and Thomas, 1987).

Similarly in the field of physical disability the nursing role is being questioned increasingly. The move towards community care has resulted in most disabled people coming within the remit of social services rather than the health service and thus many disabled people have lost contact with the service of nursing. Even such personal care as washing and dressing, which until recently were considered to be within nursing's responsibility, are now more commonly being carried out by social service care assistants. Residential forms of care too are increasingly unlikely to offer nursing as a service.

Many nurse theorists and researchers would argue nevertheless that there is, or perhaps should be, a unique role for nursing within the area of disability. Depending on one's particular nursing perspective this might involve a focus on helping, caring, interpersonal relationships, reducing stress, encouraging adaptation, developing self care, or helping the individual to develop and grow through the disability experience (Peplau, 1952; Henderson, 1966; Roy, 1974; Leininger, 1980; Parse, 1981; Orem, 1991). But in all cases, whatever the theoretical framework adopted and wherever the nursing takes place, nursing (unlike other disciplines) stresses a holistic approach where all aspects of the individual from spirituality to physiology are considered and balanced.

Nonetheless, despite sexuality being well accepted as an integral part of a holistic view of care, disabled people are still frequently perceived by nurses (as by many others in society) as being somehow asexual. This has resulted in a lack of privacy in institutional settings and a lack of advice with regard to contraception and general sex education, which prevents people from giving expression to their sexual feelings and needs (Ryan and Thomas, 1987; Lonsdale, 1990).

Advocacy has also been offered as an area where nursing can perform a useful function (Copp, 1986; UKCC, 1992). However power is already unevenly distributed in the nurse/client relationship and nurse advocacy, with its close links to paternalism and control may not in fact be desirable. Indeed, disabled people themselves are increasingly campaigning for strategies to facilitate and encourage self-advocacy (Whittaker, 1991).

Finally it could be argued that nurses have needed to see disabled people as dependent and helpless to justify our own employment. Ryan and Thomas (1987) add that it is in the interest of health professionals to emphasize the abnormality of disabled people to legitimize their own continued dominance and control of large areas of service provision as professionals. Nonetheless Ryan and Thomas (1987) also note that nurses have frequently been scapegoated by the media and researchers in their criticism of services, preventing deeper analysis of the responsibilities of society at large.

Abberley (1989), although referring mainly to social work, suggests that the caring professionals must actively recruit and train significant numbers of disabled people because professionals' attitudes towards disability will only change sufficiently to allow for real change in practice when they are able to work alongside rather than purely for disabled people.

Conclusion

Disability is a social construct that is reinforced by social policy. Many of the current difficulties faced by disabled people are caused by social constraints and barriers. The person in a wheelchair is disabled by society's refusal to provide accessible buildings and transport. The deaf person is disabled because no provision is made for alternative methods of communication.

The rise of the institution as a mechanism both of social provision and social control has played a key role in structuring perceptions and experiences of disability and in facilitating the exclusion of disabled people from the mainstream of social life. Clearly, disabled people are bound to be disadvantaged in a competitive society which values independence and physical and intellectual skills and which rewards the economically productive. If the values implicit in the Welfare State, or indeed the 'less-welfare state' remain focused on the principle that those who do not work should be less highly rewarded than those within the labour force, the situation will not change.

All the literature in this area appears to identify a basic set of needs that until now have been barely addressed by social policy: physical access to the community; improved mobility; an income that does more than cover the bare necessities; some kind of work or a meaningful way of occupying time; independent living in a suitable domestic environment; prevention of discrimination and, perhaps most importantly, equal rights to personal choice and control. The challenge is not only to provide services to meet these needs but also to provide them in a manner that does not create dependency or devalue the disabled person.

The aim of all policy and practice concerned with disability should be to promote the best quality of life for all disabled people. To understand adequately the oppression of disabled people through policy and practice there is a need for both macro and micro analysis (Abberley, 1989). Such analysis reveals two main principles on which future policy and practice should be based: equal rights for disabled people and that all people, including all disabled people, should be regarded as of equal value in the society and for the society. To this end, as a nurse, we must stop seeing disability as an individual problem that requires individual adjustment and instead put our collective efforts into curing the current disablement of our society.

Discussion points

1. How might social policy be used to achieve a non-disablist and non-disabling society?
2. What role should nursing and nurses play in disability services and provision?

Further reading

Blaxter, M. (1976) *The Meaning of Disability*, Heinemann, London
Although Blaxter's research is now over twenty years old and there have been changes in the pattern of services and provision, it still offers a useful insight into the needs of physically disabled people and many of the problems they face in obtaining adequate help to meet these needs.

Barnes, C. (1991) *Disabled People in Britain and Discrimination*, Hurst and Co, London
Barnes outlines comprehensively the full extent of discrimination that disabled people in Britain encounter currently and argues for urgent governmental action to promote and protect equal rights.

Boylan, E. (1991) *Women and Disability*, Zed Books, London
This book was first compiled as a contribution to the International Year of Disabled Persons and has recently been updated by the United Nations. It offers a very readable insight into the special problems disabled women face in the Third World.

Cumberbatch, G. and Negrine, R. (1992) *Images of Disability on Television*, Routledge, London
A fascinating study which uses content analysis of television programmes to demonstrate how negatively disability is portrayed on television. The authors put the case for better use of this medium to promote positive attitudes in society.

Daunt, P. (1991) *Meeting Disability: A European Response*, Cassell Educational, London
Daunt gives a useful perspective on disability in Europe, presenting both the current cross-national reality and offering guidelines for future action.

Oliver, M. (1990) *The Politics of Disablement*, Macmillan, Basingstoke
Oliver, a disabled sociologist, argues cogently and vehemently for a social theory of disability as an alternative to current individualistic, bio-medical approaches.

Ryan, J. and Thomas, F. (1987) *The Politics of Mental Handicap*, 2nd edn. Free Association Books, London
Ryan and Thomas offer a superb analysis of why we so often deny people with learning disabilities their humanity and want to shut them away. A diary chronicling 'care' in an institution for people with learning disabilities in the early 1970s forms a very poignant and compelling section.

References

Abberley, P. (1989) Disabled people, normality and social work. In *Disability and Dependency* (ed. L. Barton) Falmer, London, pp. 55–68

Barnes, C. (1991) *Disabled People in Britain and Discrimination: A Case for Anti-Discrimination Legislation*, Hurst and Co, London

Barton, L. (ed.) (1989) *Disability and Dependency*, Falmer, London

Berthoud, R. (1991) Meeting the costs of disability. In *Disability and Social Policy* (ed. G. Dalley) Policy Studies Institute, London, pp. 64–100

Brown, M. and Payne, S. (1991) *Introduction to Social Administration in Britain*, 7th edn, Unwin Hyman, London

Copp, L. A. (1986) The nurse as advocate for vulnerable persons. *Journal of Advanced Nursing*, **11**, 255–263

Cumberbatch, G. and Negrine, R. (1992) *Images of Disability on Television*, Routledge, London

Dalley, G. (ed.) (1991) *Disability and Social Policy*, Policy Studies Institute, London

Daunt, P. (1991) *Meeting Disability: A European Response*, Cassell Educational, London

Department of Health (1989) *National Health Service Review Working Papers*, HMSO, London

Department of Health (1992) *The Patient's Charter*, HMSO, London

Finkelstein, V. (1993) From curing or caring to defining disabled people.

In *Health, Welfare and Practice: Reflecting on Roles and Relationships* (eds J. Walmsley, J. Reynolds, P. Shakespeare and R. Wolfe) Sage, London, pp. 139–143

Griffin, T. (ed.) (1992) *Social Trends 22*, HMSO, London

Henderson, V. (1966) *The Nature of Nursing*, The Macmillan Co., New York

Leininger, M. M. (1980) Caring: a central focus of nursing and health care services. *Nursing and Health Care*, **1**, 135–143

Locker, D. (1983) *Disability and Disadvantage: The Consequences of Chronic Illness*, (i) p. 197, Tavistock, London

Lonsdale, S. (1990) *Women and Disability: The Experience of Physical Disability Among Women*, Macmillan, Basingstoke

Miller, A. (1985) Nurse patient dependency: is it iatrogenic? *Journal of Advanced Nursing*, **10**, 417–424

Nursing Times (1993) Readers' letters. *Nursing Times*, **89**, 16

Oliver, M. (1990) *The Politics of Disablement*, Macmillan, Basingstoke

Orem, D. E. (1991) *Nursing: Concepts of Practice*, 4th edn, McGraw-Hill, New York

Parse, R. R. (1981) *Man–Living–Health: Theory of Nursing*, John Wiley and Sons, New York

Peplau, H. E. (1952) *Interpersonal Relations in Nursing*, GP Putnam's Sons, New York

Roy, C. (1974) The Roy adaptation model. In *Conceptual Models for Nursing Practice* (eds J. Riehl and C. Roy) Appleton-Century-Crofts, New York

Ryan, J. and Thomas, F. (1987) *The Politics of Mental Handicap*, (i) p. 29, 2nd edn, Free Association Books, London

Townsend, P. and Davidson, N. (eds) (1992) *Inequalities in Health: The Black Report and the Health Divide*, Penguin Books, Harmondsworth

United Kingdom Central Council for Nuring, Midwifery and Health Visiting (1992) *Code of Professional Conduct*, 3rd edn, UKCC, London

Whittaker, A. (1991) *Supporting Self-Advocacy*, King's Fund, London

11

Class and social policy

Pippa Gough

Introduction

In this chapter we examine those issues to do with class and social policies. We start by trying to reach some understanding of the concept of social class – a discussion which draws on the mass of sociological literature dedicated to exploration of the intricacies of this term. The discussion here is, by necessity, partial and summarized and a guide to further reading is given at the end of the chapter. We then move on to explore Marxist theory, which is arguably the starting point for any theoretical understanding of class societies, before proceeding to elaborate this analysis by exploring Weber's perspective on class, which introduces issues of status and power into the class equation.

Having laid the theoretical foundation, we then switch the focus to the Marxist critique of Social Policy, more popularly known as the 'political economy approach' to analysing welfarism. This critique examines the goals of welfare within a capitalist system and suggests that the lessening of inequality and the maintenance of capitalism are irreconcilable objectives.

An exploration of class as a basis of power shows that economic inequalities are inseparably tied up with the distribution of power and the ability to wield power. Within this framework nurses' access to power from the platform of class is also discussed. Finally, the relevance of using a class perspective in any discussion of social policies is examined. Although class is not a popular concept for the 1990s, it will be argued that some mileage can still be obtained from this approach in making sense of policy impact and outcomes.

What is meant by social class?

Discussions on the existence and definition of social class, the facts of class inequality and the way class oppression operates have long been the subject of sociological inquiry and debate. Much of this material is covered in detail in sociology texts (for example, Bilton *et al.*, 1987; Joseph, 1986; Giddens, 1989; Haralambos, 1990) and it is not the intention here to duplicate these arguments in full. Rather this section will summarize some of the key issues purely to provide the context for a discussion of the inter-relatedness of class, Social Policy and social policies and the relevance of these to nursing.

Society is often described by sociologists as being 'stratified', or split into a patterned structure of unequal groups. This structure is stable, engrained and persists across generations. It presents in numerous forms, the most important of which are those structures depicting societal divisions based on class, gender, race, age, ability and sexuality. The exact nature of these unequal groups and the relationships between them are varied and complex – for example it can be argued that an individual's economic position may also be a result of that individual's race, gender and/or able-bodiedness. The concept of stratification therefore is never straightforward and can be confused (Bilton *et al.*, 1987).

Everybody is affected by stratification. Opportunities for health, longevity, educational success, access to employment, adequate housing and political influence are all unequally distributed within the stratified structure of society.

Societies where economic relationships are of primary and pervasive importance, such as Western industrial societies like Britain, are known as *class societies* and the term *classes* in this instance is used to describe the different unequal groups within those societies. Within this frame of reference Dearlove and Saunders (1984i) define class briefly as 'a group of people who broadly share the same economic or market position and thus enjoy similar life chances'. Bilton *et al.* (1987i) elaborate this definition and suggest that class is 'a group sharing a similar position in a structure of objective, material inequalities, produced by a particular system of economic relationships characteristic of a particular mode of production'.

In other words, our whole understanding of class and the way our class position is determined is dependent on the way work, that is, the 'mode of production', is organized in the society in which we live. Different societies have different ways of organizing production and this creates different kinds of social class and class structure. Within each structure, inequality is the result of one class dominating and exploiting the other. Bilton *et al.* (1987) give the example of societies in which argicultural production is primary, which might be organized on the basis of master–slave relationships, as in ancient Rome. In such a society your social class would either be that of the exploited and oppressed 'slave' or the dominating, exploitative 'master'. Another example is the lord/serf relationship of feudal Europe. It can be argued that modern Western (and increasingly Eastern) societies are based on the capitalist/proletarian, or ruling/working class, relationship – a view which reflects the thinking of one of the major theories of stratification known as Marxism.

Marxist theory

Marxism, named after Karl Marx (1818–1883), a famous nineteenth century sociologist, is one of the most hotly-debated social theories within the discipline of Sociology. It has been denounced, rejected and most recently said to have been overtaken by history (a view which is explored in greater depth later in the chapter). It remains, however, one of the most powerful and wide-ranging analyses of economic relationships that has been available to students of politics and sociology.

According to Marx, class divisions and class relations underpin and explain all aspects of society. Economic and material benefits, high social status and political influence all derive from the structure of classes. In other words, Marxism suggests that all inequality can be explained from an understanding of class. This interpretation has come to be severely criticized by feminist and antiracist writers who argue that gender and race inequalities cannot be reduced simply to the platform of class – that other bases of oppression are operating also (Williams, 1989).

Marx's theory of class identifies two main classes within capitalist society: a class consisting of those people who own the means of production (factories, machinery and so on) known as the capitalists or bourgeoisie; and a class of those who own nothing but their labour power and survive by selling their skills in the open market. These are known as the proletariat or workers.

Within a capitalist society, that is, one based on accumulation of profit, there is competition among the bourgeoisie, with each owner of production trying to capture the greater market share by selling goods cheaper than his competitor. This competition squeezes out the smaller producer. Karl Marx argued that, in time, this process would slowly reduce the size of the bourgeoisie, with power becoming concentrated in the hands of fewer and fewer producers. Increased market competition and the need to maintain profits would force down the wages of the workers, leading to increasingly impoverished occupational and living conditions – a situation Marx termed 'immizeration' (Joseph, 1986).

Ultimately, within a capitalist system, one class (the majority) ends up doing all the productive work for minimal return, while a minority class dominates them and pockets all the profits produced.

The Marxist perspective suggests that the State, the judiciary and legal system, societal beliefs and values and even religion all serve the interests of the ruling class, maintaining its position and hiding the reality of peoples' oppression. Thus people come to accept their oppressed position as being natural and preordained – a situation which in Marxist terminology is known as 'false consciousness'.

Marx, however, argued that the increasing immizeration of the working class would eventually lead to a greater collective awareness of the workers' true position in society (that is, as the oppressed) and to their identification with other workers. False consciousness would disintegrate and true class consciousness (an objective understanding of the unnatural exploitation of the working class) would ultimately spark the revolution which would overthrow capitalism and lead to a utopian society based on classlessness. Within this brave new world all property would be owned collectively and distribution would be based on need, rather than on the ability to pay. This type of societal arrangement has been termed 'communism' (Joseph, 1986).

Marx contended that this process was inevitable within all capitalist societies whose mode of production created the dichotomy of ruling versus working class. This polarization, Marx predicted, would always have its roots in conflict and oppression and as such was ultimately highly unstable, particularly in times of crisis such as economic slumps or war.

Over the years many criticisms have been levelled at Marx and his views of class, not least of which is the fact that increasing immizeration of the proletariat has not taken place. Society, far from becoming more and more polarized, has in fact coalesced into a large and undefined middle class, to the point where some argue that this is the predominant class of industrial societies (see Lockwood, 1958 and Goldthorpe *et al.*, 1980, both cited Joseph, 1986). Furthermore, worldwide revolution has not taken place, as predicted. The only recent 'revolutions' appear to have occurred within the communist countries of Eastern Europe, as they race, wisely or unwisely, to embrace capitalism. Additionally, Marx's emphasis on the ownership of productive wealth fails to provide adequate explanations as to all the differences in rewards and in consciousness within the mass of the population who are not capitalists. As Bilton *et al.* (1987) explain, every middle-class employee is certainly not a member of the bourgeoisie but neither are they true proletarians. In order to cope with these discrepancies the views of another famous sociologist, Max Weber, are often employed in addition to, or instead of, those of Marx and it is this approach that is examined next.

Weber's theory of class

Max Weber (1864–1920), one of the founding fathers of sociology, provides a more complex analysis of class than Marx. He argues that class is not based solely on the ownership or non-ownership of the means of production. This Marxian view ignored the fact that even among those who did not own property, there was a rich mix of skills and different skills have different market values. In Weber's view there were four, rather than two, main classes – an account which embraced the existence of 'middle' classes (Joseph, 1986).

Weber elaborated his analysis by suggesting that class was only part of stratification, highlighting the importance of 'status' and 'power'. From this perspective there are three basic forms of advantage which privileged groups may enjoy (Bilton *et al.*, 1987):

1. life chances, such as wealth and income, health, education and job security (class)
2. social standing, that is prestige and consequent high self-esteem (status)
3. political influence, that is the ability of one group to dominate others (power).

Weber suggested that these three elements are conceptually distinct. Inequality in one of these areas may not always result in inequality in others and should not be assumed. Rather, there is an interplay between status, class and power resulting in situations where a person may be high in one area and low in another. For example, consider the case of a typical vicar, whose stipend and consequent material wealth may be limited but whose social standing and political influence are likely to be high in comparison. Another example is that of the black, female nurse manager, whose material life chances may be reasonable, but whose social status and political influence, within a sexist and racist society, may be severely curtailed.

Both of these theories of class are useful in analysing situations of social policy. Joseph (1986), for example, adopts a Weberian approach to examining the impact of education policies on schools, teachers and pupils and a Marxian-type analysis for exploring 'industrial relations'. It is the Marxist critique of the Welfare State as a whole which is explored next. Much of this discussion has already been covered in the last chapter.

The Marxist critique of welfare

As highlighted in chapter 3, it is only since the 1970s that a class perspective, in this case a Marxist critique, has been applied with any recognition and coherency, to the Welfare State. Such analysis, often termed the 'Political Economy' approach, represents the application of Marxist political and economic theory to the development of welfare within a capitalist system (O'Connor, 1973; Doyal, 1979; Ginsburg, 1979; Gough, 1979). Very briefly, within this approach capitalism is criticized as being fundamentally in conflict with and antagonistic to the welfare needs of the working class – capitalism requires a working class in order to maintain the mode of production. Welfarism within a capitalist system, therefore, can never truly aim to wipe out the disadvantage and oppression of the working class, as inequality is the very basis for capitalism's existence. From this perspective, the provision of welfare within a capitalist state represents an irreconcilable conflict.

Within Marxist terms, the basis of power is property, that is the ownership of the means of production. The owners or bourgeoisie also have a monopoly on political power and thus control the military, the church, the economy, the legal system and, ultimately, societal beliefs and values. As Joseph (1986) explains, from this perspective, the government and the State are purely a tool of the ruling class, the executive managing the affairs of the bourgeoisie. The Welfare State, as a creation of government, is not impartial, therefore. Rather it exists as an agent of capitalism.

Gough (1979, cited Williams, 1989) summarizes the main goals of welfare and social policies within capitalism, under three headings:

1. Accumulation: that is, the Welfare State aiding the maintenance of conditions favourable for the accumulation of capital. An example here is the use of the private sector to provide essential welfare interventions, such as residential care.
2. Reproduction: that is, the way the Welfare State ensures a healthy, educated workforce that has adequate food and shelter, but at the same time using the provision of these life essentials to discipline and control the workforce. Thus education helps to provide the skills needed to maintain capitalism, as well as socializing future workers into an acceptance of their position.
3. Legitimation/repression: the maintenance of political stability, social harmony and social control. The growth of the post-war Welfare State is identified as the main means by which successive governments have sustained credibility with the electorate.

In other words, this critique focuses on the services of social policy to capital – for example, its meeting of social expenses, the reproduction of labour power and its function of social control.

There are, however, a couple of further considerations that compound this analysis (Gough, 1979 cited Williams, 1989). Firstly, each of these functions can in fact be in conflict with one another. For example, social control programmes, such as hostels for the homeless or Youth Training Schemes (YTS), can use up public money which could well have been ploughed back into the private sector. On the other hand, YTS enhances accumulation through the provision of a cheap labour force, but this in turn could call the government's credibility into question.

Secondly, welfare cannot simply be seen as a function of the State to maintain capitalism. Consideration must also be given to the fact that welfare provision has come about as a result of a class struggle to improve social and economic conditions for the working class. Welfare is not simply a tool of the bourgeoisie and neither should nurses, teachers, social workers and so on, be viewed merely as the agents of social control. Ultimately the capitalist system is forced to concede welfare reforms as a result of working-class struggle. On the other hand, however, this may also be for the sake of political stability, or because it also suits the needs of capitalism to provide welfare.

So when exploring 'class' as an issue within the arena of social policy and the provision of welfare, it is necessary to consider whether the ultimate goal of welfare is truly the obliteration of poverty and disadvantage. Marxist critique would suggest otherwise and points to the primacy of capitalism as an explanation for the continued existence of poverty and inequality within our society after nearly fifty years of the Welfare State. This inequality is the most visible manifestation of the way that power is exercised from within the hierarchy of class. The next section considers the domination which groups can achieve in our society through the ownership of capital and the ability to monopolize key positions in the labour market.

Nursing, the State and social class

Hugman (1991) identifies nursing, along with social work and the remedial therapies, as being one of the 'caring professions' that became closely allied to State welfare during the nineteenth century. At this time, massive industrialization created a large and mobile workforce in the country. Although it represented much-needed labour power, this mobility was seen to be a threat to the stability of society in that it encouraged the break up of families and created urban poverty, homelessness and epidemic disease. One way of responding to this contradiction was a growth in State interventions in the lives of the working classes, by nurses and social workers. Primarily, this was to look after the health of the labourers and their families in order to ensure as active a contribution to production as possible, as well as to administer punitive measures to those not seen to be working as they might. Under this system of intervention the labels of 'deserving' and 'undeserving' of State help were quickly adopted (this is discussed in more detail in chapter 1). Caring, although humanitarian in origin, thus became inextricably tied up with notions of control and, in particular, State control. Hugman (1991) argues that, as a result of this caring, within a capitalist context, has become a key element in the legitimation of the Welfare State – the friendly face of State intervention (this draws on the work of Gough, 1979, discussed above). The contradiction of this role in the mainte- nance of capitalism and the relationships the caring professions have with different social classes have been key issues in the development of nursing within the NHS.

Critical histories of nursing reiterate this theme of the professionals' role as agents of the State (Dingwall, 1988; Maggs, 1989, cited Hugman, 1991). From this perspective the role of the State is seen to be one of considerable control and influence over the practice and development of the caring professions. Profes- sional nursing can be seen to have originated out of middle-class concerns about the productive labour of the working classes and the desire to promote the moral value of the work ethic. However, as Hugman (1991) points out, the role of the professional within welfare is somewhat more complex than this one-dimensional view. There is room to understand the nurse's role as often promoting the demands of the labour movement and the working classes for better living conditions and quality of life. In this way, nurses can be seen to serve the interests not only of the dominant but also of the dominated classes. Moreover, Gough (1979, cited Hugman, 1991) emphasizes the interests shared between the professionals and their client group against the State, and stresses the commonality of their class position, that is as employed workers.

So the class position of nurses is defined on the one hand by their position as State agents, that is allied to the dominant classes, and on the other hand as employees and thus belonging to the dominated and oppressed. Hugman (1991) points out that although members of the nursing profession were originally recruited from the working classes, the development of training, career hierarchies and a degree of professional autonomy do in fact separate nursing from the working class as it is popularly perceived and locate it, more appropriately within the large and amorphous middle classes. Additionally, Hugman (1991) goes on to argue that working-class clients/patients themselves perceive caring professionals as middle class, despite the collective and personal origins of the professional and the fact that the professional continues to sell his/her labour power to earn a living.

> This class difference is bound up with the exclusion of the working-class clientele from both professional knowledge and the way in which that knowledge is used to accomplish the everyday work of an occupation. The very claim to knowledge establishes an element of class position and adds to the legitimacy of professional power. (Hugman, 1991i)

This issue of power has been placed at the centre of understanding nursing, caring and the State. In the next section we will therefore examine this concept further from the platform of class and how this may be applied to an analysis of nursing.

Class as a basis of power

As we have seen above, distribution of power and the ability to wield power in Britain often have something to do with class and economic inequality – although, as we have seen in the previous chapters, power can also be a function of gender, race, age, ability and so on. Sociologists, however, in trying to pinpoint what it is in industrialized societies that causes inequalities of power between people, have traditionally started from an analysis of class relations.

Dearlove and Saunders (1984) suggest that this analysis needs to draw on both Marxist theory and Weberian approaches to understanding the concept of class. Therefore this discussion will need to address not only divisions based on ownership, or lack of it, of key property resources (the means of production), but also occupational divisions stemming from the labour market which denote status as well as differences in income. In other words, class power has something to do with power and influence arising from property ownership and something to do with power and status in the labour market. These two aspects will now be examined in more detail.

Ownership of property
Empirical evidence shows that wealth within Britain is clearly distributed unequally, with the majority of property and key resources concentrated in relatively few hands (see, for example, Bilton *et al.*, 1987; Joseph, 1986). This ownership of property can arguably increase an individual's power in relation to others and, as a result, improve that individual's life chances. Dearlove and Saunders explain that:

> To establish a property right in something, whether it be a teddy bear or an office block, is to exclude others from the right to use and enjoy its benefits. To own property is to claim exclusive rights of use, benefit, control and disposal, and such rights are crucial when it comes to achieving one's objectives in the world. (1984ii)

However, many forms of property ownership are of little significance when it comes to an analysis of class or economic domination within society. Large sections of the population, for example, own cars. Although this may improve their quality of life compared to the person who is dependent on public transport, as a power base this type of ownership is not the key to ruling the world. If a car owner chooses to sell this car, the impact on society as a whole is virtually non-existent.

On the other hand, as Dearlove and Saunders (1984) argue, the way a multinational corporation chooses to close down and dispose of factories or land does have a significant impact on the rest of society – consider for instance the uproar over the recent loss in Britain of Leyland DAF vehicle manufacturers or the shutting down of numerous coal mines by the government. The resulting unemployment, poverty, dependence on State welfare and the future standard of living for everyone within such communities will be affected by that decision. Some forms of property ownership, therefore, have more significance than others, with most of the power accruing to those owners of productive resources such as land, factories and money investment.

Ownership of capital has changed during this century. Firstly, economic power has tended to become concentrated in a relatively small number of giant corporations and, secondly, the locus of power within these companies has shifted from those who own them to those who manage them, leading to a division between property ownership and economic control. These trends have significant implications when considering class as a basis of power. Questions arise as to which class is now the more powerful – the propertied class or the managerial class. This is not to suggest that the relationship between property ownership and economic power is now totally severed, but rather that this relationship has become more complex (Dearlove and Saunders, 1984). What remains a certainty is that ownership and control of private property remain a very strong and lasting power base in our society and no analysis of domination can afford to ignore this.

But what does this discussion of property ownership or economic power have to do with nursing and nurses? Generally it can be argued that nurses, from the platform of nursing, are never really in the position of owning capital or being part and parcel of the propertied class. This is simply because renumeration is usually poor and market position weak. This is not to say that individual nurses are not wealthy, but it is unusual for this to be the case as a result of pursuing nursing as a career. Neither are nurses ever in a position (to any great degree) of managing key property resources. Historically, nurses have always suffered restricted access to positions of managerial control – an explanation for which has its roots in gender inequalities and the lowly status of caring. When considering class as a basis of power in the context of nursing, therefore, the spectre of a powerful managerial class, which does not necessarily include nurses, has considerable significance.

Health service managers are not the owners of the health services, but can wield considerable economic power within them – often to the detriment of the professional power of nursing. Much of this managerial control was wrested from an embryo nursing management structure during the Griffiths reorganization of 1984 (DHSS, 1983) and the introduction of 'general management'. Likewise the recent reforms wrought by the NHS and Community Care Act 1990 and the move to Trust status has again served to oust nurses from positions of managerial power and the ultimate control of key property resources. As a result the allocation of scarce health resources is rarely informed by the values underpinning nursing.

Position and status in the labour market

Another source of class power recognized by Weber is the ability to monopolize opportunities and positions in the labour market, usually through the possession of particular skills which are, or are perceived to be, in short supply and high demand. It is precisely these skills that can command high renumeration and good conditions of employment.

Dearlove and Saunders (1984) point out that income levels and perceived scarcity of skills are closely associated with different types of occupations. For example, professional workers (doctors, lawyers and so on) earn twice that of skilled workers (electricians, plumbers) who, in turn, earn three times as much as unskilled manual workers (dustbin collectors, cleaners). These income inequalities have a direct effect on other areas of life such as the ability to qualify for a mortgage, buy into private transport, schools and medical care. Unequal life chances as a spin off from unequal incomes (arising from monopoly of job opportunities) are therefore cumulative and this helps to perpetuate inequalities across the generations.

The pattern of the unequal distribution of income reflects the way in which different occupational groups exercise differential power in the labour market – consider here the unequal power between doctors and nurses who are both involved in similar jobs yet command very different rewards and conditions of work. This power is exercised as a form of what Weber called 'social closure'. That is a 'process by which social collectivities seek to maximize rewards by restricting access to resources and opportunities to a limited circle of eligibles' (Parkin, 1979, cited Hugman, 1991ii). This closure or maximizing of class power can be exercised either through a process of exclusion or usurpation. Exclusionary strategies for exercising power can be identified when powerful occupational groups gatekeep and limit entry to an occupation, thus maintaining their scarcity and high renumeration.

Professionalism is a classic example of exclusionary tactics, with particular reference to law and medicine. These groups gain the monopoly of market opportunities via credentials, qualifications and usually through a system of being licensed by the State to practise. Much of this process enhances public legitimacy and in turn feeds into the demand for higher status and income.

Within this context, the question arises as to why nurses, who undoubtedly operate an increasing degree of exclusionary control as described above (consider the educational entry gate to nursing, the recent move to higher education and the maintaining of a professional register), continue to have such a diminished power base as a profession – especially *vis-à-vis* doctors. Explanations for this situation are complex but much of the answer lies in the fact that nurses are rarely in the position of being seen as owning 'skills in short supply'. Consequently, they do not successfully monopolize market opportunities for giving care and are therefore afforded little in the way of status and power.

At the root of this is the fact that nursing as a profession is highly gendered, a situation which according to Porter (1992) affects nurses in a number of interconnected ways. Firstly, because the skills of caring are primarily seen as mundane women's work (that is, any women can do it, it does not require special training!), nursing is devalued in terms of labour market position and renumeration. This is not the case for medicine or law. Secondly, because nursing continues to be juxtapositioned alongside the predominantly male-oriented occupation of medicine, the sexual division of labour is starkly contrasted and gender rather than occupation determines the inequalities. Many of these arguments are explored in more detail in chapter 6, when gender as a basis of power is considered in the context of nursing and policy.

Nurses, however, are not a homogenous group and caution must be exercised when making general statements about the class position of the nursing profession as a whole. Within nursing, some nurses operate exclusion more successfully than others and are thus more upwardly socially mobile within the class hierarchy. A prime example of this is the development of a predominately male managerial elite within nursing. Although forming only 9 per cent of the total nursing workforce, male nurses fill a disproportionately high percentage of senior posts (Dolan, 1993) – reasons for which are various and are discussed further in chapter 6. While this is obviously not an explicit conspiracy against female nurses, such sexist organizational practices, allowing promotion of men over women, have an exclusionary ring to them. Additionally, in terms of class, it can be argued that nursing is one of the main vehicles of social mobility for men.

Pascall (1986) argues that all social welfare services involve a gender hierarchy. The professionalization of care, and its removal from the private, domestic sphere into the public world of paid work, has made room for men at the top. Nursing is no exception. Pascall goes on to say that, in class terms, this does not imply that men actually do the caring work when this becomes paid work, as this remains the role of grass-roots, working-class female employees. Rather it is the high spots that are occupied by men. Stacey and Price (1981, cited Pascall, 1986i) suggest that 'throughout all the known world and in history, wherever public power has been separated from private power, women have been excluded'. Ultimately, the professionalization of nursing could mean the erosion of women's power.

Current moves to upgrade nurse education, as embodied by the Project 2000 reforms (UKCC, 1986), could be said to be indicative of nurses becoming more exclusionary in an attempt to increase their professional power base. However, in contrast, these exclusionary tactics are not open as a course of action to the less qualified members of the caring workforce, namely health care assistants, now nearly as numerous as qualified nursing staff and predominantly female. This new division of labour within the health service workforce has dimensions not only of class and gender but also of race, with overseas nurses and nurses from black populations playing an important part in this rationalization (Pascall, 1986).

Within the current climate of financial constraint and the purchaser/provider scenario, these unqualified women may fast be becoming the 'nursing' workforce of the future (see, for example, the Value For Money Unit Report (NHSME, 1992) on skill mix in the District Nursing service). Within the brave new world the fact that a small group of qualified nursing elites may have secured class power on an exclusionary basis will be of no consequence to the decimated profession. As long ago as 1977, Carpenter (cited Pascall, 1986) was warning that the stratification of nursing work into basic nursing tasks, clinical nursing and managerial control was profoundly against both the interests of the majority of nurses and ultimately of a quality service for patients. This warning has been steadfastly ignored.

Usurpationary stategies for exercising class power, on the other hand, occur when less powerful and less privileged groups come together in an attempt to improve their material position through collective bargaining, pressure and organization. The activities of trade unions representing the rights of the working class are a typical example of this, although now in a more limited form than a decade ago. As an expression of power the process of usurpation is always negative, that is it is always the power not to work or co-operate. Usurpationary closure never implies domination. The ability to dominate is to secure the compliance of others without encountering resistance. This is an ability that, arguably, less powerful groups do not have.

From the nursing perspective it is interesting to consider the viability of class power through usurpationary strategies. As a large oppressed group, it would seem reasonable to assume that nurses should be able to exercise considerable usurpationary power as a way of increasing occupational opportunities and income. Historically, however, this has not been the case. Possible reasons for this lack of skill in collective action include the fact that usurpationary strategies are often undermined by a tension between collective and individual interests. Within a predominantly female profession, where the status of caring and consequent job esteem and worth is low, a nurse may well consider her own job is not important enough to strike for. This links into ideas of dependency on other (male) sources of income – where the secondary (female) job is only useful as pin money and does not necessarily represent a career. Moreover, the Royal College of Nursing has always been fervently opposed to its members taking strike action. Its lastest guidance on the matter (RCN, May 1993) pursues this non–militant line vigorously, arguing that industrial or strike action in the health service is always ultimately harmful to patient care.

Usurpation as collaboration, rather than as militant collective action is, however, a more feasible option for nurses – as demonstrated within the Nursing Development Unit (NDU) movement (Wright, 1992). Here the empowerment of nurses is based on the promotion and development of nursing as a therapy in its own right, worthy of organizational support and resources. New nursing practices generate new nursing knowledge, the use of which in turn enables nurses to articulate and demonstrate their value. This type of collaborative, collective action could well secure the nursing power base of the future.

Overall, though, the picture painted intimates that class is not an adequate basis for nursing power or professional influence within either the organizational hierarchy or the policy arena. Health policies still fail to reflect the nursing voice. Nurses continue to be subordinated, caught somewhere between exclusion and usurpation, between the working and the middle class. They can (and increasingly do) operate exclusionary control but are at the bottom of the pecking order in exclusionary groups, with women in nursing marginalized more than men. Additionally, nurses have a long history of being singularly unsuccessful with usurpationary strategies to secure and enhance their position in the labour market – although the NDU movement may change that. Consequently, power within the professional field and the ability to monopolize occupational opportunities and income, in a Weberian sense, are as yet fundamentally denied to nurses.

Is a class perspective relevant in the 1990s

Although it is possible to develop a class perspective of nursing, of which only the main issues and themes have been raised here, the appropriateness of a class analysis in today's world has to be questioned. How relevant or useful is a discussion of class to Social Policy and policies today, especially in the face of critiques that suggest that Marxism and the dichotomous society are no longer a credible theory. On the face of it, a class analysis appears to be rapidly losing popularity, aided not only be the rejection of communist ideology and culture in Eastern Europe but also the frequent assertions from the ideological platform of individualism and the New Right, that we are all moving towards a 'classless society'.

For nurses and other workers in the health services, however, this statement, in the face of rising ill health due to increasing poverty and social inequalities, is problematic. Both the Black report and the Health Divide (Townsend, 1992) point to an unquestionable link between class and morbidity and mortality (see chapter 4). Poverty in Britain is becoming more widespread (Townsend and Davison, 1992). Nurses see the impact of class position on health every day of their working lives and arguably upon their own health as well. In fact, much of nursing practice is developed in response to these class patterns of illness and early death, with health visiting being a prime example. The concept of social class, therefore, still has a major importance and relevance for nurses in the shaping and development of nursing practice – but is this still the case for welfare provision as a whole?

Historically, much critical analysis of welfare, especially since the 1970s and the development of the Marxist critique within Social Policy (see chapter 3), has had its origins in an examination of the relation of social policies to work, that is the social and economic organization of production and the resulting stratification of society. As we have seen, this critique highlights the role of welfare institutions in maintaining the needs of capitalism for a literate, healthy workforce on one hand, and the struggles of the working class to improve their conditions on the other. Williams (1992), however, points out that in Social Policy we are now moving into a different age wherein the focus is far less on proletarianism and traditional class politics and far more on the emerging politics of identity based on ethnicity, gender, age and/or sexuality. This shift she argues is fundamentally connected to the massive change in methods of production within our society. Williams (1992) makes this link by examining the extensive changes in welfare policy and provision in Britain today, which she suggests are characterized by fragmentation, uncertainty and contradiction.

Fragmentation has occurred with the rise of a mixed economy of welfare, with individualism, contracting out, privatization and provision of service from a multiplicity of sources including the voluntary, private, public and informal sectors. Within this diversity there is often a desperate need for co-ordination and coherency of services. A trend is becoming discernible whereby the skills of those who work in welfare service are being broken up in line with the fragmented market. In nursing, for instance, we can identify the segmenting of nursing into component parts with the less skilled 'tasks' going to lower-paid, less-qualified, part-time and contracted-in workers. In the face of this, much grass-roots work has become very creative in order to cope with the changed circumstances, but projects of this type often remain small scale and localized. Additionally, many of these local projects are in competition with each other for funding – a situation which prohibits collaboration and dissemination of progressive working practices.

Connected to fragmentation Williams (1992) suggests there is also uncertainty and change. Within the current economic climate long-term funding is rarely secured for any welfare services within the public, private or voluntary sectors. Managers and politicians are working to short-term objectives, commonly tied in to performance-related pay and minimal fixed-term contracts. Strategic planning of provision tends to be shelved, often resulting in an upsurge of short-lived, precarious projects that raise the expectations of the user, then fail to deliver. Work and the delivery of services are constantly being redefined and altered and it is the less powerful groups of workers that are unable to manage this change proactively in order to secure satisfactory job conditions and reward. Uncertainty and change also exist for the service user, often left wondering whether there will be a service and who will provide it. In addition, Williams (1992) identifies uncertainty of the ethos and purpose of welfare. Universalism has been criticized but not necessarily replaced by the overarching commitment to individualism, family, self-help and the market. The situation is more fluid, more complex and more contradictory.

These contradictions go to the heart of today's Welfare State. Most obvious is the paradoxical way fragmentation of welfare services on the ground has led to an increasing centralization of State power at the top. Williams (1992) points out that this is particularly so in education with the increased control of central government over resources which it distributes to grant-aided schools and academic institutions, Within the health and social services there is a similar picture whereby the incorporation of private and voluntary sectors has required increased State powers to supervise and regulate. Other contradictory developments include the effects of the New Right's reliance on individualism and the squeeze on public services on the one hand, while public commitment to equity and collective provision is burgeoning on the other. The outspoken and sometimes violent public demonstrations against the poll tax can be seen as a vivid example of this

(Williams, 1992). The emphasis on monetarism and the free market throughout the 1980s has created a dramatic increase in poverty and an intensification of inequalities of gender, race, age and disability. This is especially so where these are compounded by class inequalities or exclusion from work. However, there has also been a growing awareness of and resistance to these unequal conditions and treatment as evidenced in the growth of self-advocacy groups, the emphasis on the primacy of the consumer, the concern with delivering a quality service and the influence of equal opportunity policies which have penetrated every corner of welfarism.

Williams (1992) argues that these processes of diversification, fragmentation, uncertainty and contradiction within welfare reflect the wider social, economic, political and cultural changes currently impacting upon Western, industrialized societies as a whole – a trend loosely termed postmodernity. At an economic level this includes the industrial changes known as post-Fordism, characterized by the move away from a mass-produced, standardized product to something far more differentiated and responsive to individual consumer demand. This diversity is also observed at a social and cultural level where the trend is away from uniformity towards the acknowledgement of hetero-geneity. The individual identity of the consumer is paramount and choice is exercised through the consumption of different-iated products. At a political level these changes are reflected in the fragmentation of traditional class politics and the emergence of a 'politics of identity', based on, for example, gender, age, ethnicity, disability and/or sexuality. This shift is exemplified by the current challenges to and rejection of the deterministic ideologies found in the former Soviet Union and the states of Eastern Europe.

These major cultural, social, economic and political transitions have found an echo in a postmodernist shift in theory and analysis. Within Social Policy this newly-formed, postmodernist theoretical position emerges from earlier critiques and rejects the structural, macro theories, such as Marxism, and any other approach that seeks to establish an overarching, deterministic, total picture. Williams (1992) suggests that the Marxist dichotomy of class is replaced by enquiry into the diversity of political and cultural identity. Non-class bases of identity are examined, local discourses unpicked and subjectivity emphasized in the retreat from structural analyses of power and function.

So what does this fragmentation of class politics mean in policy terms and is it relevant? The answer is undoubtedly yes. The growing importance of the development of identity politics means that demands upon welfare provision will revolve around meeting the specific needs of particular groups. This is in contrast to pressing for universal provision to cover the needs of all (Williams, 1992). In fact the development of consumer-led provision has already found reflection in nursing, in the recent growth of Primary Nursing in this country. As a way of organizing the delivery of care, Primary Nursing embraces all the characteristics of postmodernity. The product, nursing, is non-standard and non-mass produced. It is highly individualized, highly differentiated and through negotiation with the client, is totally responsive to consumer demands. In other words it echoes precisely the current shifts in welfare.

Conclusion

In this chapter we have been concerned with an examination of the concept of class, power, policy and nursing. We have explored both Marxist and Weberian approaches to this subject and have considered the access of nursing and nurses to power from the platform of class – a discussion which by necessity, drew on analysis of gender as an axis of inequality.

Questions have also been raised about the relevance of a class analysis of welfare in the 1990s. In respect of nurses being able to identify class-related causes of ill-health and to develop their practice accordingly, class remains of vital importance. However, further examination of the deeper political, economic and societal trends involving a shift from uniformity to diversity, revealed how the overarching, structural analyses based on class were now being replaced by the new policies of identity. In translating this rejection of proletarianism into policy terms, the need to move in the direction of universal services which ultimately are capable of meeting diverse and differentiated needs becomes paramount. This is arguably the only way forward for nursing as well.

Discussion points

1. Are male nurses of a higher social class than female nurses? Why might their social classes be different?
2. Does the Welfare State support a class system or work to dismantle it? What part do nurses play in this process?

Further reading

Abbott, P. and Wallace, C. (eds) (1990) *The Sociology of the Caring Professions*, Falmer Press, London

Dearlove, J. and Saunders, P. (1984) *Introduction to British Politics*, Polity Press, Cambridge and Basil Blackwell, Oxford

Miliband, R. (1969) *The State in Capitalist Society*, Weidenfeld and Nicholson, London
Considered a classic. This book offers what is thought to be the most comprehensive Marxist analysis of politics and the State in Britain.

Salvage, J. (1986) *The Politics of Nursing*, Butterworth Heinemann, Oxford

References

Bilton, T. Bonnett, K., Jones, P., Stanworth, M., Sheard, K. and Webster, A. (1987) *Introductory Sociology*, 2nd edn, (i) p. 36. Macmillan Education Ltd, Basingstoke and London

Dearlove, J. and Saunders, P. (1984) *Introduction to British Politics*, (i) p. 169; (ii) p. 174. Polity Press, Cambridge and Basil Blackwell, Oxford

Department of Health and Social Security (1983) *NHS Management Inquiry Report* (Griffiths Report), HMSO, London

Dolan, B. (1993) Gender and Change. In *Project 2000: Reflection and Celebration* (ed. B. Dolan), Scutari Press, London, pp. 75–88

Doyal, L. (1979) *The Political Economy of Health*, Pluto Press, London

Giddens, A. (1989) *Sociology*, Polity Press, Cambridge

Ginsburg, N. (1979) *Class, Capital and Social Policy*, Macmillan, London

Gough, I. (1979) *The Political Economy of the Welfare State*, Macmillan, London

Haralambos, M. and Holborn, M. (1990) *Sociology: Themes and Perspectives*, 3rd edn, Unwin Hyman, London

Hugman, R. (1991) *Power in Caring Professions*, Macmillan, London

Joseph, M. (1986) *Sociology for Everyone*, Polity Press, Cambridge and Basil Blackwell, Oxford

National Health Service Management Executive (1992) *The Nursing Skill Mix in the District Nursing Service*, HMSO, London

O'Connor, J. (1973) *The Fiscal Crises of the State*, St James's Press, New York

Pascall, G. (1986) *Social Policy: A Feminist Analysis*, (i) p. 27. Tavistock Publications, London and New York

Royal College of Nursing (1993) *Industrial Action by Other Unions. Your Questions Answered*, RCN, London

Townsend, P. and Davidson, N. (1992) *Inequalities in Health: The Black Report and the Health Divide*, Penguin Books, Harmondsworth

United Kingdom Central Council (1986) *Project 2000: A New Preparation for Practice*, UKCC, London

Williams, F. (1989) *Social Policy: A Critical Introduction*, Polity Press, Cambridge and Blackwell Publishers, Oxford

Williams, F. (1992) Somewhere over the rainbow: universality and diversity in social policy. In *Social Policy Review 4* (eds N. Manning and R. Page) Social Policy Association, London, pp. 200–219

Wright, S. (1992) Exporting excellence. *Nursing Times*, **88**(**39**), pp. 40–42

12

Policy for and of nursing

Pippa Gough, Sian Maslin-Prothero and Abigail Masterson

Introduction

There are numerous themes which run through this book which cannot be ignored when discussing social policy and nursing, namely those aspects of inequality and oppression in respect of class, gender, race, disability and age. What has become apparent is that the Welfare State and associated social policies, rather than remedying the ills of society, as was the initial aim of collectivist and universal provision, have conversely often served to reinforce these areas of disadvantage. Nursing as part of this establishment must also take its fair share of blame.

Throughout the book we have aimed to explain the ways these inequalities interact and interlink. In each case an examination of nursing as a profession and an activity has provided a more than adequate platform for this analysis, presenting as it does a rich history within which the ideologies of sexism, imperialism, capitalism, ageism and so on, have all played their part. The contemporary product is a complex profession reflecting these myriad influences. This can be detected in the make-up of the nursing workforce, the way nursing care is often delivered in partial and biased ways and also in the way the profession has been characterized unremittingly throughout its history by a lack of power.

This trend of powerlessness has led to nurses being unable to challenge adequately the public policy agenda, which has persistently neglected issues directly concerning our practice and education – even to the extent of us being unable to control and direct the future shape of our own profession. The effect of this with regard to the care we are then able to provide is that we can rarely influence proactively the allocation of scarce health resources in line with the values that underpin nursing. These values include holism, choice, partnership, empowerment and individuality. This legacy of being restricted to managing change purely reactively raises fundamental questions with regard to our grasping the opportunity to enhance our power through our practice.

This chapter aims to shift the focus away from the policy analysis of nursing, which has been developed to some extent within each preceding chapter, onto different theoretical ground. Although it is useful to develop and discuss a policy of nursing there is also a pressing need for nurses to develop their own analysis for policy – we need a wider perspective of our place in and as part part of the public, voluntary and private services. We believe this policy for nursing is the only way of enabling the profession to reach its fullest potential. Nurses need to start to use and influence policy to their own ends, that is in terms of professional direction and delivery of care. Through the evolution of a 'policy acumen', distilled from a policy analysis concerned with the nature of nursing itself, nurses can grasp the nettle of power within the health arena. A clear statement developed from this approach has the potential to provide the platform from which to educate the public on nursing's values, beliefs and tenets as well as the shared and independent functions of nurses. It could also serve to inform the public about major health problems, concerns and issues for which nurses can be the ideal advocates and care givers.

A policy analysis for nursing

This policy for nursing is as yet uncharted terrain and what we offer here are purely the first small steps into what we hope will prove to be a paradigm shift in nursing. Kleffel (1991) describes a paradigm as the shared knowledge, commitments and values that exist among a professional group. When facts can no longer be explained, questions solved or research framed by the paradigm, an anomaly exists. Discovery, as in the case of this book, begins with the awareness of the anomaly, or in this instance the awareness of the need for nurses to become more policy efficient and effective. When the anomalies subverting the existing paradigm can no longer be ignored, new investigations begin that lead the profession to a new basis for practice. When the shift is completed, the nurse will be working within a new world, with different parameters and different ways of doing and thinking (Kleffel, 1991).

We have decided that one way of beginning to map this new theoretical territory is to examine the four metaparadigms of nursing as described by Fawcett (1989) namely: person, health, environment and the nature of nursing. The rationale for using this particular framework lies in the profession's acceptance of these four metaparadigms as the legitimate domain of nursing. Additionally they provide a useful tool for exploring all aspects of policy. Through this examination we hope to offer a glimpse of an alternative world view for nurses – a world view which can more helpfully inform our practice, our knowledge base and our actions within the wider policy context. We will now examine each of the metaparadigms in depth.

Person

The most central concept within the domain of nursing is the person. In nursing theory 'person' is used to refer to those individuals, families or groups, either sick or well, who are in need of nursing care (Bergman, 1983). In addition the metaparadigm of person encapsulates not only nursing's views about patients and clients but also beliefs about nurses themselves as people. The most consistent philosophic component of the concept of person in contemporary nursing is holism, that is the belief that the person is more than the sum of the parts and should not be viewed in isolation from his/her context (Chinn and Kramer, 1991).

The nurse's view of self as a professional is greatly influenced by the image of nursing and nurses as portrayed by the public, the profession itself, mentors and role models (Leddy and Pepper, 1989). Nursing throughout its history as we have discussed in other chapters of this book has been controlled and shaped by dominant groups in the policy-making arena. Nurses thus in common with other oppressed groups have internalized personality characteristics of self-hatred and low self-esteem (Leddy and Pepper, 1989). Nursing must overturn this oppression to be able to realize its full potential as a force in health and health care.

Attention to the personal self is also crucial to accessing the intrinsic power of nursing. Perhaps the most important gift a nurse can bring to the nurse/patient relationship is herself and in order to do this nurses have to value themselves and nursing. Personal self-concept is effected by interpersonal relationships and a person's view of self controls the roles he or she will be able to assume. The dual socialization of female nurses as women and nurses thus contributes to the powerlessness of nursing (Leddy and Pepper, 1989).

Bevis (1978) has identified four main philosophical views of person that have existed in nursing and still remain influential – asceticism, romanticism, pragmatism and humanist existentialism.

Exploring asceticism first, early nurses, she argues, often gave up home, family and fortune to devote themselves to the care of others in holy orders. From Nightingale onwards there was less stress on total self-denial but there was still a strong emphasis on devotion to duty and a pervasive belief that nursing was a 'calling'. The patient was viewed as a spiritual being with salvation and oneness with God being the aim of care.

Romanticism turned this focus on spirituality and selflessness into a doctrine about always doing the best for the client, and having loyalty to the doctor and the training school. Romanticism thus supported a dependence on medicine and a lack of autonomy, assertiveness or independence for both nursing and nurses.

Post World War II shortages of staff, increased workloads and medical development thrust nursing into pragmatism, that is nursing became centred on practicality and utility. Nurses relinquished their direct care-giving responsibilities and developed into supervisors of untrained staff. Doctor's needs rather than patients needs became paramount. Hospitals were organized around medical specialities and patients were seen as diagnoses and collections of signs and symptoms rather than people. The focus was on the problem rather than the person and cure rather than care.

Finally, the rise of humanism in nursing led to nurses viewing patients and clients more holistically, as unique individuals capable of making choices and directing their own care. This has coincided with an increasing emphasis on accountability for decisions made both in terms of patients and clients and nurses themselves. Such accountability is felt to be an important step on the route to autonomy. True autonomy would mean that nurses would have control over their own profession and work functions (Leddy and Pepper, 1989). Nursing however lacks a collective professional identity and has been characterized by internal dissension and rivalry with each subgroup focusing on its own interests. If nursing were to develop a collective self-concept and present a united front our enormous potential political power might at last be realized.

So what does this mean for the development of a policy for nursing? Firstly a focus on the person from a humanist perspective is the route to autonomous action for nurses. Therefore if we expand our knowledge base in line with this perspective within this domain of nursing we could achieve part of the shift in thinking necessary to prompt the emergence of a new paradigm. This paradigm is a policy for nursing.

Health

As nurses one of our central roles is to promote health, assess health need, enable health facilitating activities and provide care. The promotion of health is one of the nine nursing competencies necessary for the first level registration laid down in Rule 18 (Statutory Instrument, 1983), and Rule 18A (Statutory Instrument, 1989). Despite this, as nurses, have we yet grasped the full meaning of the concept of 'health', let alone its implications for practice?

Dictionary definitions are pure lexicography and unhelpful in informing our practice. Alternatively there are a variety of models and theories regarding the concept of health and health beliefs. These range from a narrow focus on an absence of disease to a multidimensional state of wholeness, and are discussed in more detail by other authors (WHO, 1946; Illich, 1976; Smith, 1981; McBean, 1991; Seedhouse, 1986). Suffice to say that health is complex, and not something that can easily be defined. There is a need to recognize the complexity surrounding the term and how its meaning varies from person to person. Health is about individuals, their access to resources and equality of opportunity (McBean, 1991). It is also about the influence individuals, families and communities can exert on their political, social and economic environment. Although the rhetoric on health is something with which all nurses can engage it would appear that this broad understanding is rarely reflected in nursing practice at any level and in any setting.

At the inception of the NHS little was known about professional and lay health beliefs and how these could affect a person's perception of their own health. With the increasing publicity surrounding the WHO definition of health (WHO, 1946) and the later emphasis on a holistic approach in 'Health for All 2000' (WHO, 1978) nurses were prompted to consider themselves as the professional group that could implement and integrate this liberating philosophy.

Nursing theorists have long viewed health as the fundamental aim of nursing rather than an adjunct that has become popular currency. Consequently health is a central concept of all nursing models. Elliot-Cannon (1990i) notes each theorist conceives health differently: 'in terms of behavioural stability (King, 1971); adaptation (Roy, 1984); wholeness (Orem, 1971); system stability (Neuman, 1974); expressions of life processes (Rogers, 1970); and behavioural equilibrium and independent functioning (Johnson, 1980)'.

It has been hoped that a wider understanding of the all-embracing and complex nature of health might result through education (UKCC, 1986). However, this education is occurring within the wrong orientation. Nurses are as yet unempowered, as a result of socialization, subservience to medicine, gender and so on, to fully realize their potential contribution as health enhancers. At present we have the knowledge but not the skills. McBean (1991) argues that without political endorsement nursing remains paralysed and an understanding of health is therefore meaningless. Thus nurses need to move beyond encouraging clients to adapt and change in order to improve their health status, to recognizing how individual circumstances – social, economic and political – impact on people's health.

Overall the approach to health in nursing is developing and

broadening. We have moved (and continue to move) from a medical model of care, with its emphasis on supporting the doctor in 'curing', towards a 'health' model. Such a model embraces a more holistic approach to care and recognizes everything taking place within a person's life – biological, social, psychological, emotional, economic, environmental and political – and how these interact and interrelate upon people's health.

Professional knowledge about health can provide us with the vision and power to develop policy from an alternative world view of nursing. We must now maximize this knowledge in terms of our practice.

Environment

Within the environmental metaparadigm a policy for nursing forces us to look beyond the parochial boundaries of any one setting for nursing care and to develop a more global perspective. It challenges nursing to embrace a broader, more comprehensive view of the environment that incorporates social, political and economic realities – a sort of critical, social reconceptualization of the world within which nursing takes place. Stevens (1989) argues that the new nursing knowledge arising from this reconceptualization can potentially be used by nurses, individuals and communities to alter oppressive social circumstances and to increase the capacity for emancipatory change.

In their day-to-day practice nurses are involved in caring for individuals and communities whose health and well-being are primarily associated with, and dependent upon, their environmental conditions. Nursing interventions are frequently required for infectious diseases, injuries sustained within the home or workplace, exposure to pollution, substance abuse, malnutrition, suicide attempts and myriad health problems caused by the oppression of ageism, sexism, racism and the unequal distribution of human rights (Kleffel, 1991).

Nurses often claim these environmental factors are a central component within their domain of practice and knowledge development. This however is not always the case. Chopoorian (1986, cited Stevens, 1989 and Kleffel, 1991) argues that nursing theories simply do not encompass explanations for phenomena such as riots motivated by racism or poverty, exploitation of the old or violence against women and children. We, like Chopoorian, cannot understand why nurses fail repeatedly to show public outrage about the origins of their clients' compounded health problems – especially as they bear witness to the most painful aspects of these problems. Chopoorian asserts that it is precisely this lack of consciousness of environment within nursing theory and a paucity of political nous that contributes to the marginal role of nursing in mainstream social, economic and political affairs. She challenges nursing to broaden its usual conceptualization of the environment as being solely the immediate milieu to which clients must adapt – the client-orientated psychosocial paradigm – and to embrace sociopolitical and economic contexts.

Kleffel (1991) found that this problem is not confined to nursing. Many disciplines have a narrow focus, limited to the immediate surroundings of the individual at the expense of action directed at change in organizational, institutional, environmental and politico-economic conditions. However Kleffel (1991) does identify some theoretical models which focus attention on environmental effects on health and behaviour and develop strategies which remove the emphasis from personal health behaviours to unhealthy environmental factors. Kleffel (1991) suggests that nurses should aim to incorporate these theoretical approaches into their work as a matter of urgency. The only way forward for nurses is to view human life and health as a multidimensional unity with the wider environment.

Kleffel (1991) describes this new approach for nursing as 'thinking upstream', that is an approach that focuses on modifying economic, political and environmental factors that are demonstrably the precursors of poor health, globally. Society is the locus of change as opposed to 'down stream' thinking in which the individual is the locus of change.

Examples of 'upstream' thinking in nursing are provided, amongst others, by Milio who as long ago as 1976 (cited Kleffel, 1991) was maintaining that the range of health choices available to the population is shaped by policy decisions in both governmental and private institutions. Rather than targeting efforts to change individual health behaviour, she advocated interventions directed at the national policy-making level. Choices that enabled the promotion and maintenance of health have to be more readily available and less costly than health damaging options, if a society is to upgrade its health status. Milio, (1976, cited Kleffel, 1991) exhorted nurses to put their energies into developing interventions which would foster a health-sustaining environment, rather than continuing to focus on helping the individual to adapt to the status quo.

Another example of 'up-stream thinking' is offered by the school of critical social nursing, derived from critical social theory and described by Stevens (1989). From within this framework the meaning of environment is expanded to incorporate critical analysis of the social, economic and political worlds of nursing individuals, families and communities. It involves uncovering oppressive social structures that constrain individuals' health, limit their life possibilities and restrict their equal and fully-conscious participation in society. Stevens (1989i) suggests this critical way of thinking may be experienced as 'a powerful new lens, a frame of reference or interpretive scheme that is different from conventional nursing scholarship yet clearly in line with nursing's holistic perspective'.

From a critical social viewpoint on the world, nurses are not afraid to challenge the legitimacy of a status quo that disadvantages and oppresses individuals and communities. Nursing interventions involve enabling clientele to identify the environmental problems which restrict their health and plan appropriate collective action to change oppressive constraints (Stevens, 1989).

Kleffel (1991) argues that the adoption by nursing of an expanded consciousness of the environmental domain represents a paradigm shift in nursing science. As described previously, nursing's current environmental paradigm is psychosocial and client-oriented. However, there is a growing awareness, particularly among health visitors with their desire to regain the public health remit, that this view of the environment is limited – it prevents nursing from examining the relationships of social, political and economic conditions that mitigate against the achievement of good health (Kleffel, 1991).

The rethinking of nursing's environmental domain will revolutionize the profession by enabling access to the wider social, political, economic and global debates where, up until now, nursing has been silent (Kleffel, 1991).

Nursing

Nursing is a complex activity that complements and augments the work of other health-care professionals. Attempts have been made since the 1950s to define the exact nature of nursing – however, its essence remains to all intents and purposes elusive (Chinn and Kramer, 1991). Such explorations are nevertheless crucial to the development of a policy for nursing. If we cannot define nursing we cannot hope to change it.

Definitions of the nature of nursing abound in the nursing literature. They range from a narrow focus on helping to those definitions that stake a claim to the entirety of caring itself (Henderson, 1978; Leininger, 1984). June Clark in the forword of the RCN's *The Value of Nursing* (1992) emphasizes that nursing is more than the tasks nurses do, yet, increasingly, government and managerial-driven value-for-money exercises look set to reduce and restrict it to just those easily-quantifiable and visible tasks.

Henderson (1978) identified that nurses' perception of nursing is frequently at odds with the public's image and thus, it seems reasonable to assume, that of the policy makers. Salvage (1983) criticized the trivial and demeaning ways that 'angels' and their work are portrayed in the media. These stereotypes include the ministering angel, the battleaxe matron, the doctor's handmaiden and the sex symbol (Bridges, 1990). Hughes (1980) stresses that such public opinion will always have an effect on the ability of the profession to provide a unique and beneficial service as, inevitably, these images will also affect the decisions of policy makers. If nurses are never seen as intellectually able or politically powerful then they will never be afforded credence in terms of key decisions.

Nursing in the UK has continually been influenced by the directions, goals and principles of government and dominant groups in the policy-making process (Robinson, 1992). Historically reasons for this marginal position can be found in the gendered nature of nursing, undeveloped intellectual potential, the juxtaposition to medicine and the invisibility of much nursing care (which we discuss throughout the book).

However, this pessimistic view of the powerlessness of nursing in the UK can be tempered somewhat if we look at the dynamic model of nursing development in the USA (Weisskopf, 1993).

Here nurses have developed strong political affiliations, view lobbying as part of their normal role and actively encourage practitioners to go into politics at all levels (Girouard, 1989). This overt political activity has even led to the development of a strong Social Policy statement from the American Nurses' Association [ANA] (ANA, 1980).

If nurses in the UK could follow this model we might be able to challenge the pervasive medical focus in health policy and develop services that enable and give legitimacy to our autonomy. This search for power however is not only about increasing the nursing voice for the good of nursing. It is also about realizing our untapped potential for enhancing health through our unique contribution. This contribution encompasses the holistic approach founded on values of partnership, empowerment and the promotion of informed individual choice.

Development of a more radical agenda for action would enable us to revisit and redefine our role as health advocates, which has remained static at the micro level of individual patient care. True advocacy as a nursing concept must encompass something wider than this, for example lobbying at all levels of policy formulation and becoming active participants in the political process.

In order to legitimize this role of advocate, nursing must be prepared 'to go public' and speak out with one voice about its shared aims for health-related social policy. Unity is vital. For too long nursing power has been dissipated through parochial, petty in-fighting between subgroups. Use of our sheer numbers can translate political will into action. This collective self-actualization is dependent on a re-conceptualization of the very nature and aims of nursing itself. It requires a shift in thinking only possible through the adoption of a new world view. Unless the profession can define itself nursing will remain a merely reactive force, shaped by other dominant groups and therefore unable to reach its full promise. A comprehensive definition of nursing and a clear articulation of its policy perspective, universally accepted by the profession, would give us clear guidance with regard to our legitimate goals, focus and parameters of work. Additionally it would give direction to the educational preparation of practitioners and identify the phenomena about which nursing knowledge should be advanced (Schlotfeldt, 1987).

Achieving the paradigm shift

The avenues open to selecting and distilling the various aspects of knowledge and skills that will enable us to become more active in the policy arena are difficult to identify with absolute certainty. Several current key initiatives and activities are, however, worth considering, namely: the Nursing Development Unit movement; the greater use of reflective practice; recent moves to promote leadership in British nursing; the improvement and restructuring of professional education and development of nurses as typified by Project 2000 (UKCC, 1986) and the Post Registration Education and Practice proposals (UKCC, 1993). Each of these will be discussed in turn.

Nursing Development Units

Essentially a Nursing Development Unit (NDU) is a clinical setting where care is given, a base from where care is co-ordinated or a clinical team that aims to achieve and promote excellence in nursing, midwifery or health visiting by evaluating practice and encouraging innovation. An NDU is committed to improving patient/client care by maximizing the therapeutic potential of nursing. A climate is developed where each person's contribution is valued and an open, questioning, supportive approach is fostered. As such an NDU is a power house for the development not only of clinical practice but also of a diversity of nursing knowledge (Black, 1992).

NDUs first arrived on the British nursing scene in the early 1980s at Oxford and Thameside. Today there over three hundred NDUs in the UK as well as a growing body of interest in Europe (Wright, 1992). Fuelling the setting up of the original units was the feeling that it was time for nursing to come out of its shell and be more open about its potential and aspirations as well as its numerous achievements. Salvage (1989) suggested that a nursing flagship, as embodied by an NDU, had the ability to become a vital force in raising morale, demonstrating the art of the possible and spreading good ideas and good practice.

In times of uncertainty and disruption in nursing and health care, as is epitomized within the current NHS, NDUs have a crucial role to play in preserving and promoting the essence of nursing. Without these demonstration sites to show us how to take nursing forward in creative, high-quality and equitable ways, the profession could well be dismantled.

The concepts that inform and drive the NDU movement are various but have one major theme, that is empowerment. NDUs are about developing partnership and sharing power with the health service user, the promotion of informed choice and autonomy, the creation, evaluation and dissemination of high-quality practice initatives and the raising of awareness of the therapeutic value of nursing in its own right. The development of new practices and new knowledge by nurses, for nurses, is at the heart of enabling the profession to achieve equal status with other health professionals, both at the point of delivery of care and at the initial planning of services and formulation of policy frameworks. Christman (1988i) argues that:

> If designed properly, the centre for excellence will assist nurses to achieve parity at the decision-making levels that influence policy, design and allocation of resources. In this way nurses can maintain a proactive instead of reactive posture in the social context of health care.

The implications are that the very nature of NDUs and the knowledge, self-worth and power derived therein, will go some way to creating the alternative world view that nursing requires to survive and grow.

Reflective practice

The emergence of a new paradigm is dependent upon the expansion of the knowledge on which nurses base their practice. Ultimately, and at its widest interpretation, this involves the development of a sharper 'policy acumen'. However, there is no guarantee that knowledge currently gleaned within a theoretical setting transfers successfully to clinical work or that it will improve the quality of care delivered. Moreover, as Benner (1984) has argued, the type of knowledge presented to nurses is often not appropriate for the complexities of clinical nursing practice – a fact borne out by Kleffel (1991) and Stevens (1989) in their discussion of nurses' limited knowledge of the socio-political environmental factors affecting health (discussed above).

Traditional ways of acquiring knowledge, based on positivism and a rigorous scientific approach, although useful, can be problematic to nursing; it assumes that all problems arising in clinical practice can be solved by scientific means and from determined academic theory (Schon, 1987). This is not the case, however, for the everyday, messy and often confusing problems that confront nurses – described by Schon (1987) as the 'swampy lowlands' of practice.

By studying various types of professionals at work, Schon (1987) identified reflection as a process of knowledge acquisition originating in practice highly suited to solving complex practice-based problems. Boud, Keogh and Walker (1985) describe reflection as an active process of exploration and analysis of action that can reveal unexpected outcomes and provide insight into values, beliefs and attitudes. These new understandings and appreciations can be activated and applied to future experiences, thus changing and improving practice in a continuous process of quality enhancement.

Reflection can also be used as a method of critical research into accepted and ritualized situations. Smyth (1986, cited Dewing, 1990) describes the power of reflection in assisting individuals to expose the understandings they have about the social dynamics of their own working and learning environments. Through this process, they can begin to challenge and change the status quo. Thus reflection is also a tool of liberation; of conscientization; a throwing off of false consciousness; a process of awareness raising that can reveal to nurses the true state of their powerlessness and the sources of their oppression. It is at this point that nurses can create change.

Leadership initiatives

In a discussion paper on the issues surrounding nursing leadership Rafferty (1993) argues that there is a legacy of neglect of leadership in the profession by both nurses and policy makers. This is currently being felt more keenly than ever as nurses struggle to carve out a role and identity for themselves within the changing structures of the NHS. Rafferty (1993) suggests that nurse leaders need intellectual, political and practical skills to take nursing forward. They need to be radical in their vision and their action to ensure that the key positions are filled by people with the calibre that the profession and the wider health service so urgently need.

At the end of January, 1993 Health Secretary Virginia Bottomley announced a bursary scheme totalling £1.25 million over two years aimed at boosting the leadership potential of nurses, midwives and health visitors – an initiative which on the surface would appear to fit very well within the emerging paradigm.

Precisely what skills and knowledge are required by nurse leaders have not been widely explored, but postgraduate degrees of various sorts are being pursued, for example Masters of Business Administration, Masters of Policy Studies and so on. Whether or not education on its own is sufficient to promote nursing leaders has yet to be seen. Although it will certainly provide the right orientation among the nurses concerned to press for and create change, it is doubtful that the structures and vested interests that have sought to subordinate nurses for so long will be so easily dismantled.

Central support has also been given publicity to strengthening the role of nurses at key decision-making levels in the form of a King's Fund College report commissioned by the NHSME (NHSME, 1993). This focuses on the urgent need to involve nurses in the process of purchasing and stresses the fact that nurses' influence on strategic planning is limited by lack of access to corporate management boards. If nurses are to make a full contribution, the report points out that greater access to this level of management is vital. The King's Fund recommends increased development and support for nurses working in this field. It also urges the creation of development opportunities for both established purchasers and those planning a career move.

The new education and professional development

Project 2000 heralded a new approach to the initial preparation of nurses (UKCC, 1986). Its broad-based curriculum has the potential to encourage the development of many of the qualities necessary for the paradigm shift. This, coupled with the new PREP (UKCC, 1993) proposals which emphasize the incorporation of policy studies as an essential facet of nursing knowledge, bodes well for the creation of a broader perspective.

Conclusion

In 1992 Professor Jane Robinson argued that within nursing:

> Seizing the initiative and determining the course of events in policy matters appears to be crucially dependent on the holding of power: power not only to ensure that an issue reaches – or fails to reach – the public agenda, but power also to define the issue in such a way as to bring about particular ends. (Robinson 1992i)

We believe that this power is not only a function of position within an organization but also concerns knowing about the way power operates and having insight into a process which is about the allocation of values; that is the policy process.

Nursing and its priorities are invisible to nearly everyone except nurses, a condition labelled brilliantly by Jane Robinson (1992) as 'The Black Hole Theory'. This theory suggests that many nurses are unable to see their work within a broad policy context. As a group they are locked into the gravitational force of its own internal preoccupations, observed and contained from without by others who lack totally any comprehension of nursing's problems and concerns. The tensions and dynamics of this situation are the social equivalent of an astronomical black hole. Robinson (1992) contends that the historical lack of critical, aware and intellectually developed nurses has contributed fundamentally to nurses' inability to escape from this black hole.

Our exploration of the four meta-paradigms of nursing which looked at ways of expanding the knowledge and boundaries of each domain, suggests perhaps one way out of the abyss.

References

American Nurses' Association (1980) *Nursing: A Social Policy Statement*, ANA, Kansas City

Benner, P. (1984) *From Novice to Expert: Excellence and Power in Clinical Nursing Practice*, Addison Wesley, California

Black, G. (1992) A difference of degree or kind. *Paediatric Nursing*, **February**, 22–23

Boud, D., Keogh, R. and Walker, D. (eds) (1985) *Reflection: Turning Experience into Learning*, Kogan Page, London

Bridges, J. M. (1990) Literature review on the images of the nurse and nursing in the media. *Journal of Advanced Nursing*, 15, pp. 850–854

Chinn, P. L. and Kramer, M. K. (1991) *Theory and Nursing: A Systematic Approach*, 3rd edn, Mosby, St Louis

Christman, L. P. (1988) A conceptual model for centres of excellence in nursing. *Nursing Administration Quarterly*, **12**(4), (i) 5; 1–4

Dewing, J. (1990) Reflective practice. *Senior Nurse*, **10**(10), 26–28

Elliott-Cannon, C. (1990) Mental handicap and nursing models. In *Models for Nursing 2*, (eds J. Salvage and B. Kershaw), Scutari Press, London, p. 77–88, (i) p. 81

Fawcett, J. (1989) *Analysis and Evaluation of Conceptual Models of Nursing*, 2nd edn, Davis, Philadelphia

Girouard, S. A. (1989) Health policy: implications for the CNS. In *The Clinical Nurse Specialist in Theory and Practice*, (eds A. B. Hanric and J. A. Spross), 2nd edn, W. B. Saunders, Philadelphia

Henderson, V. (1978) The concept of nursing. *Journal of Advanced Nursing*, 3, pp. 113–130

Hughes, L. (1980) The public image of the nurse. *Advances in Nursing Science*, **2**(3), pp. 55–72

Illich, I. (1976) *Limits to Medicine. Medical Nemesis: The Expropriation of Health*, Marion Boyars, London

Kleffel, D. (1991) Rethinking the environment as a domain of nursing knowledge. *Advances in Nursing Science*, **14**(1), 40–51

Leninger, M. M. (1984) *Care: The Essence of Nursing and Health*, Charles B. Slack, New Jersey

McBean, S. (1991) Health and health promotion – consensus and conflict. In *Nursing: A Knowledge Base for Practice*, (eds A. Perry and M. Jolley), Edward Arnold, London, pp. 52–92

NHSME (1993) *The Professional Nursing Contribution to Purchasing: A Study by the King's Fund College*, DoH, London

Rafferty, A. M. (1993) *Leading Questions: A Discussion Paper on the Issues of Nurse Leadership*, King's Fund Centre, London

Robinson, J. (1992) Introduction: beginning the study of nursing policy. In *Policy Issues in Nursing*, (eds J. Robinson, A. Gray and R. Elkan), Open University Press, Milton Keynes, pp. 1–8

Robinson, J., Gray, A. and Elkan, R. (eds) (1992) *Policy Issues in Nursing*, Open University Press, Milton Keynes

RCN (1992) *The Value of Nursing*, RCN, London

Salvage, J. (1983) Distorted images. *Nursing Times*, **79**(1), pp. 13–15

Salvage, J. (1989) Nursing developments. *Nursing Standard*, **22**(3), 25

Schlotfeldt, R. M. (1987) Defining nursing: a historic controversy. *Nursing Research*, **36**(1), pp. 64–67

Schon, D. (1987) *Educating the Reflective Practitioner: Towards a New Design for Teaching and Learning in the Professions*, Josey Bass, London

Seedhouse, D. (1986) *Health: The Foundations of Achievement*, John Wiley, Chichester

Smith, J. A. (1981) The idea of health: a philosophical inquiry. *Advances in Nursing Science*, **3**(3), pp. 43–50

Statutory Instrument (1983) *The Nurses, Midwives and Health Visitors Rules Approval Order*, HMSO, London, (SI no 873)

Stevens, P. E. (1989) A critical social reconceptualization of environment in nursing: implications for methodology. *Advances in Nursing Science*, **11**(4), (i) 61; 56–68

UKCC (1986) *Project 2000: A New Preparation for Practice*, UKCC, London

UKCC (1990) *The Report of the Post-Registration Education and Practice Project*, UKCC, London

UKCC (1991) *Report on Proposals for the Future of Community Education and Practice*, UKCC, London

UKCC (1993) *Proposals for the Standards for Post Registration Education and Practice*, UKCC, London

Weisskopf, M. (1993) The looming battle turf in the health care system. *The Washington Post National Weekly Edition*, May 24–30, p. 14

WHO (1978) *Health for All 2000*, WHO, Copenhagen

Wright, S. (1992) Exporting excellence. *Nursing Times*, **88**(39), pp. 40–42

Summary

Pippa Gough, Sian Maslin-Prothero and Abigail Masterson

As stated in the introduction, the aim of this book has been to stimulate within the nursing profession an interest in and awareness of the fundamental importance and relevance of the discipline of Social Policy to the everyday practice of nurses, midwives and health visitors and the organization of their work.

This book represents, therefore, an attempt to contribute to the growing knowledge base for nursing through the identification and exposition of that knowledge that may usefully be seen as providing a bridge between the worlds of nursing and Social Policy.

Much of this bridge building has been done by exploring pertinent issues within the policy arena and determining how these relate to and impact upon nurses and their delivery of care. This attention on 'issues' rather than 'services' as a way of understanding and interpreting policy is deliberate. For example, in preference to focusing on the welfare service of health, we have chosen instead to explore health and nursing issues in relation to class, gender, welfarism and families, ethnicity and race, disability, age and so on. By using this format we have avoided a traditional policy analysis which splinters people's lives into different services and interventions such as housing, education or social security, for example. Instead our analysis reflects a holistic approach, which is arguably the entire raison d'etre of nursing today.

In chapter 1 we explored the nature of Social Policy and discussed why this discipline has a crucial part to play in enabling the emergence of a new paradigm concerned with a policy for nursing. Much of the chapter was given over to an introduction to the history of social policy formulation in Britain, highlighting areas of special interest to nurses and nursing. Discussion points aimed to elucidate why it is necessary to take a historical perspective to understand fully the present NHS, and the wider Welfare State, and nursing's role within it.

The focus for chapter 2 was the process of social policy formulation and implementation. The key players in this process were identified, including statutory, voluntary and private bodies as well as influential vested interests or pressure groups, for example the medical profession, pharmaceutical companies and so on. The invisibility, marginalization and powerlessness of nursing throughout the policy process was stressed.

There is no doubt that, even in its present-day, reduced and somewhat dismantled form, the State and its policies still have a profound impact on the whole of people's lives. Chapter 3 therefore was dedicated to a detailed examination of State action and various political perspectives on welfare and power. The position of nursing and nurses in relation to the distribution of power was examined at macro and micro levels in order to provoke an awareness of the way power operates. This offers a greater understanding of the historical and current position of nurses in influencing the policy agenda. Questions were raised as to the political values and beliefs informing the development of nursing as well as the extent to which nurses are part of the professional covert operation of power in relation to users of health care services.

Chapter 4 examined the policies surrounding the creation and continued development of the NHS. The various reorganizations since 1948 were chronicled in some detail. Particular emphasis was placed on how these reorganizations have affected and shaped nursing and the care nurses give. Key themes and policy issues emerged which centred on the changing political ideologies which have switched the focus of the service from firstly, one provided wholly by the State to that of a mixed economy of care, and, secondly, a concentration on expensive, 'high-tech' care to an increasing emphasis on health promotion and care in non-institutional settings. The impact on nurses and nursing of these progressive changes is mixed and it was argued that the true potential of the profession, in terms of new ways of delivering care, has yet to be fully realized.

Caring and the way in which social policies define and impact on the caring role were the central themes of chapter 5. The multidimensional nature of caring and the way the responsibility for this falls predominantly on women in both the public and private domain was examined. In addition the legitimacy of the profession's claim that caring is the foundation of nursing was debated. This argument was linked into the way in which nursing has been affected by the ideology which underpins and defines caring and caring roles. It became apparent that nurses are often in the perfect position to recognize the strain that carers are under yet, paradoxically, may add to the burden of care by failing to recognize these difficulties. Nurses urgently need to address their ignorance of social policies and their impact. They must wake up to the fact they can promote change and enhance the position of carers by adopting a more radical agenda and lobbying governments to create sensitive and appropriate social policies.

Chapter 6 drew on much of the material offered in the previous chapter and took a women-centred perspective on policy, concentrating on gender as a basis for a system of domination of women by men. This routinized subordination, as well as assumptions made about women's dependence on men, is reflected not only in the way policy is formulated and implemented but also in the way the discipline of Social Policy is conceptualized and its knowledge base constructed. Once again nurses' lack of power was demonstrated. Nursing is a women-dominated profession and traditionally women do not possess power. Consequently nurses' ability to influence decision making and the allocation of health resources has been compromised.

An overview of the current state of the family in terms of theory and practical issues and the way these link to policy was given in chapter 7. Key to this discussion was an examination of intra-family relationships as well as those relationships between the family and society as a whole. The ways in which these 'private' and 'public' facets of the family interconnect have been claimed as legitimate areas for concern and intervention by the caring professions. Issues around nurses developing partnership in care with families, as opposed to the more traditional policing role for nurses, were addressed. Contrary to the political and professional focus on the individual and individualism, a community-development approach was offered as the way forward for nurses. This means that models of care need to include proactive involvement in the planning of policy and services for the family by nurses.

Chapter 8 was concerned with an examination of the issues surrounding social policies and race. It opened with a full discussion of the complexity of terminology surrounding race and ethnicity, racism, racial discrimination and racial prejudice. The composition and origins of the UK population and the link with oppression of immigrant black populations were discussed and the need for appropriate support and provision of care for black populations highlighted. The implicit racism of much of the social and health policy examined raised questions as to how this may impact on nurses and nursing practice. It was seen that nursing education and nursing services have consistently failed to provide appropriate services to Britain's black community. This situation will only be remedied by the black population's involvement in the planning and provision of health and other welfare services, and by constantly challenging racism wherever it occurs.

The focus for chapter 9 was exclusively older people. Ageism as an ideology was examined and the way this influences the policy process and marginalizes the needs and demands of this growing group highlighted. It was seen that over the last decade care of older people has changed from increasing intervention by the State to involve policies which are far more selective – viewing the role of the State as that of 'enabler' rather than provider. The private and voluntary sectors are expected, with statutory agencies, to provide a basic minimum of services within the competition of the market. Again it was argued that it is only by understanding the ageist framework within which health care for older people is planned and organized that nurses can respond more effectively to the needs of the health-service user.

Chapter 10 tackled issues concerned with disability and policy, a major theme of which was a view of disability as a social construct, reinforced fundamentally by welfarism. In a competitive society which values independence and physical and intellectual skills and which rewards economic productivity, disabled people are bound to be disadvantaged. It was argued that the rise of 'the institution', in which nurses have played a large part, as a mechanism of both social provision and social control, has been key to structuring both the perceptions and experiences of disability. Nurses were called upon to dismantle their view of disability as an individual problem that requires individual adjustment and to put collective effort instead into curing the disablement of society.

An examination of the concept of class, power, policy and nursing was the concern of chapter 11. Both Marxist and Weberian approaches to this subject were considered and the access of nursing and nurses to power from the platform of class was discussed. Questions were also raised about the current relevance and usefulness of a class analysis of welfarism to the postmodern age, especially in the face of the emerging 'politics of identity' and rejection of proletarianism. In policy terms, the need to develop services which are universal but which are also capable of meeting diverse and differentiated needs were highlighted. In this Tomlinson era, this is particularly the case for nursing – if we fail to take notice of the wider political and socio-economic trends, then the profession will cease to exist in any coherent way.

In chapter 12 we turned our attention to the as yet unformed and undefined theoretical terrain of a policy for nursing. Up until this point the material presented throughout the book had concentrated purely on trying to assemble a policy analysis of nursing; to knit together an analysis of social policy issues with a nursing perspective. Although this has been important, our original intention, as stated at the start of this book, has always been more ambitious – that is to pursue a policy *for* nursing; to develop an analysis which informs and shapes nursing practice as well as the future direction and priorities of the profession.

As a starting point for this investigation we chose to examine the four domain concepts or metaparadigms of nursing, described by Fawcett (1989), from a 'policy platform'. This examinatiom exposed a large gap in nursing's knowledge and skills, that if addressed could broaden the scope of legitimate nursing activity within each of these domains. In other words the 'policy acumen' described in the introduction was highlighted as being vital if nurses were to provide care more autonomously and comprehensively and in line with nursing values. The new knowledge and skills offered the potential of developing an alternative world view – a possible shift in our beliefs, values and commitments and thus heralded the emergence of a new paradigm for nursing.

In 1992 Robinson suggested that nurses were caught within the social equivalent of an astronomical black hole – locked into the gravitational force of our own internal preoccupations, contained and controlled by outsiders who don't or won't understand our priorities and aspirations. According to Robinson (1992) there was only one way out of this historical trap: education and the development of critical, aware and intellectually able nurses who 'are not afraid to take their seat at the various policy-making top tables and to make a creative contribution to the planning, delivery and evaluation of health care' (Robinson, 1992ii).

This book, which offers the beginning of a discourse about a policy *for* nursing, is our contribution to the development of an escape from the Black Hole.

References

Fawcett, J. (1989) *Analysis and Evaluation of Conceptual Models of Nursing*, 2nd edn, F. A. Davis Company, Philadelphia

Robinson, J. (1992) Introduction: beginning the study of nursing policy. In *Policy Issues in Nursing* (eds J. Robinson, A. Gray and R. Elkan) (i) p. 3; (ii) p. 5. Open University Press, Milton Keynes, pp. 1–8

Index